IMAGES
of America

FLINT HILLS

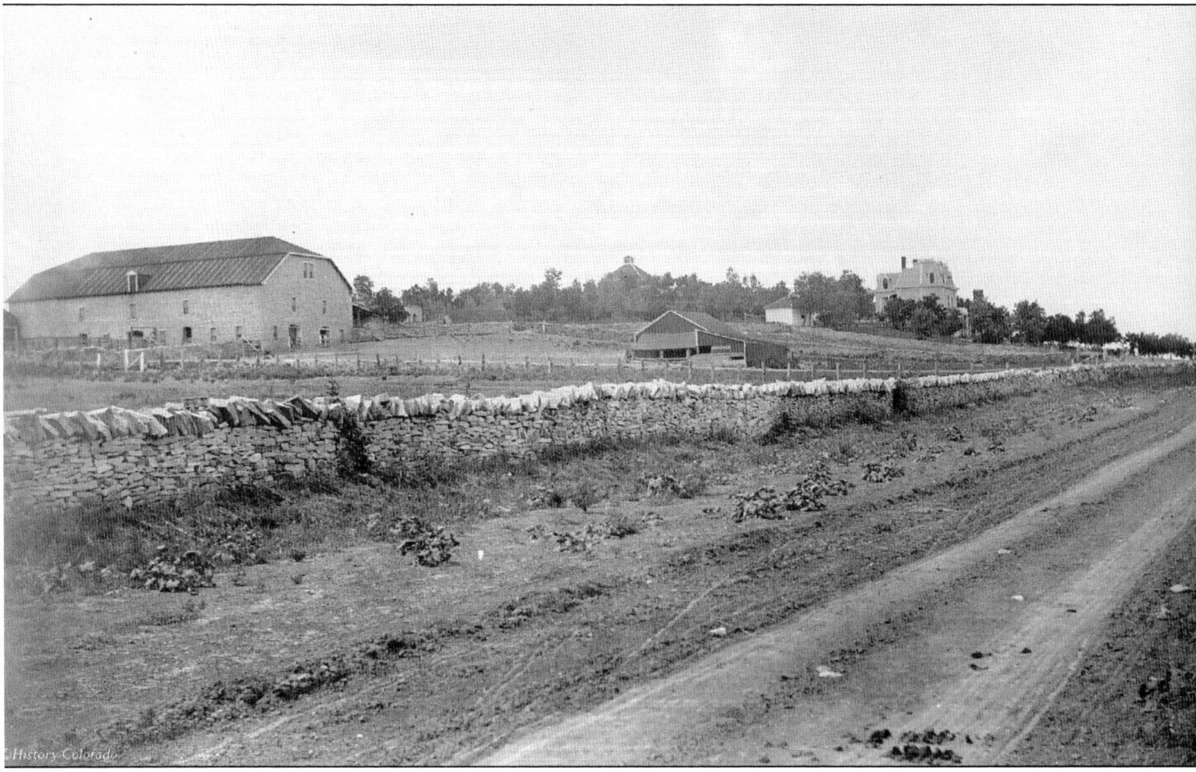

This view of the Stephen F. Jones ranch at Strong City comes from the collection of William Henry Jackson, famed photographer of the American West, who captured this image of the ranch in the mid-1880s. Stoneworkers for David Rettiger completed work on the house, barn, and 45 miles of stone fence on the Jones estate in 1881. Jones and his family lived here until they moved to Kansas City in 1888, selling the Spring Hill Farm and Stock Ranch in Chase County to neighbor Barney Lantry. Today, this property is part of the Tallgrass Prairie Preserve. (Courtesy History Colorado, William Henry Jackson collection scan 20101808.)

ON THE COVER: Fred Howard, left, and E.C. Crofoot of the Crofoot Feed Lot in Strong City inspect a group of 281 Z Bar steers purchased from the Davis Ranch in August 1955 heading for an Iowa feedlot. For 35 years, Howard was the ranch manager for the Chase County Davis Ranch, or the Z Bar Cattle Company, as it was known in later years. (Courtesy Fred Howard II.)

IMAGES
of America

FLINT HILLS

Greg A. Hoots

ARCADIA
PUBLISHING

ISBN 978-0-7385-8313-6

Published by Arcadia Publishing
Charleston, South Carolina

Printed in the United States of America

Library of Congress Control Number: 2010940834

For all general information, please contact Arcadia Publishing:
Telephone 843-853-2070
Fax 843-853-0044
E-mail sales@arcadiapublishing.com
For customer service and orders:
Toll-Free 1-888-313-2665

Visit us on the Internet at www.arcadiapublishing.com

I dedicate this book to Fred Howard II,
a true friend of the Flint Hills.

Contents

Acknowledgments

I would like to thank all of the organizations and individuals that have assisted me in the preparation of this book. This book presents photographs from many sources, far more than previous titles I've authored for Arcadia Publishing. Simply, there were so many contributors with so many great photographs that, with the space provided here, I am unable to thank every individual. However, I would like the contributors and readers to know that my thanks are extended here and expressed in the image credit that appears after the caption for each photograph.

I would like to add a note of acknowledgment to five special contributions that were made by organizations and individuals. First, I would like to thank the Wabaunsee County Historical Society in Alma and its curator, Alan Winkler, for the generous contribution of photographs and the use of their museum facility in Alma. Second, I would like to acknowledge the great assistance I received from Carla Gallmeister and Charley Klamm at the Chase County Historical Society Museum and Library and for the use of their photographs. The museum and photograph collection in Cottonwood Falls is impressive. Third, a sincere thanks to Bonnie McClintock at the Morris County Historical Society Research Center in Council Grove. Bonnie was so helpful and knowledgeable, providing me with so many photographs of Council Grove. Fourth, a special thanks goes to Heather Brown of the National Park Service at the Tallgrass Prairie Preserve for the wonderful contribution of photographs and material on the Davis Ranch. The photograph collection was priceless. And finally, I want to acknowledge and give a sincere thanks to Phyllis Scherich of the Merrill Ranch in Comanche County, Kansas. Not only did Phyllis provide me with a wonderful collection of photographs from the Davis Ranch, but she is an accomplished researcher, and her assistance is duly noted.

I would also like to thank Ted Gerstle, my editor at Arcadia Publishing, for his support and encouragement during the writing of this book.

Finally, I want to thank my wife, Cheryl, who is always supportive of my writing and publishing efforts.

Introduction

The Kansas Flint Hills region spreads over a dozen counties in the northeast and east central section of the state, boasting thousands of acres of native prairie grass. At one time, before the settlement and development of the frontier, between 150 million and 250 million acres of prairie existed in North America. Now, less than four percent of that amount still survives the onslaught of agriculture and civilization, and most of that remaining prairie lies in the Flint Hills of Kansas. Images of America: *Flint Hills* takes a photographic journey back in time through the region, tracing the paths of two scenic byways, looking into the past of several towns in the area. This volume also tells the story of the greatest cattle ranch in the history of Kansas and looks at the real cowboys of the Flint Hills, both at work and at play.

Chapter one follows the path of the Native Stone Scenic Byway, which winds along the Mission Creek and Mill Creek Valleys, resplendent in beauty, rich with history. The byway begins three miles south of mile marker 350 on Interstate 70, in southwest Shawnee County, and passes through the unincorporated town of Dover, Kansas, before entering Wabaunsee County. Along the route, travelers pass through the ghost town of Keene before arriving in Eskridge, a small town of 500 residents about 40 miles southwest of the state capital of Topeka. Five miles to the east of Eskridge sits Lake Wabaunsee, a spring-fed reservoir that provides drinking water for 2,000 residents in the region and excellent recreational facilities for both fishermen and water-sports enthusiasts. The byway then transverses 15 miles of ranch land bordered by miles of native stone fences before arriving in Alma, the seat of government in Wabaunsee County. The route, 48 miles in length, features historic limestone commercial buildings, homes, fences, and bridges before returning to Interstate 70 at mile marker 328. Once in Alma, the traveler may follow the tour of homes provided in this book, seeing over a dozen historic views of homes in the "City of Native Stone."

Chapter two features photographs from Council Grove, Kansas, located in Morris County at the intersection of K-56 and K-177 Highways. Council Grove claims a rich history as a frontier town from the fact that during the years that the Santa Fe Trail was a major passageway for westward bound travelers, the town was the last point where supplies could be purchased between Independence, Missouri, and Santa Fe, New Mexico. Council Grove boasts two dozen historic sites, which visitors can view on a self-guided tour. Today, Council Grove is home to some 2,400 residents and serves as the seat of government for Morris County. Nestled in the heart of ranching country, tourism found an increasing role in the city's economy as it became the beginning point for the Flint Hills Scenic Byway.

Chapter three follows the Flint Hills Scenic Byway, which begins at Council Grove and follows K-177 Highway, passing through the Tallgrass Prairie Preserve, the historic towns of Strong City and Cottonwood Falls, and the cattle-producing region at Matfield Green and Bazaar before ending at Cassoday. The Chase County twin cities, Cottonwood Falls and Strong City, are steeped in history, and ample photographic evidence of that fact is provided in this chapter. Cottonwood Falls has long claimed a metropolitan flair, from its impressive French

Renaissance–style limestone courthouse to Kansas's first interurban, horse-drawn trolley system connecting it with Strong City. The elegance and decorum of the past are still very visible in Cottonwood Falls today, from the architecture of the restored buildings to the cobblestone streets. The Flint Hills Scenic Byway received scenic byway designation from the Kansas Department of Transportation in 1995, and in 2005 the route was designated a National Scenic Byway by the Federal Highway Administration.

Chapter four examines the history of the greatest cattle ranch in the history of Kansas, the Davis Ranch. Amassed by George Davis, a man who was no rancher at all, the empire overshadowed all of the spectacular ranches that together comprised the Davis Ranch or, as it was later known, the Z Bar Ranch. The Tallgrass Prairie Preserve at Strong City is comprised of land that was once an integral part of the Z Bar ranching giant. As vast as the 10,000-acre ranch at Strong City is, it is hard to believe that the Davis Ranch, at its peak, had more than eight times that much ranch land in Kansas alone, along with about 10,000 additional acres in western Missouri. As a ranching operation, George Davis's Z Bar was the model for success.

Chapter five presents photographs of cowboys in the Flint Hills working at their vocation and enjoying the competition of rodeo sports. Throughout the Flint Hills region, the ranching and farming industry drives the economy. It has been that way for a century and a half, and it remains so today. While substantial changes have occurred in the last 50 years in cattle ranching, the business is still one that is very much driven by the cowboy. Changes in cattle marketing and in consumer demand for beef have led the evolution of the industry, but the basics of the cow-calf operation are unchanged. Rodeos have been the cowboy's playground and a source of entertainment for millions of spectators worldwide. This chapter includes historic photographs of the greatest rodeo in the state, the Flint Hills Rodeo in Strong City, and also tells the story of one man's dream come true, Lester Marten's Rodeo Arena at Alma.

I have designed this book to be a handbook for travelers in the Flint Hills as well as a volume for study for those seeking historic photographs and information about this pristine section of the American prairie. Take this book with you as you drive down the two scenic byways located in the Flint Hills. While some buildings disappear and others appear, and while change seems to erode the character of the landscape, one will find so much unchanged in the Flint Hills. And it is that pristine quality of the landscape that makes this region a true national treasure. Enjoy your time in the Flint Hills.

One

Native Stone Scenic Byway

The Native Stone Scenic Byway received that designation by the Kansas Department of Transportation (KDOT) in 2006, making it one of nine scenic byways in the state. The road to becoming a byway was not an easy one. Efforts to establish a scenic byway through Wabaunsee County's steeply rolling hills, along its winding roads, began in 1994. Efforts to coordinate and establish a route for the byway met with delays and indecision. One of the organizers who worked diligently to establish consensus for the route that was ultimately chosen was Debra Shufflebean, then owner of the Sage Inn Bed and Breakfast. A dozen years after the effort began, the route was approved by the KDOT, designating the 48 miles of K-4 Highway and K-99 Highway as the Native Stone Scenic Byway.

The Native Stone Scenic Byway begins, or ends, depending on the direction of travel, at the intersection of Southwest Glick Road and K-4 Highway in southwest Shawnee County. Not only is the scenery gorgeous at this point along K-4 Highway as it winds through Mission Creek Valley to the southwest, but the area is also rich in history. This intersection, in the triangle that is created as K-4 takes one of its characteristic 90-degree turns, was the location of Carl and Margaret Daniel's store and gas station. The station was an icon along K-4 Highway. Margaret Daniel recalled that she and husband Carl, back from military service in World War II, were looking for a place to settle down and make a living. They were out driving along K-4 Highway and came upon the station, which had been abandoned during the war. The weeds, she recalled, reached to the eaves of the roof. She said Carl asked her how she thought this place looked, and she replied it looked good to her. They purchased the station, and for years, "Carl and Margaret's" was a very well known stopping point for travelers along K-4 Highway.

The highway itself is rich in history. The section of K-4 Highway from Topeka to Dover was the first paved section of highway in the state of Kansas. There was some controversy and debate in the mid-1910s as to whether paved roads would be successful in Kansas. Some doubters thought that the roads would simply fall apart from the stress of the harsh climate fluctuations and demands placed by agriculture equipment. The Kansas State Highway Commission spent much effort in promoting the idea of "365-day roads." K-4 Highway was an example of how road building could work in Kansas. The terrain along K-4 would be a challenge. Rough, rocky outcrops and low-lying bottomland prone to erosion, along with the need to bridge Mission Creek at two points, would prove to the detractors that paved roads would work in Kansas. The State Highway Commission brought a quartzite-based aggregate rock from Lincoln, Kansas, to mix in the concrete, hoping to ensure hardness. The concrete mixing and stabling of mules and equipment were headquartered on the bend just across the highway from where Carl and Margaret Daniel's store would later be. The project was a great success, and that section of K-4 Highway proved that 365-day roads were the future of the state.

The road winds to Dover, located on Mission Creek on the Shawnee and Wabaunsee County line. The town is rich with history, as it was the site of an early stagecoach stop and a ford across Mission Creek for travelers who were venturing to the American West. Alf Sage built his first stagecoach stop in 1865, expanding it into a full-size inn by 1878. The Dover community was once a busy business center featuring a bank, two dry goods stores, two gas stations, a garage, a livery, and other enterprises. Community businesses still flourish in Dover today, including a bed-and-breakfast, a café, a tractor sales and repair business, and several other businesses in the outlying area.

One and a half miles west of Dover, a traveler on the byway can turn to the south, driving a mile on the gravel to Echo Cliff Park. The park, maintained by volunteers, is located on the bank of Mission Creek and features a pedestrian bridge over the creek. Echo Cliff has been a spot for picnic goers, swimmers, and fishers for decades.

Seven miles west of Dover, the traveler arrives in Keene, Kansas, once a thriving community but now a ghost town with only a few residences surviving. Keene once boasted a store and gas station, its own school, a blacksmith shop, and a community hall. From August 15, 1877, to May 15, 1901, Keene had its own post office.

Eleven miles southwest of Keene, Highway K-4 leads to Eskridge, a town platted by the Atchison, Topeka & Santa Fe Railway as it was expanding its lines across Kansas. In 1880, the AT&SF had formed the Manhattan, Alma & Burlingame Railway to provide rail service to the coal fields discovered near Burlingame. Eskridge grew with the coming of the railroad. In fact, the town moved about a mile to accommodate the location selected for the railroad depot. Eskridge boasts several historic buildings constructed between the 1890s through the early 1910s.

Four miles west of Eskridge, travelers on the byway discover Lake Wabaunsee, a spring-fed lake nestled high in the Flint Hills, created by public works projects during the Great Depression. Beginning as a transient work camp created by the Kansas Economic Recovery Committee in 1934, the bulk of the construction of the lake fell into the hands of the Works Progress Administration (WPA) in 1936. The south shore of the lake contains a community with over 200 private homes. The north shore has a public beach, camping and picnic sites, a boat ramp, permit office, the Lodge restaurant, and a small community of private owners of the old barracks quarters. The 415-acre lake offers fishing, boating, and other recreational opportunities. The lake itself is owned by the City of Eskridge.

Six miles west of Lake Wabaunsee, the traveler reaches the junction of K-4 and K-99 Highways. The scenic byway turns north on K-99, winding north for nine miles toward Alma. Along that route, one passes miles of stone fence built by early settlers as the open range was eliminated in the state. A section of stone fence located on the west side of the road was restored by volunteers. Six miles north of the junction, travelers pass the Sump Barn, a huge hay barn built in 1905 by Henry Sump that is located on the east side of the road. The barn, constructed of native walnut with a native limestone basement, is known for its unique paint design, a red background with white encircled stars on every door.

Two miles north of the Sump Barn, the byway traveler arrives in Alma, the "City of Native Stone." The city's business district is lined with historic limestone buildings constructed with stone quarried locally. Alma, with a population of 800, is the largest town in Wabaunsee County and serves as the county seat. The byway traveler finds the historic Wabaunsee County Courthouse, constructed in 1931, one block west of K-99 Highway. The town contains over 400 residences, including many historic homes.

The byway continues north on K-99 Highway for three miles to its end at Interstate 70. Two miles north of Alma, travelers can view a second section of stone fence reconstructed by volunteers, organized by the Native Stone Scenic Byway Committee.

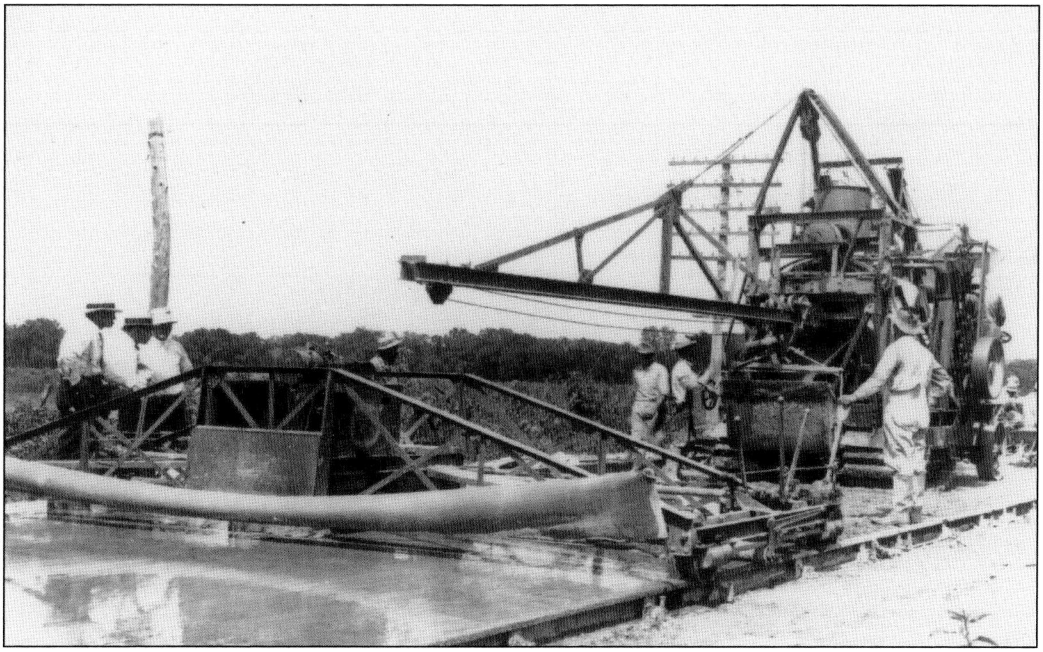

Workers pour concrete on the first paved highway in Kansas, K-4 Highway. The first section of pavement ran from US Highway 75 in Topeka, along what is now West Twenty-first Street, and then along what was formerly called the Southwest Trail to the pavement's end in Dover. The 20 miles of road was controversial, as many people did not believe that 365-day roads would survive the Kansas climate. (Courtesy Kansas State Historical Society.)

Carl and Margaret Daniel's station and store was located at the intersection of Southwest Glick Road and K-4 Highway. The couple purchased the station after World War II, operating it for almost 30 years while farming the Mission Creek bottom ground nearby. Carl and Margaret's was a landmark on K-4 Highway. Everyone who traveled the road regularly stopped at the store. The station was demolished in 1974. (Courtesy Margaret Daniel.)

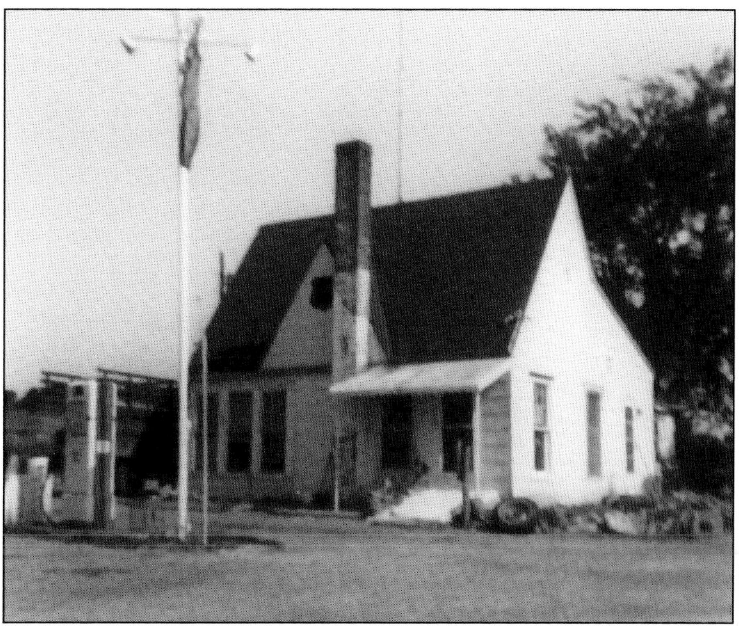

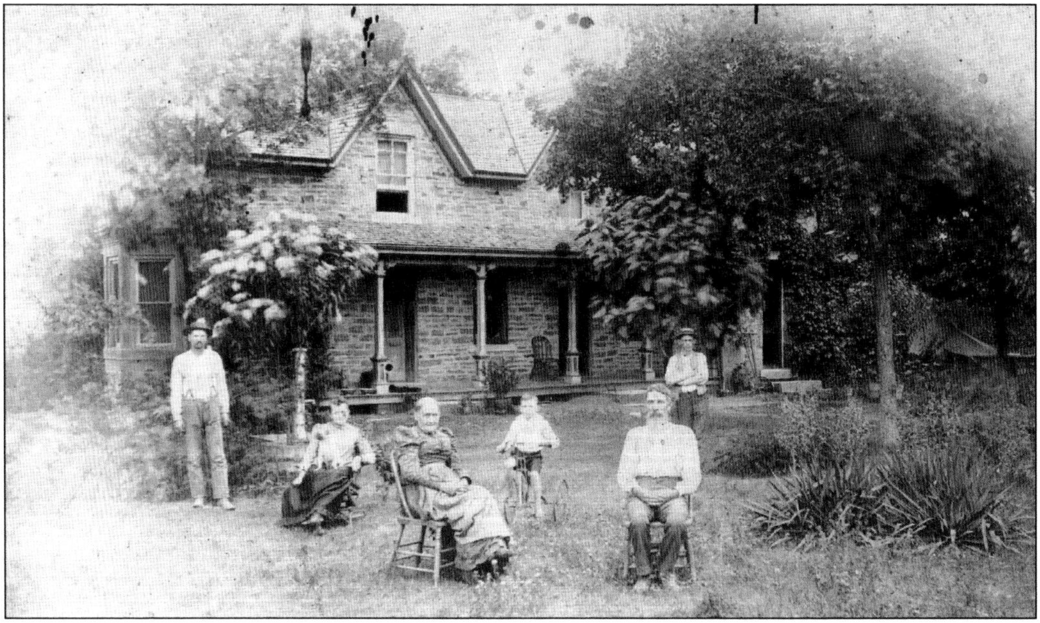

Alfred Sage (front right) and other unidentified members of the Sage family pose in front of their residence and stagecoach stop located at 13553 Southwest K-4 Highway, Dover. The first section of the Sage Inn was constructed in 1865, and it was expanded to the size seen here in 1878. Today, the six-bedroom house is used as a bed-and-breakfast. (Courtesy Joann Hepworth.)

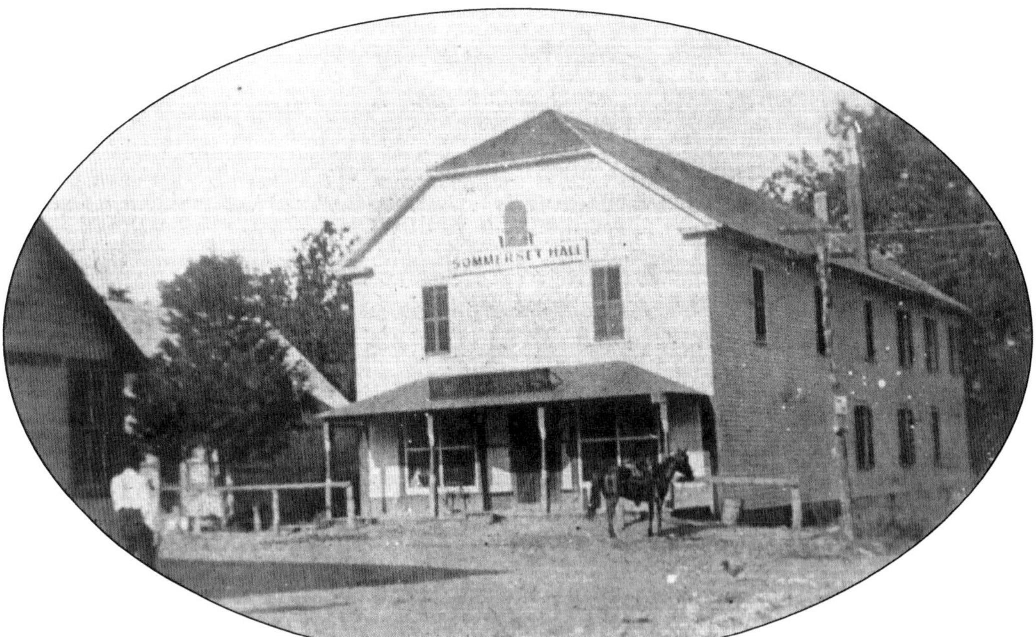

Sommerset Hall was constructed by Alf Sage as a store in the late 1880s in Dover at 5701 Southwest Douglas Road. The Odd Fellows lodge moved into the upstairs hall in 1902 and purchased the building in 1905. Today, it houses the Sommerset Hall Café. (Courtesy Chester Todd.)

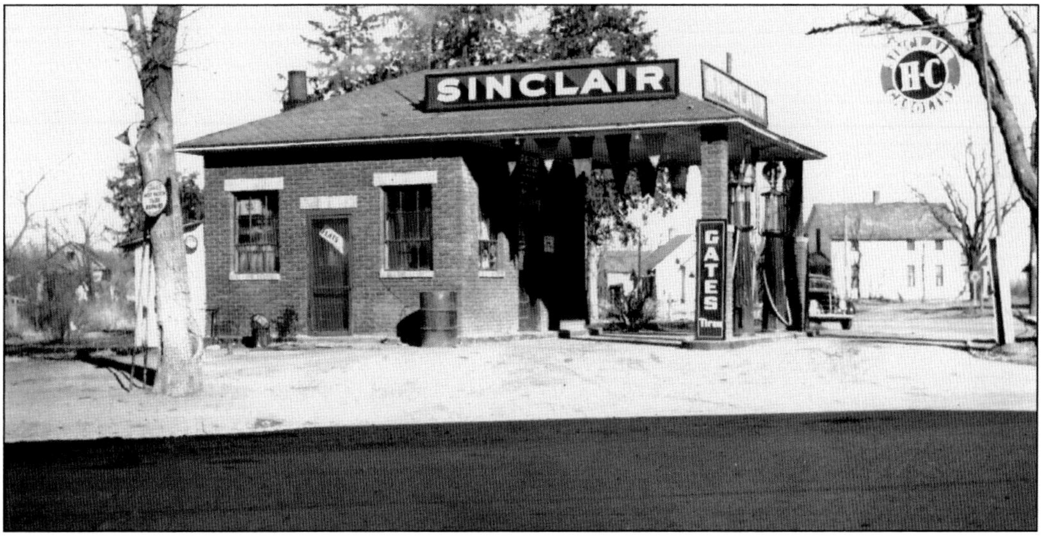

This Sinclair gas station was located at the northwest corner of K-4 Highway and Southwest Douglas Road in Dover. Built by Arthur Bowker in 1928, the station was being operated by Marvin Gurtler when this photograph was taken in the late 1930s. Today, this building still stands on the corner, just in front of the Sage Inn Bed and Breakfast, and is now part of that property. (Courtesy Wayne Gurtler.)

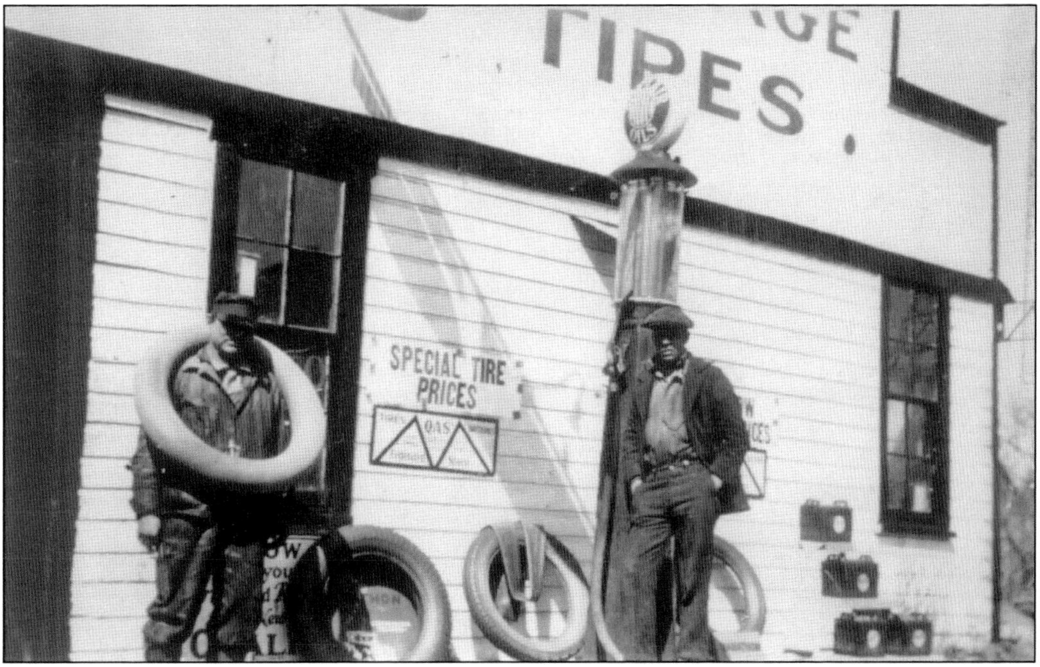

Walter Black, left, and Ed Fisher, proprietor of the Southwest Trail Garage, pose for this 1930s photograph. This garage was constructed by Arthur Bowker, who also built the station seen at the top of the page. The garage was located where the Maple Hill Fire District No. 4 is located today, at 13547 Southwest K-4 Highway in Dover. (Courtesy Chester Todd.)

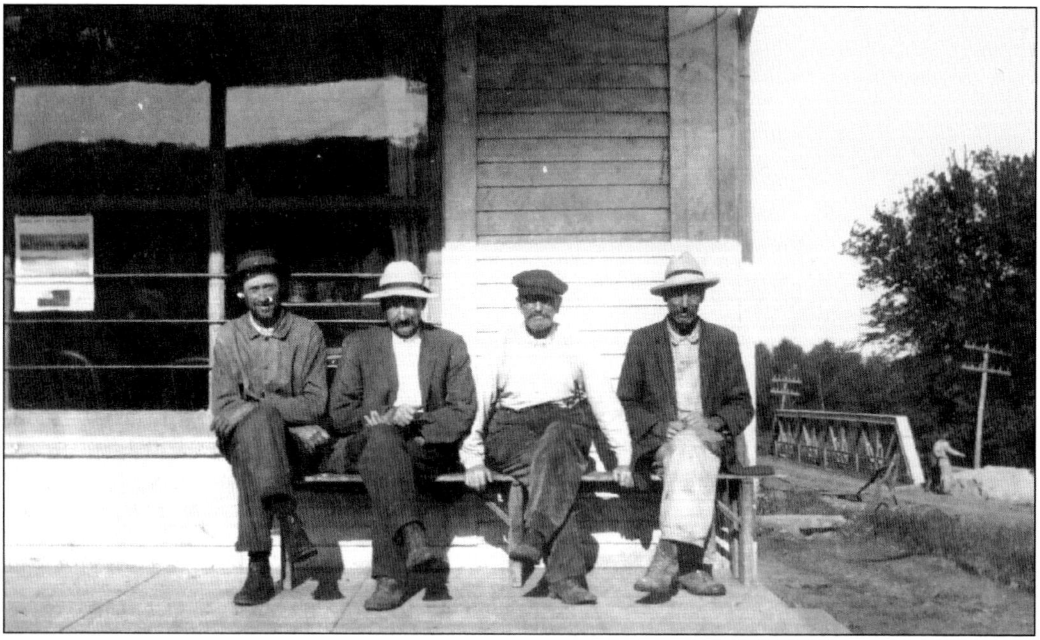

Four unidentified men "press the bench" in front of the Sommerset Inn store in Dover around 1930. To the right, one can see the steel bridge that crossed the first channel of Mission Creek. Just out of sight in this view is the arched concrete bridge seen on the opposite page. For over 125 years, this building has been a center of the Dover community and remains so today. (Courtesy Joann Hepworth.)

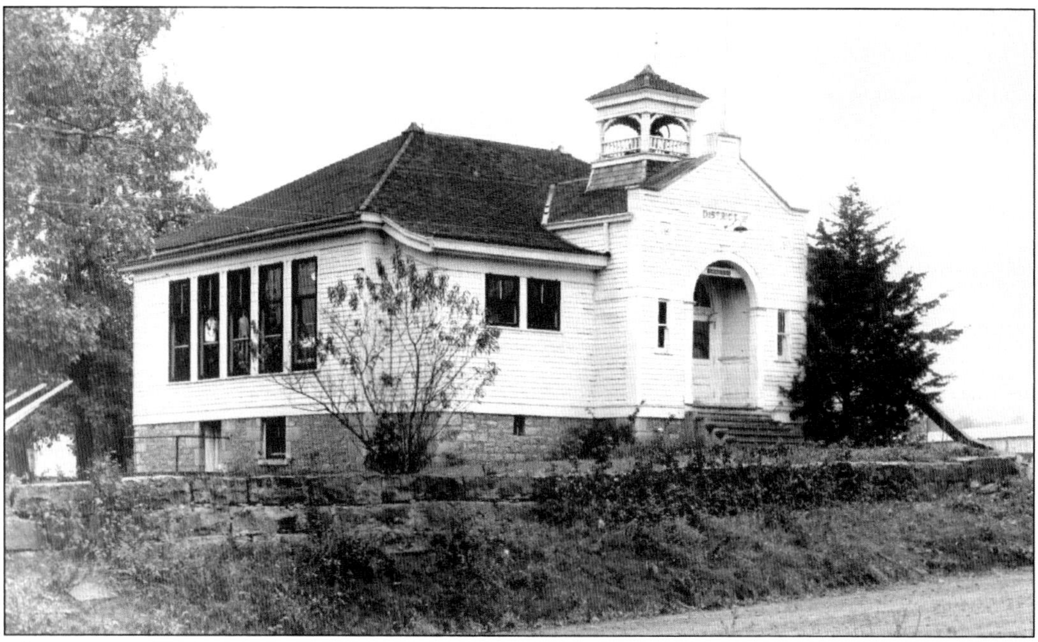

The Dover School District 15 School is pictured here, located at 5748 Southwest Douglas Road. This building replaced the one-room stone schoolhouse that sat on the same lot. In 1956, Dover built a new school just to the south of the old District 15 building, which was sold. It is now a private residence. (Courtesy Chester Todd.)

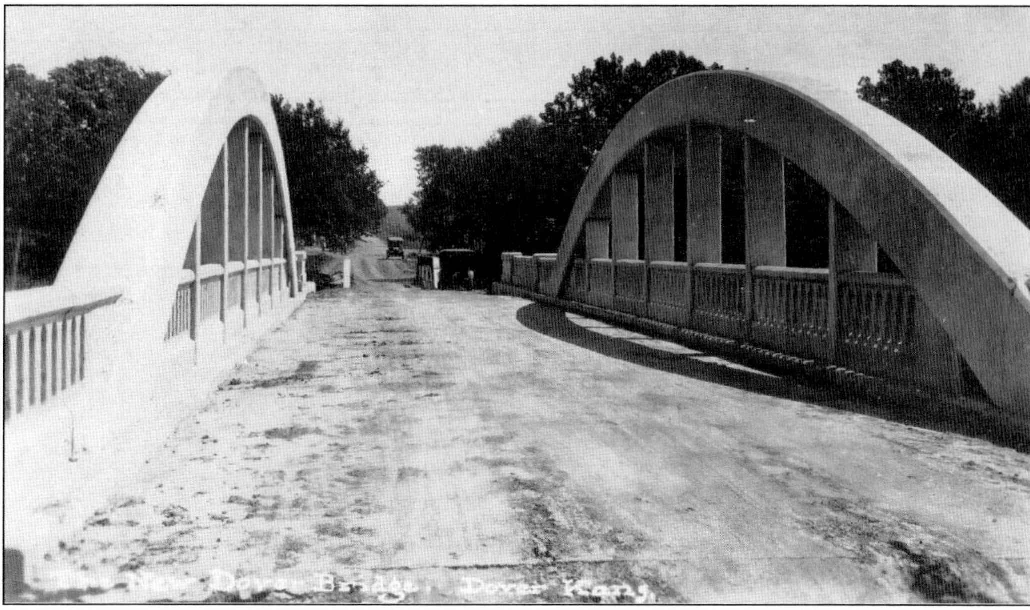

Above, the new concrete arch bridge across Mission Creek at Dover is seen in this c. 1924 real-photo postcard. Originally, the stream had two branches that were spanned at Dover. One can see the steel bridge just east of the new concrete bridge in this view. Below, "A little hard luck while erecting the steel bridge, Dover, Kans" is the caption for this Zercher Photo real-photo postcard. The steel bridge apparently collapsed during its construction in the early 1920s. This particular crossing over Mission Creek was a long-standing one for travelers, even before the first bridge was constructed. It was the site of a shallow ford where wagons and horses could cross the creek. (Both, courtesy Greg Hoots.)

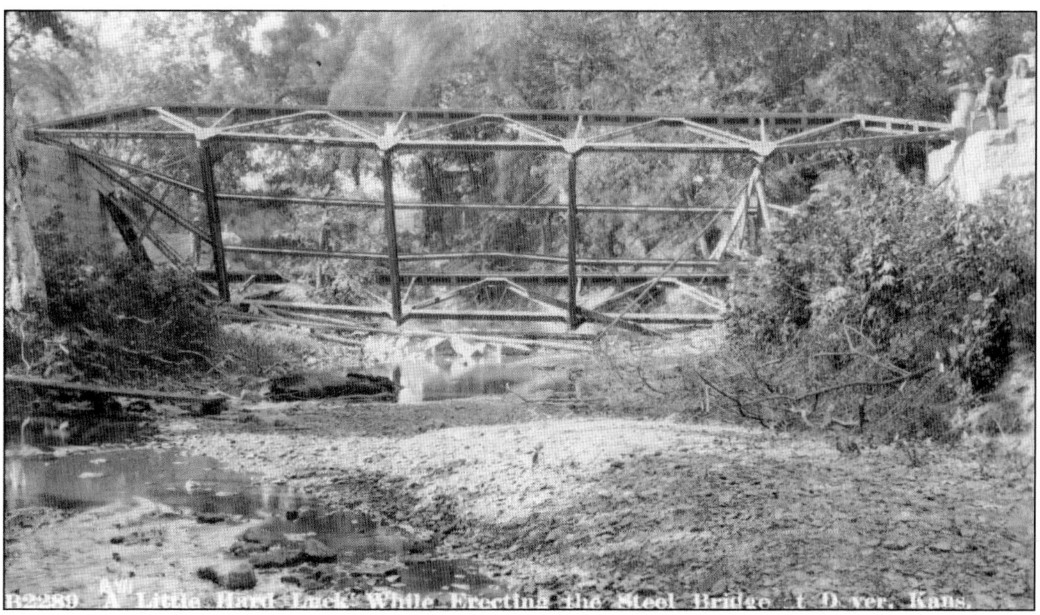

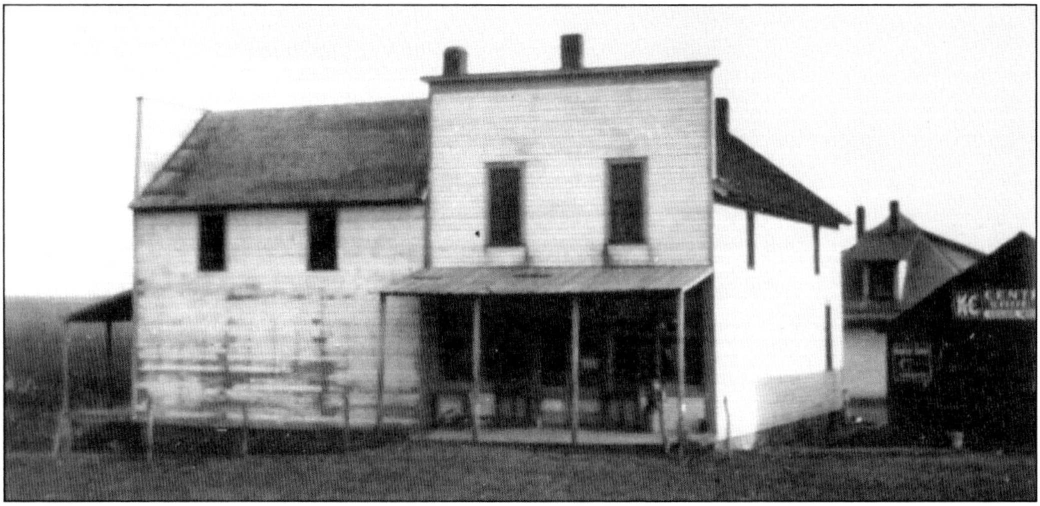

The Keene store was located at 15026 Southwest K-4 Highway, Keene, Kansas. Seen here in about 1920, the store at that time had a full, two-story addition and storefront, which faced the east, as well as the more recognizable front section facing north. This business opened at Keene in 1874, and the building succumbed to fire in 1996. (Courtesy Ida Thomas.)

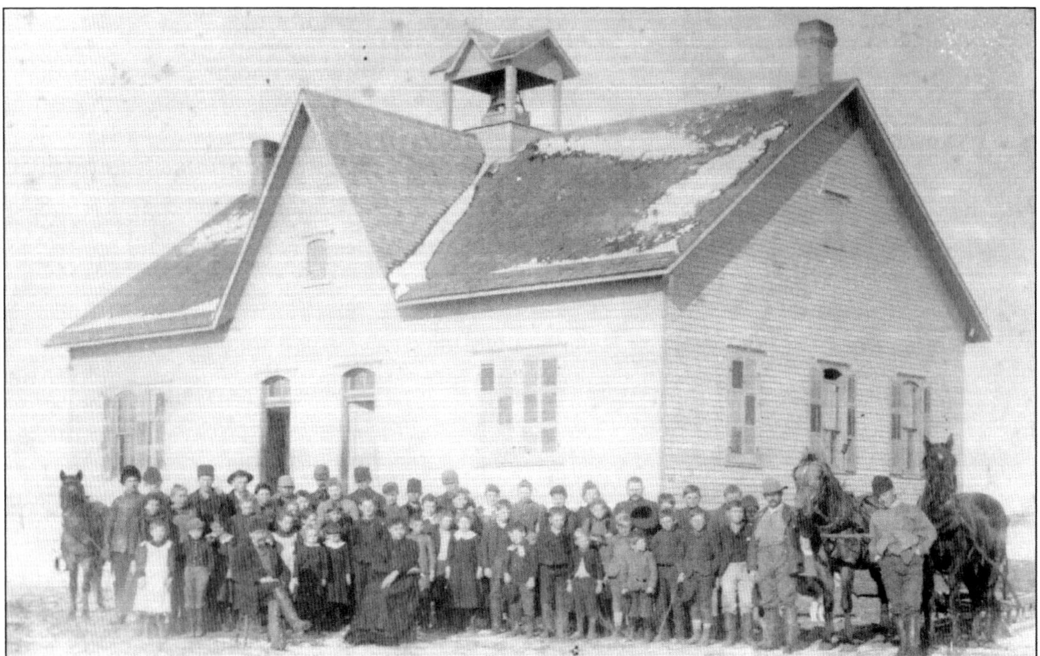

Over 40 students and several adults pose in front of the Keene School, District 56, in this c. 1900 winter scene. The school was located at the northwest corner of Southwest K-4 Highway and Windy Hill Road. This building was sold for demolition and was removed in the 1970s by Gary Kemble of Eskridge. (Courtesy Wabaunsee County Historical Society.)

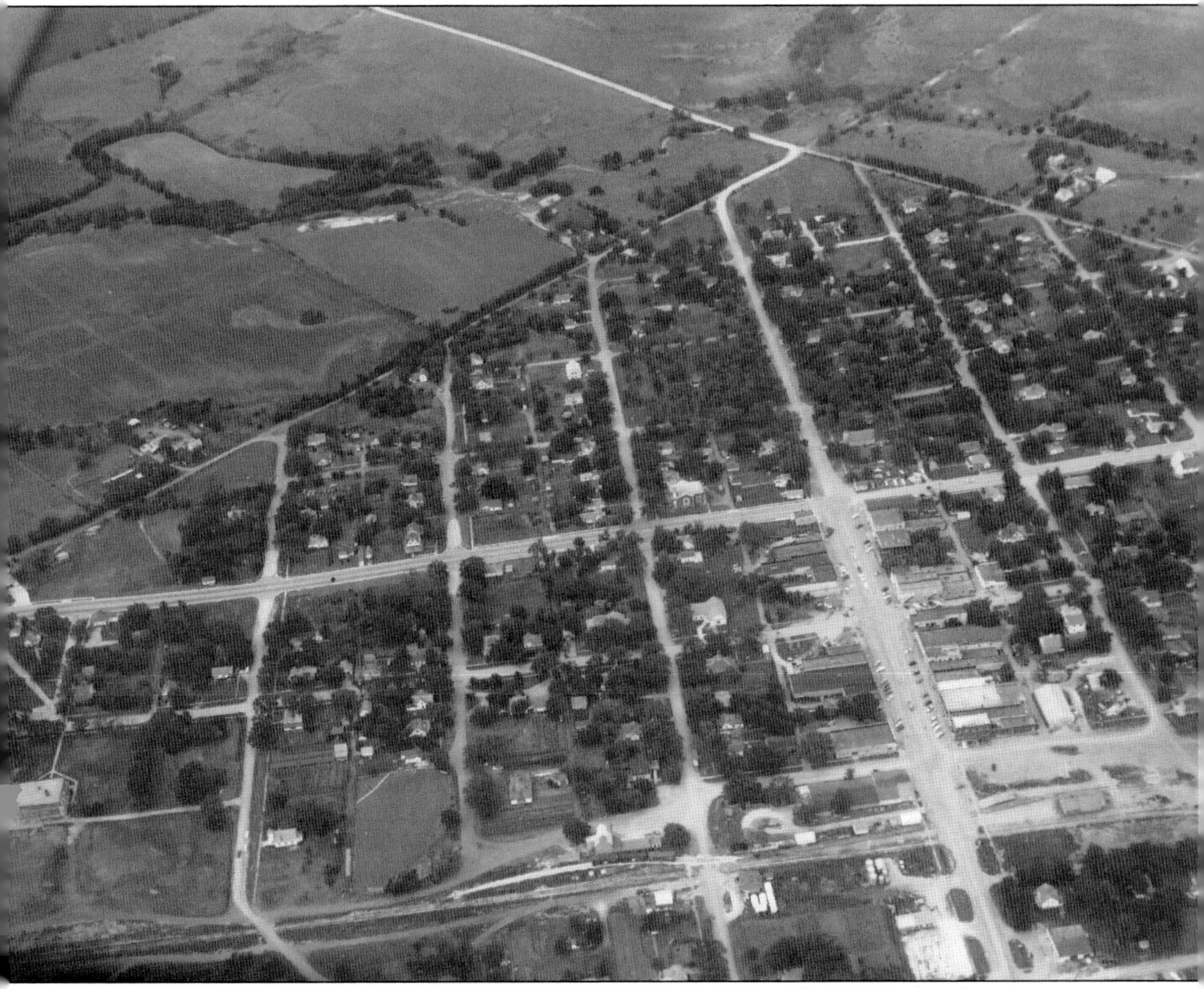

This c. 1955 aerial photograph of Eskridge was taken by longtime resident and aircraft enthusiast Dean Dunn. The Atchison, Topeka & Santa Fe railroad tracks can be seen running horizontally at the bottom of the photograph, with Main Street running vertically. The town was platted at a 45-degree angle, relative to the county section lines. The Manhattan, Alma & Burlingame Railway platted the town to run parallel to the railroad tracks as they passed through the area. As a point of reference, the old Eskridge Grade School is seen at the lower left corner of the photograph. (Courtesy Dean Dunn.)

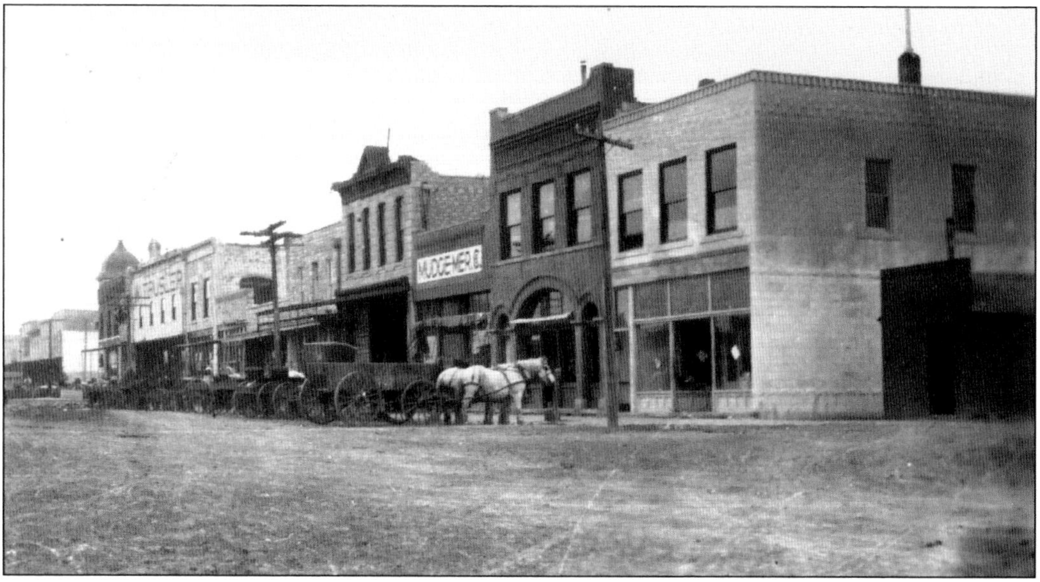

This early-1900s view of the west side of Main Street in Eskridge was taken before the 1913 fire that destroyed nine buildings. The Earl Building, ninth from the right, was the southernmost of the nine buildings destroyed by the fire; however, it was rebuilt and today houses the Eskridge Branch Library. (Courtesy Wabaunsee County Historical Society.)

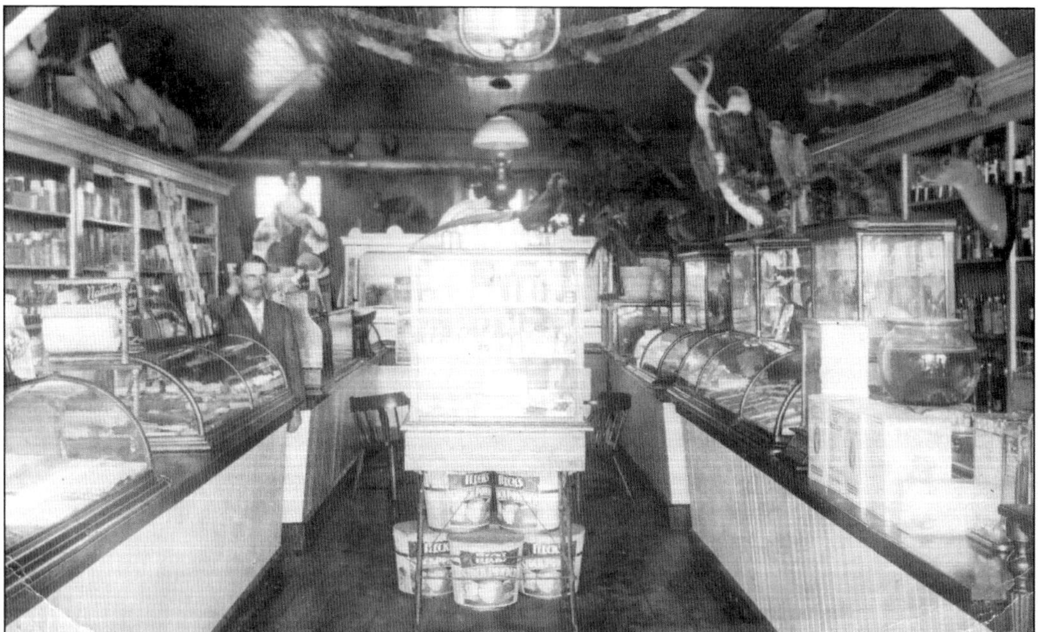

E.E. Brown's drugstore in Eskridge was the last example of a patent medicine drugstore in the town. It is believed to have been destroyed in the 1913 fire. One cannot help but also notice the prominent display of mounted wildlife in the store, including a bald eagle at the right. (Courtesy Greg Hoots.)

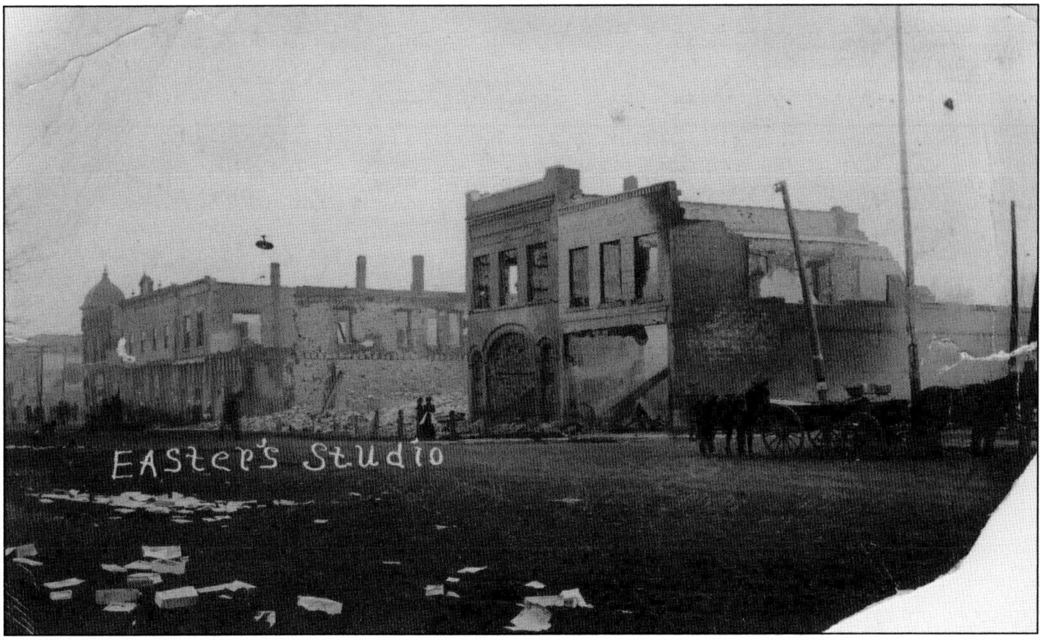

These two views by Easter Studio show the aftermath of the 1913 fire on Main Street in Eskridge. In the view above, at the far left of the image, one can see the new Waugh building, the old Waugh building, and the Trusler Building, the only three structures that were not gutted by the flames. The photograph below, an unusual view, shows the block destroyed by the fire in a view taken from the alley in the rear. The same section of this block was devastated by an earlier blaze in 1895, also burning all structures down to the Trusler Building. (Both, courtesy Inez Dunn)

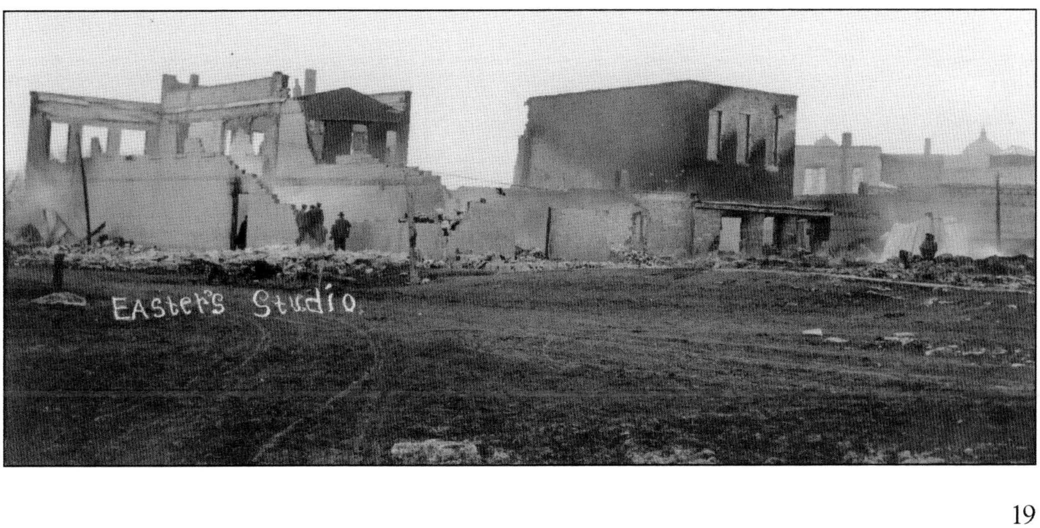

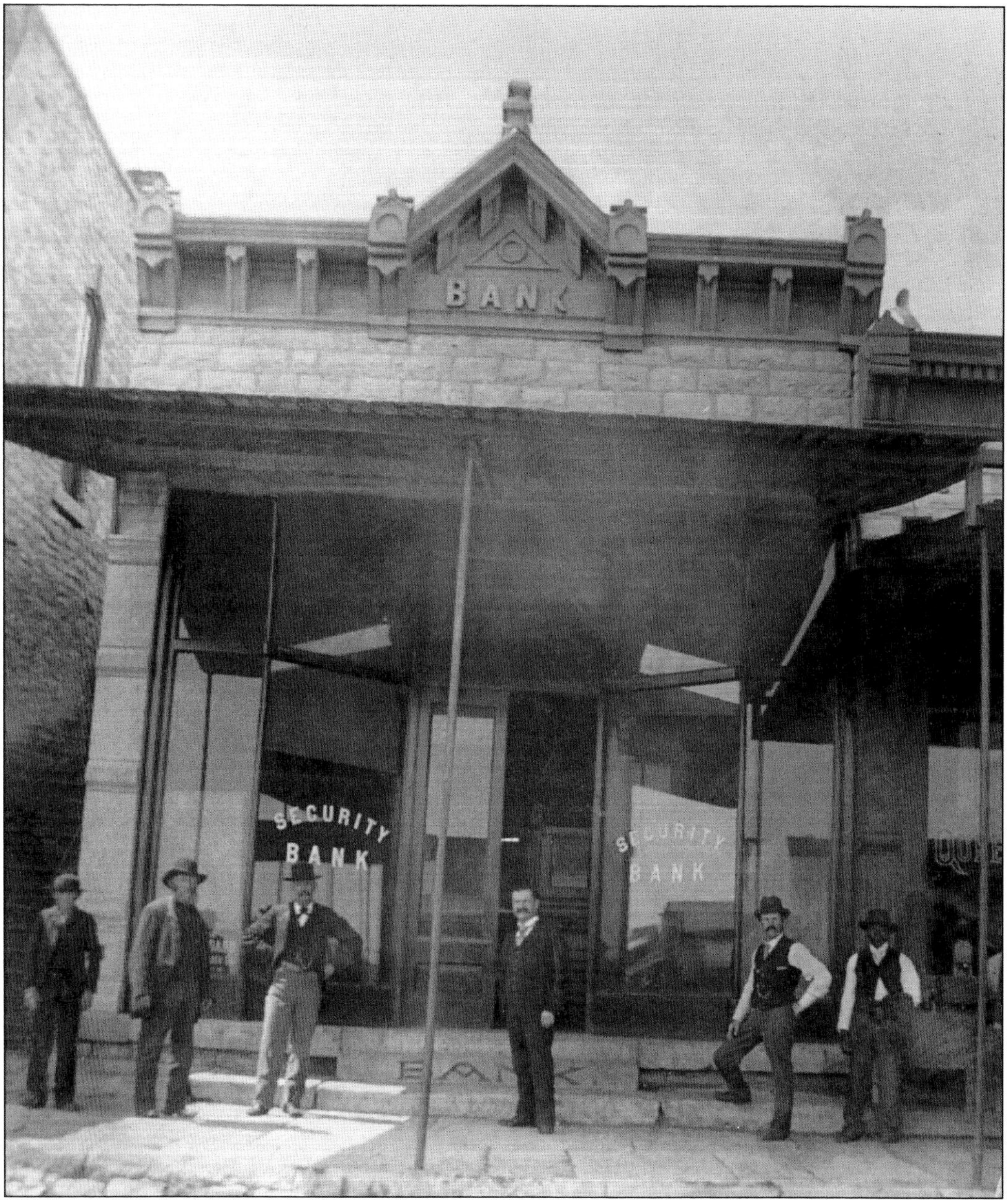

The Security Bank, seen here in the late 1880s, was located at 121 South Main Street in Eskridge. Founded by brothers John Y. Waugh and George G. Waugh in 1884, the bank became known as the Security State Bank by 1900. No one is identified in this photograph; however, the man standing in the center of the doorway is believed to be George Waugh. In this view, one can see Mattie Trivett's dry goods store, just to the left of the bank building. Trivett's store burned in late January 1906, and within days the Waugh brothers purchased her lot for $2,000 as a site for a new bank building. The Security State Bank merged with Eskridge State Bank in 1959 and moved all operations to the latter, at the north end of the block (see page 23). This building was refaced with brick after World War II and still stands today in Eskridge. (Courtesy Bruce Waugh.)

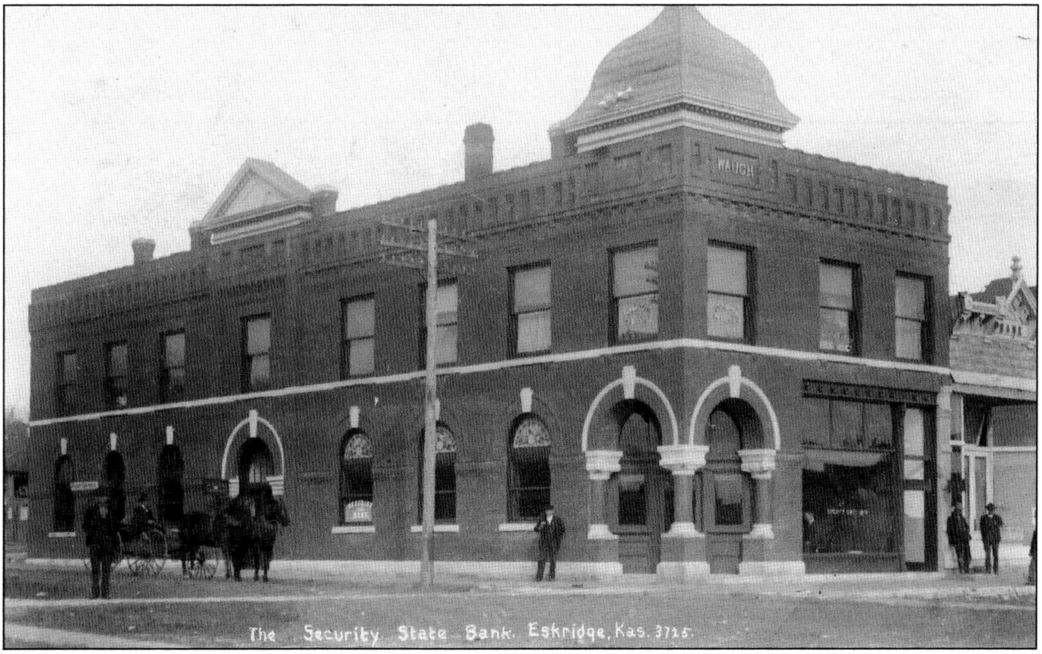

The Waugh Building has been a cornerstone of the Eskridge business district for over a century. When the building opened in November 1906, Dr. William Walker and a dentist, Dr. A.H. Reynard, established offices on the second floor. On November 1, 1906, the post office moved into the Waugh Building, where it remained until moving into a new structure across Main Street in 1962. (Courtesy Waugh Law Office.)

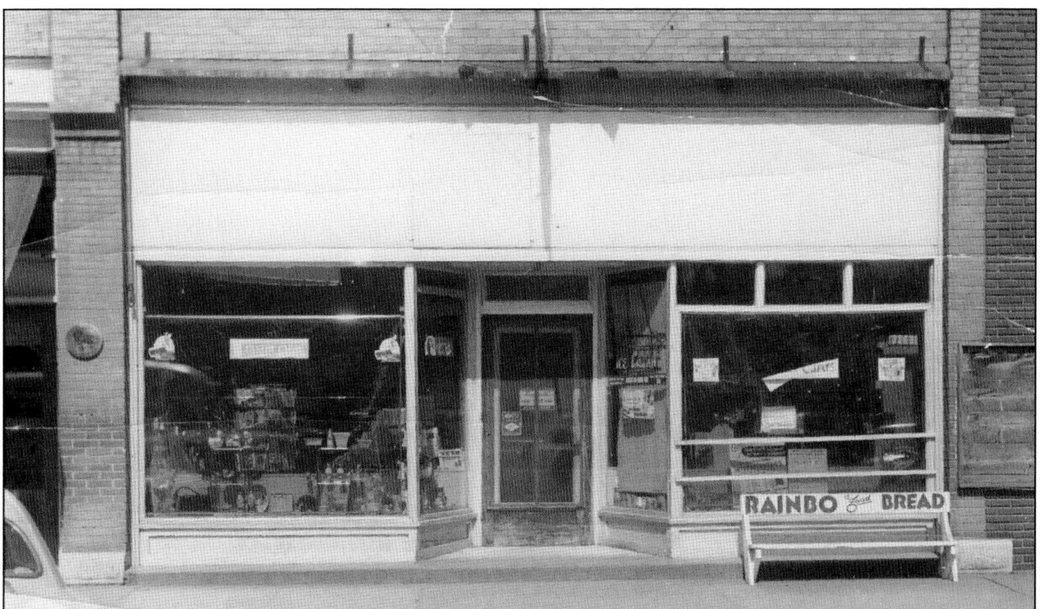

Preston Dunn's Rexall drugstore was located in this building at 111 South Main Street in Eskridge. Dunn had moved to Eskridge with his parents in 1898 as a five-year-old. He was Eskridge's first college-trained pharmacist, having graduated in 1915. After serving in World War I, Dunn returned to Eskridge and operated drugstores there for over 40 years. (Courtesy Dean Dunn.)

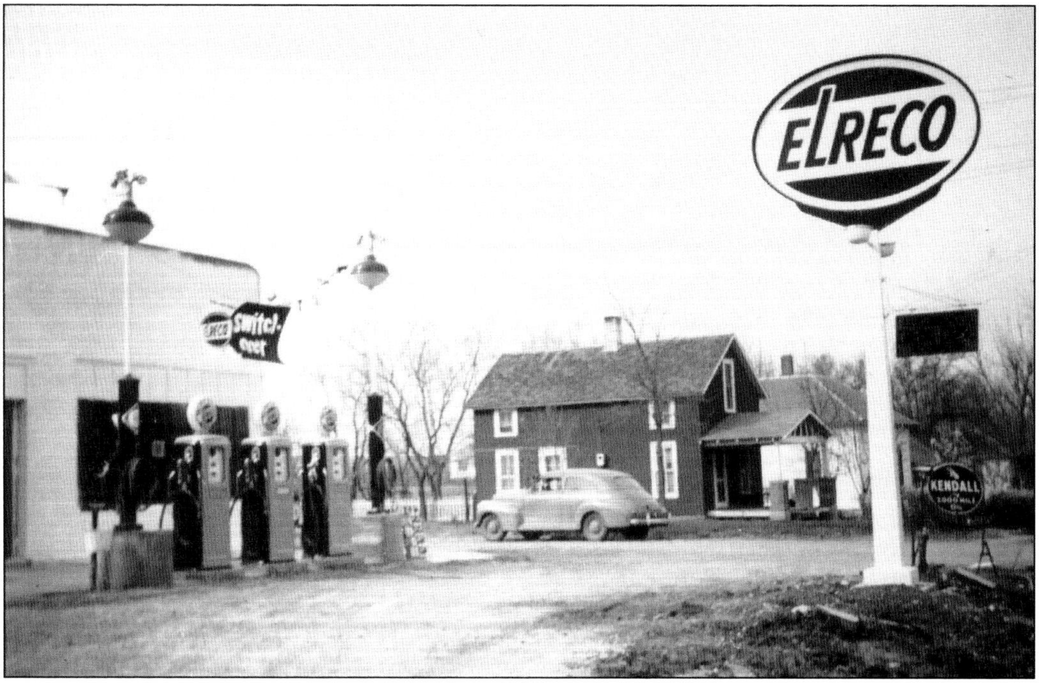

The Elreco station was located at 107 North Main Street in Eskridge and was owned by Robert Archer when this early 1955 photograph was taken. Later that same year, Dale and Hazel Kemp purchased the station and owned it for 55 years. Elreco was a brand owned by Eldorado Refinery Corporation, which was purchased by Fina Petroleum in the mid-1950s. (Courtesy Bob and Carol Kraus.)

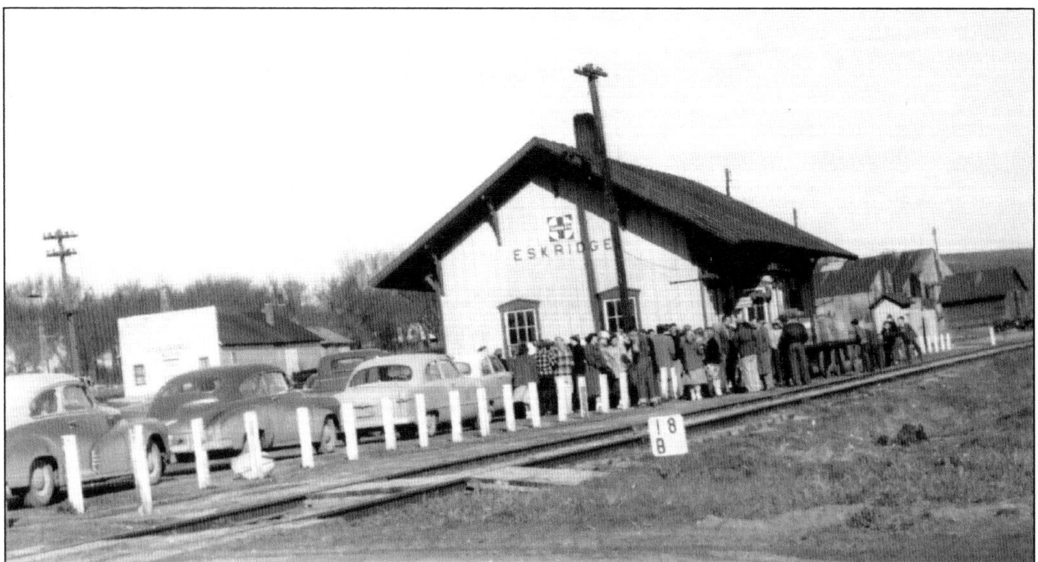

A crowd has gathered for the arrival of a train at the Atchison, Topeka & Santa Fe depot in Eskridge in this early 1950s photograph. The depot was located on the lot where the Flint Hills Bank of Eskridge sits today. To the left, one can see the Star Grange Building that stands today at First and Cedar Streets. (Courtesy Eskridge Branch Library.)

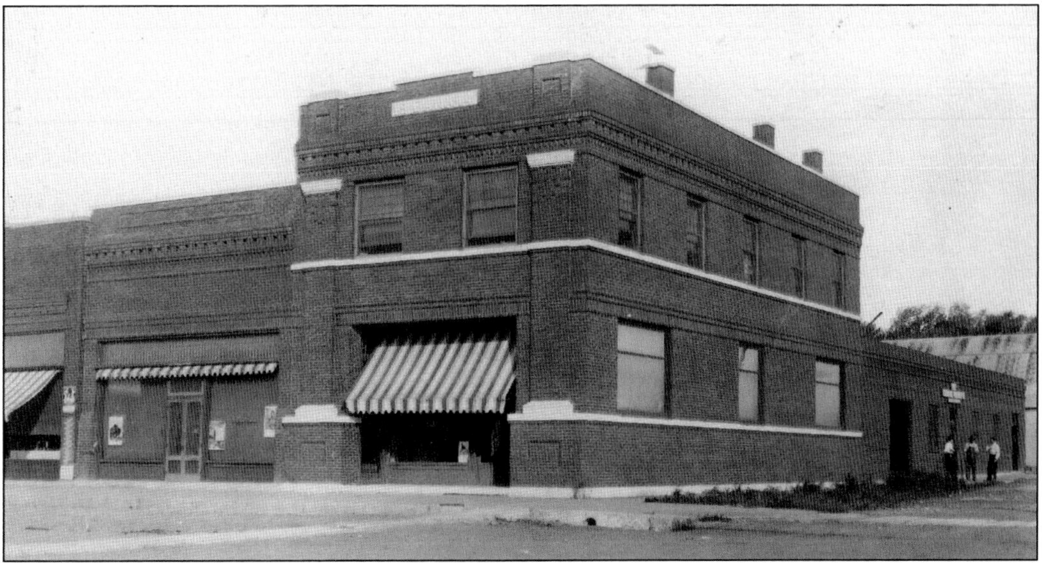

The Eskridge State Bank constructed this building in 1914 after fire destroyed their bank in 1913. Located at 101 South Main Street, the bank operated in this structure until it was declared insolvent in 1985. The Flint Hills Bank of Eskridge acquired the assets and liabilities of the failed institution. (Courtesy Bob and Carol Kraus.)

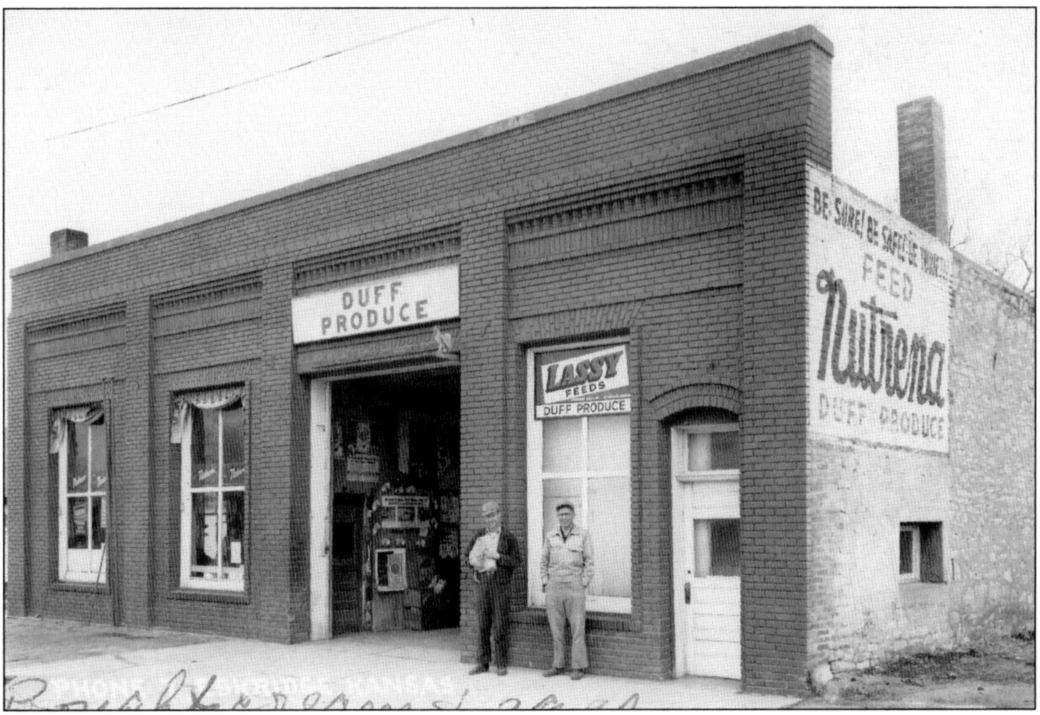

Duff Produce was located at 100 South Main Street on the lot where an early Eskridge hotel had once stood. In this c. 1925 view, Dale Shawgo and Warren Duff are seen standing in front of the business that marketed produce and feed. In the 1930s, Duff sold gasoline at a pump in front of the building. Currently, the structure is a warehouse for Eskridge Lumber Company. (Courtesy Bob and Carol Kraus.)

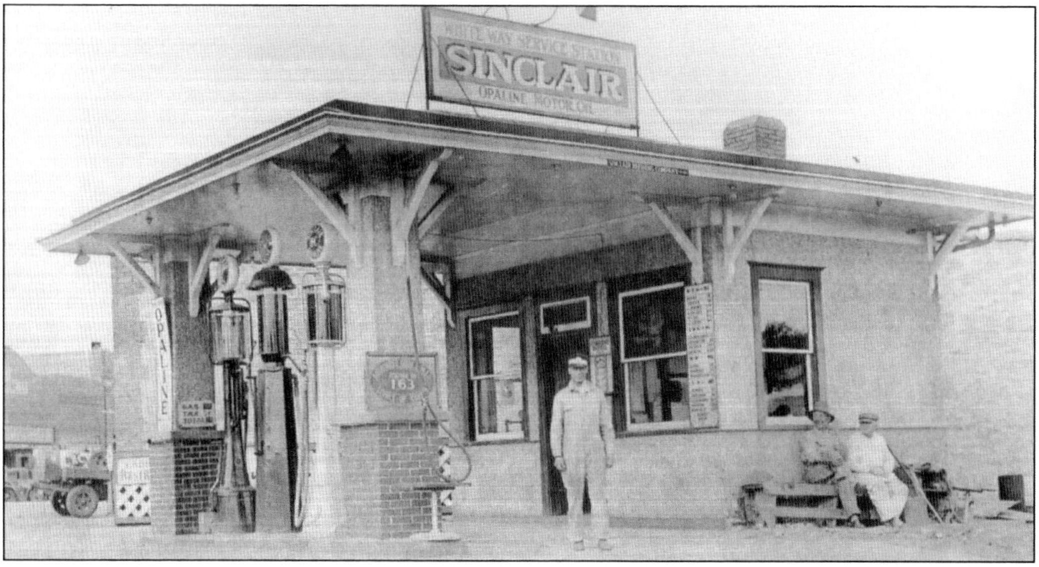

Cloice Meeker is seen standing in front of his Sinclair Station, located at 122 Main Street in Eskridge, with two unidentified men resting on a bench. The Sinclair station was located directly across from the Waugh Building and north across Second Avenue from Wall's Standard Station. This station was demolished in 1962 to make way for the new post office. (Courtesy Wayne Johnson.)

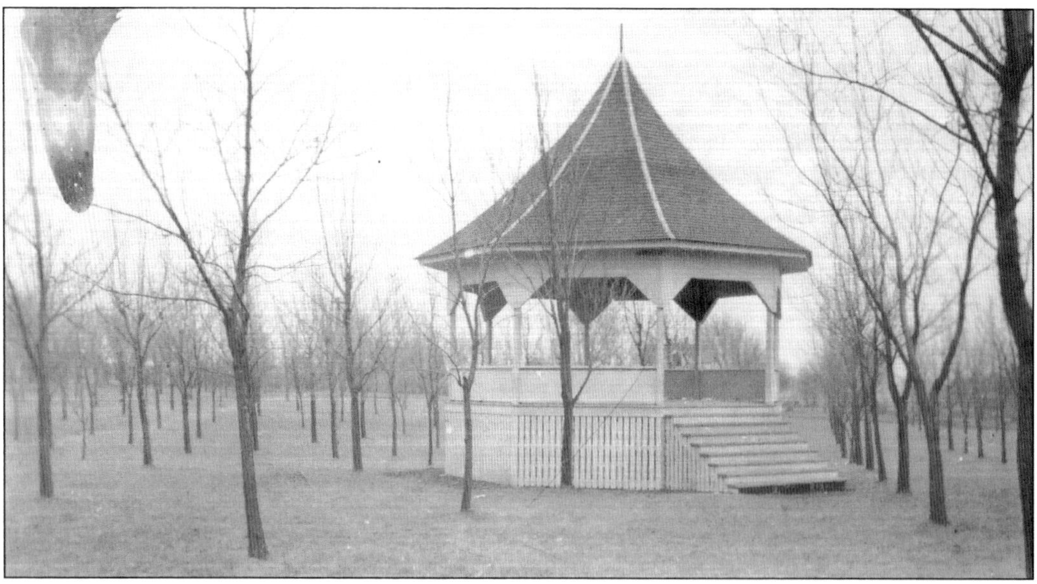

The city park has been located in the 400 block of Main Street in Eskridge for the last century on land donated by John Y. Waugh, who built a home across the street. The gazebo bandstand is seen in this c. 1910 real-photo postcard along with many newly planted trees. The gazebo still stands today, along with a new Veteran's Memorial on the Pine Street side of the park. (Courtesy Greg Hoots.)

This c. 1950 view of Main Street in Eskridge looks to the north from Third Avenue. K-4 Highway was a brick street as it passed through Eskridge. In 1950, there were three car dealerships, five gas stations, two grocery stores, and a hardware store on Main Street. (Courtesy Dean Dunn.)

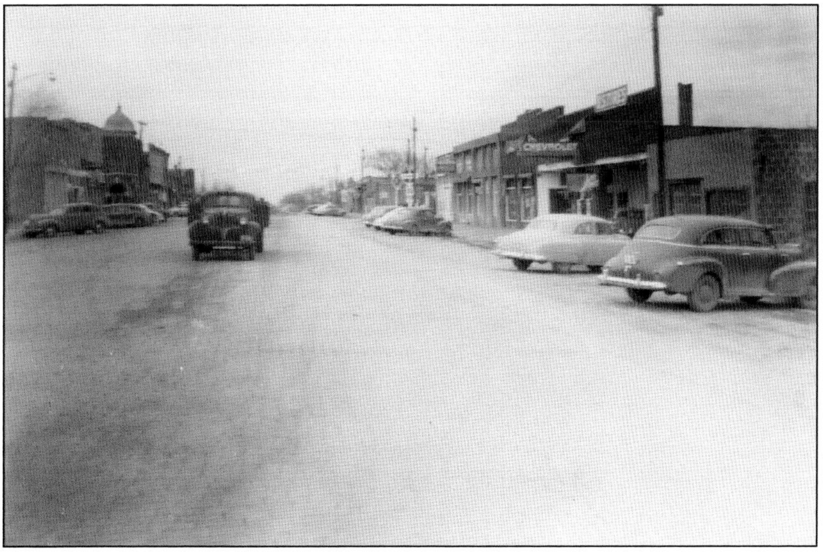

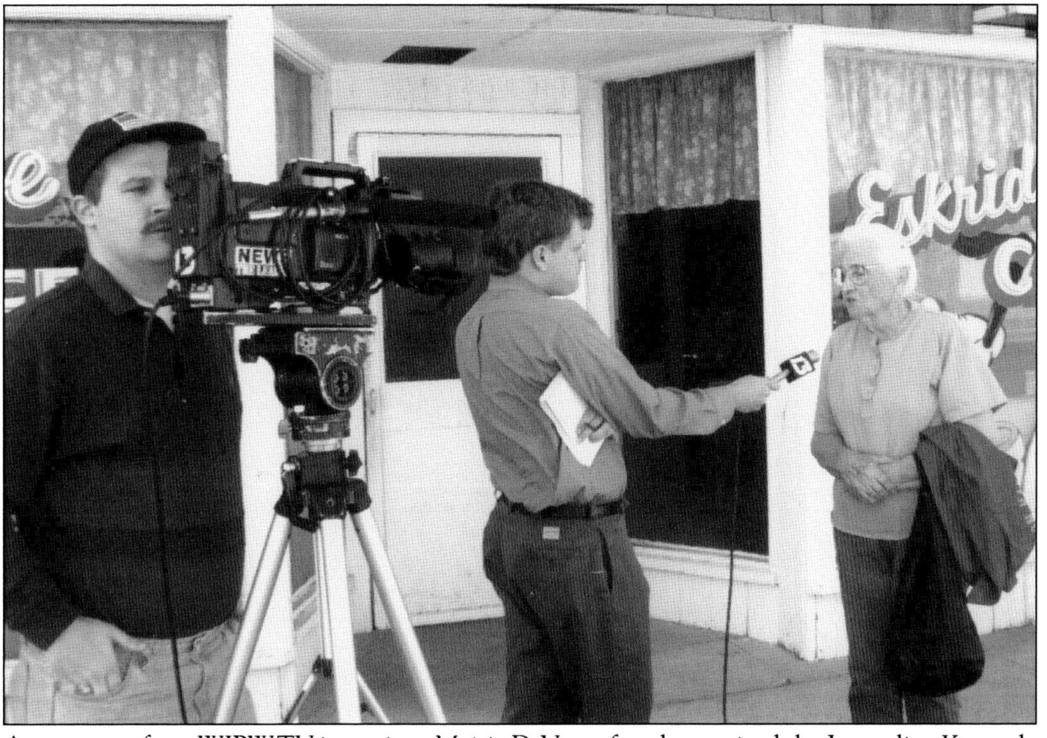

A news crew from WIBW-TV interviews Maisie DeVore after she received the Jacqueline Kennedy Onassis Award from the Jefferson Awards for Public Service for her efforts to construct a city swimming pool in Eskridge. DeVore collected over six million aluminum cans to raise money to construct the pool. To honor DeVore, the Kansas Department of Transportation renamed K-4 Highway in Wabaunsee County Maisie DeVore Highway on July 14, 2009. (Courtesy Benetta Foster.)

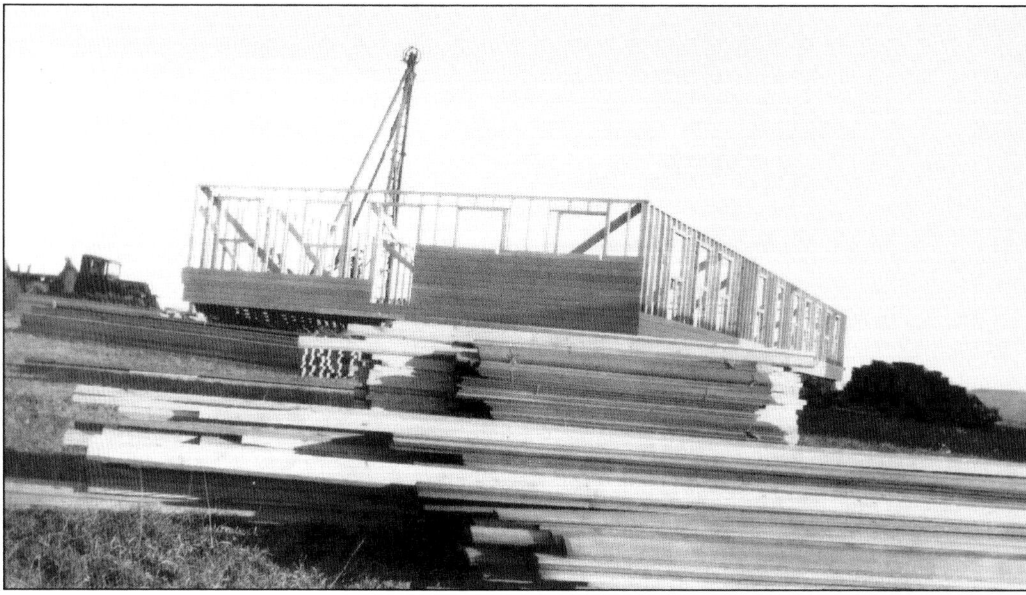

In this December 1933 photograph, workers from Rinner Construction Company, Topeka, constructed the first barracks buildings at the Kansas Economic Recovery Committee's Lake Wabaunsee transient work camp. In early 1934, the first KERC workers arrived to occupy these buildings while doing site preparation for the lake. In August 1935, the camp closed, and in January 1936 the Works Progress Administration assumed control of the lake construction project. (Courtesy Wabaunsee County Historical Society.)

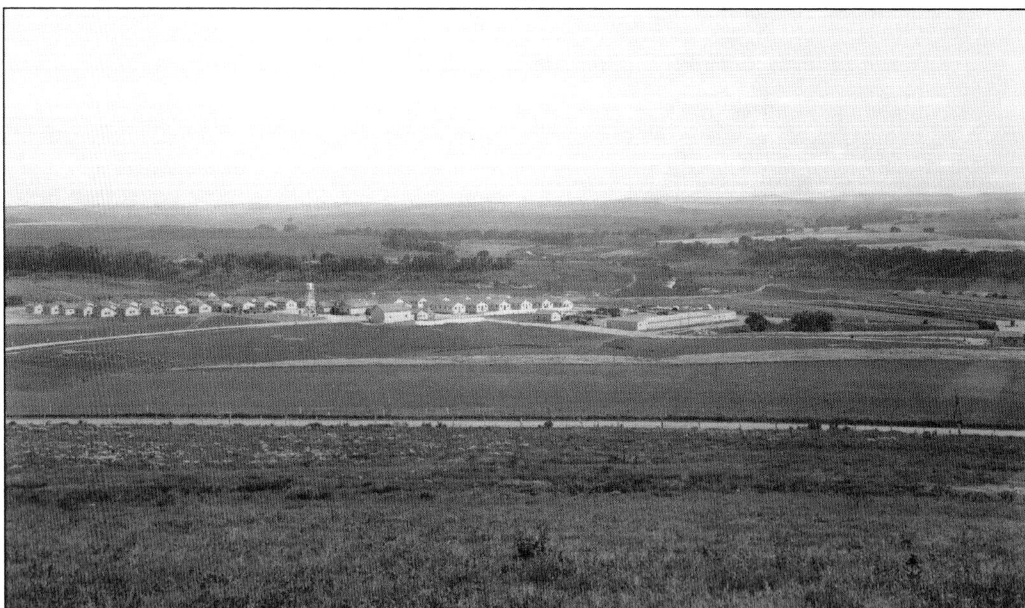

Nearly 60 buildings filled the Lake Wabaunsee camp operated by the Works Progress Administration as it assumed control of the project in January 1936. In this view from summer 1936, heavy machinery can be seen behind the complex grading the lakebed. On December 31, 1936, the dam construction was complete. By October 1937, fish were being stocked in the lake. (Courtesy Kansas State Historical Society.)

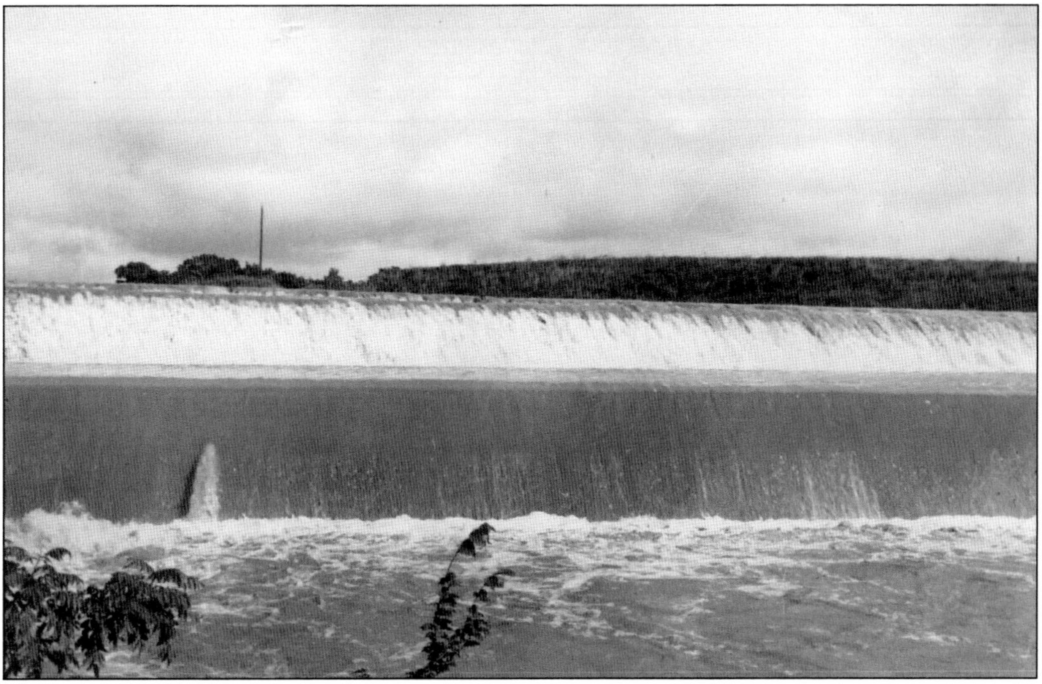

On June 12, 1941, heavy rains filled Lake Wabaunsee for the first time, sending water over the road at the spillway and into the overflow at the south branch of Mill Creek. Floodwaters damaged the hand-laid rock spillway many times over the years until it was replaced in 1999. (Courtesy Dean Dunn.)

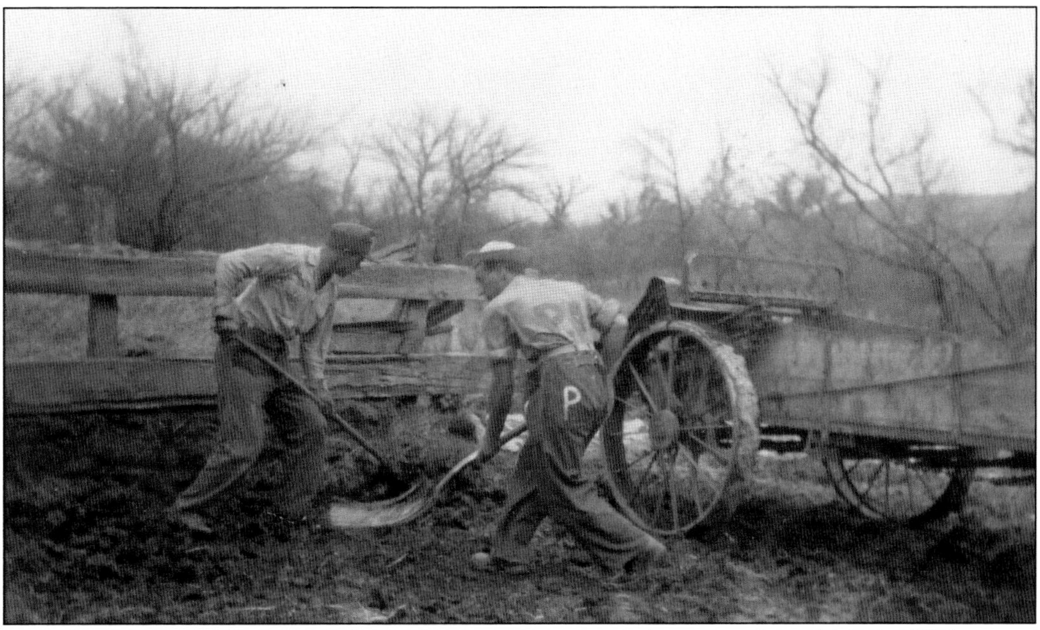

German prisoners of war were housed at work camp no. 5, operated at the Lake Wabaunsee barracks from July 1, 1944, until December 1, 1945. Prisoners were used as labor for area farmers as well as for county road and bridge crews. Here, two unidentified prisoners shovel manure into a spreader on a Wabaunsee County ranch. (Courtesy Wabaunsee County Extension Service.)

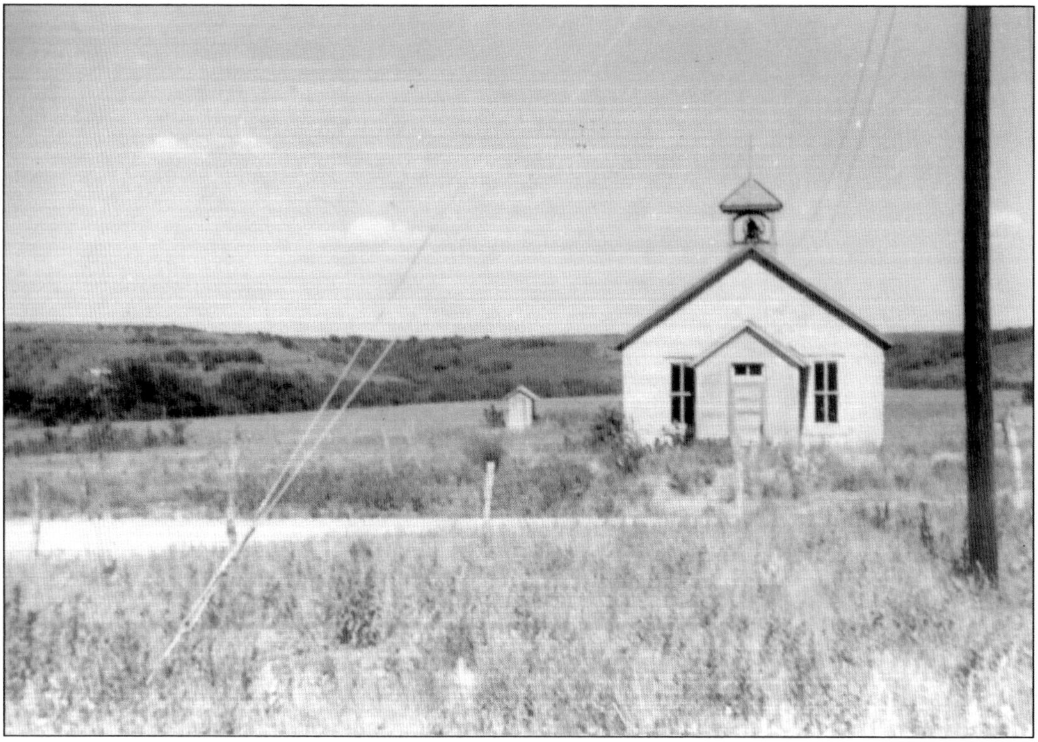

School district 45, also known as the Sunbeam School, was located at the junction of K-99 and K-4 Highways, nine miles south of Alma. The Kansas Department of Transportation maintains a supply depot at this location today. (Courtesy Wabaunsee County Historical Society.)

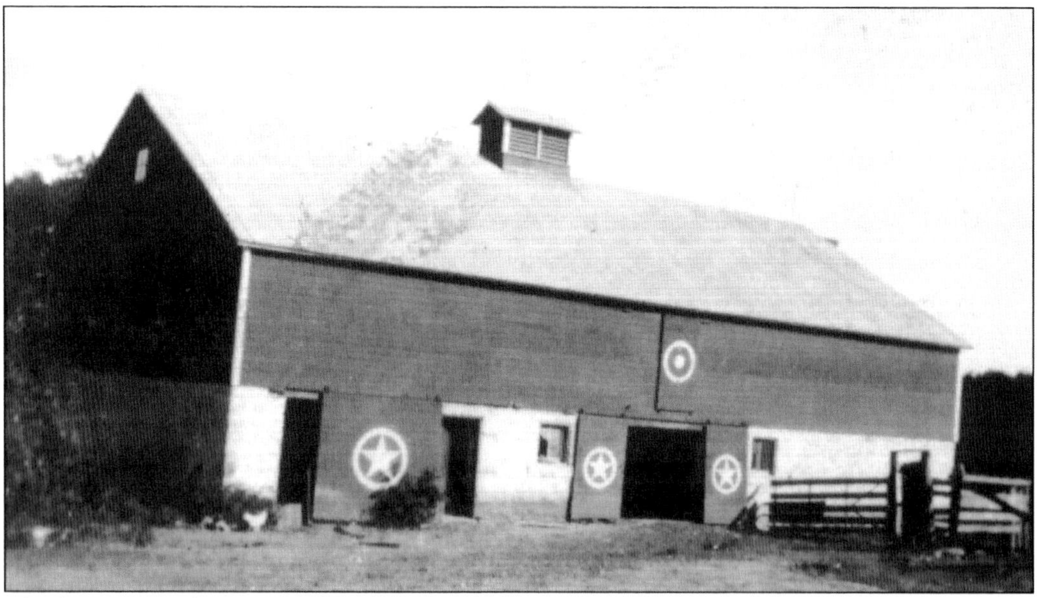

This barn sits on the east side of K-99 Highway, approximately four miles north of the K-4 Highway junction, on the Fred Steinmeyer farm. Constructed around 1900, the barn shared a paint scheme with the Sump barn located 2.5 miles to the north. Another view of this barn is seen on page 118. (Courtesy Keith Schultz.)

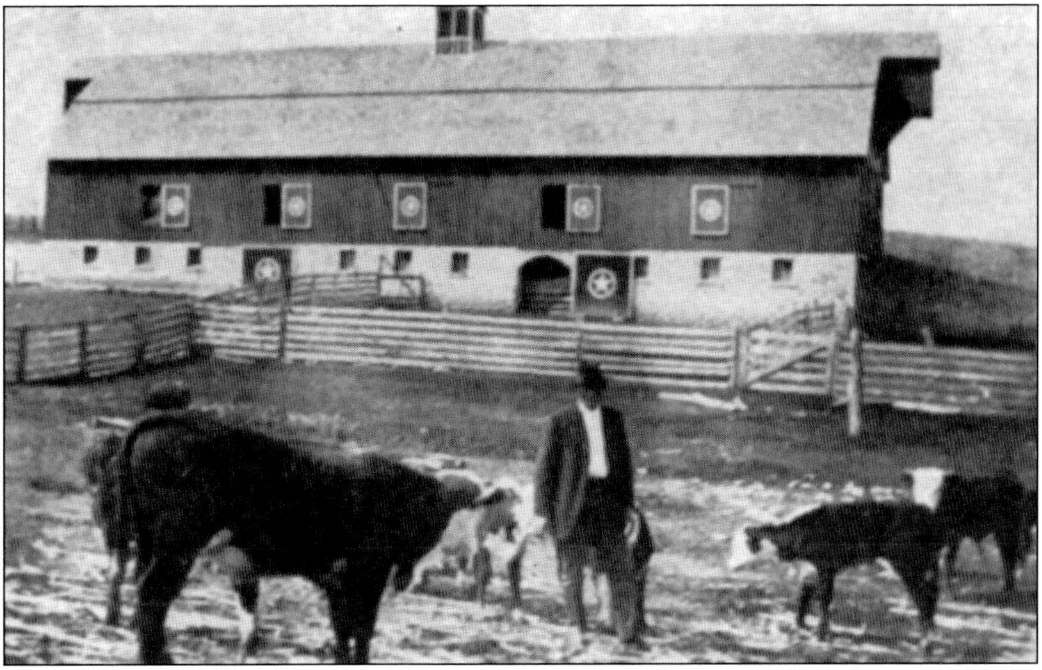

Henry Sump is seen in front of his barn located on the east side of K-99 Highway, two miles south of Alma. Built in 1905, the barn is constructed of solid walnut, milled on the site. Likewise, the foundation is made of native cut limestone. Sump died at his ranch in 1920, struck by lightning while driving a team of horses pulling a manure spreader. (Courtesy Wabaunsee County Historical Society.)

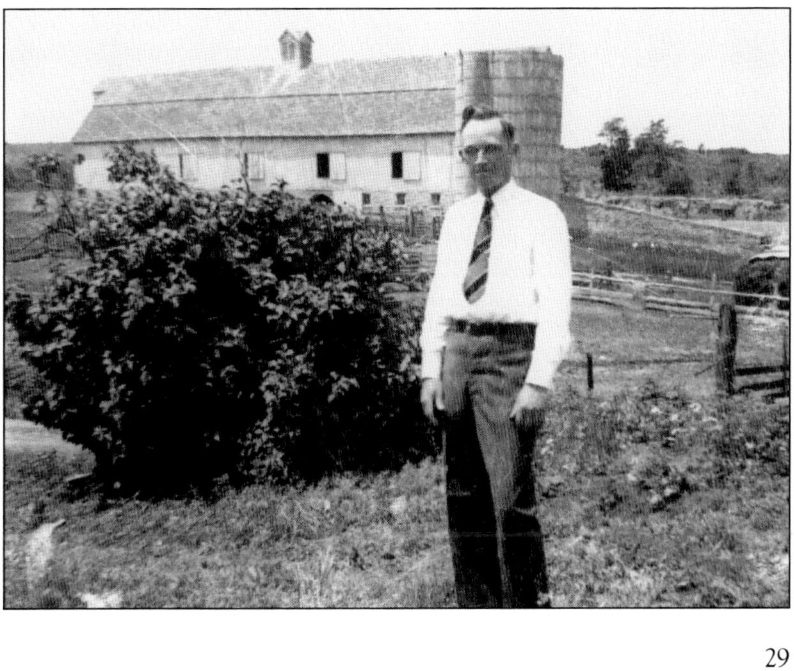

Galyn Gronquist is seen in this spring 1942 photograph just prior to his overseas tour with the Army Air Force. The Sump barn is painted white in this image. Sometime after this photograph was taken, owner Fannie Thowe had the barn repainted with the familiar red-with-white-stars design. (Courtesy Juanita TenEyck.)

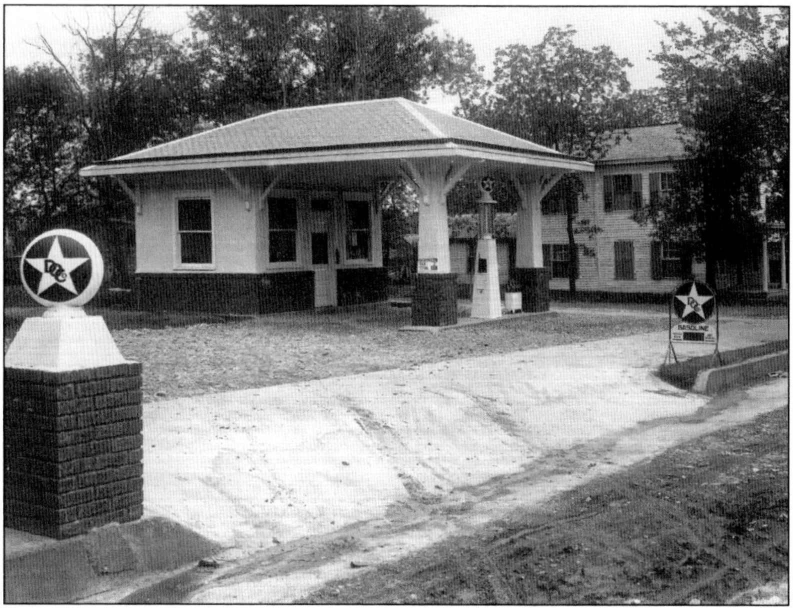

This gas station, located at 200 Missouri Street in Alma, sold Derby Oil Company products at the time of this 1920s photograph. Derby Oil Company, based in Wichita, Kansas, was a popular brand in the Midwest. The station was one of a half-dozen places that sold gasoline in Alma in the 1920s. (Courtesy Kansas State Historical Society.)

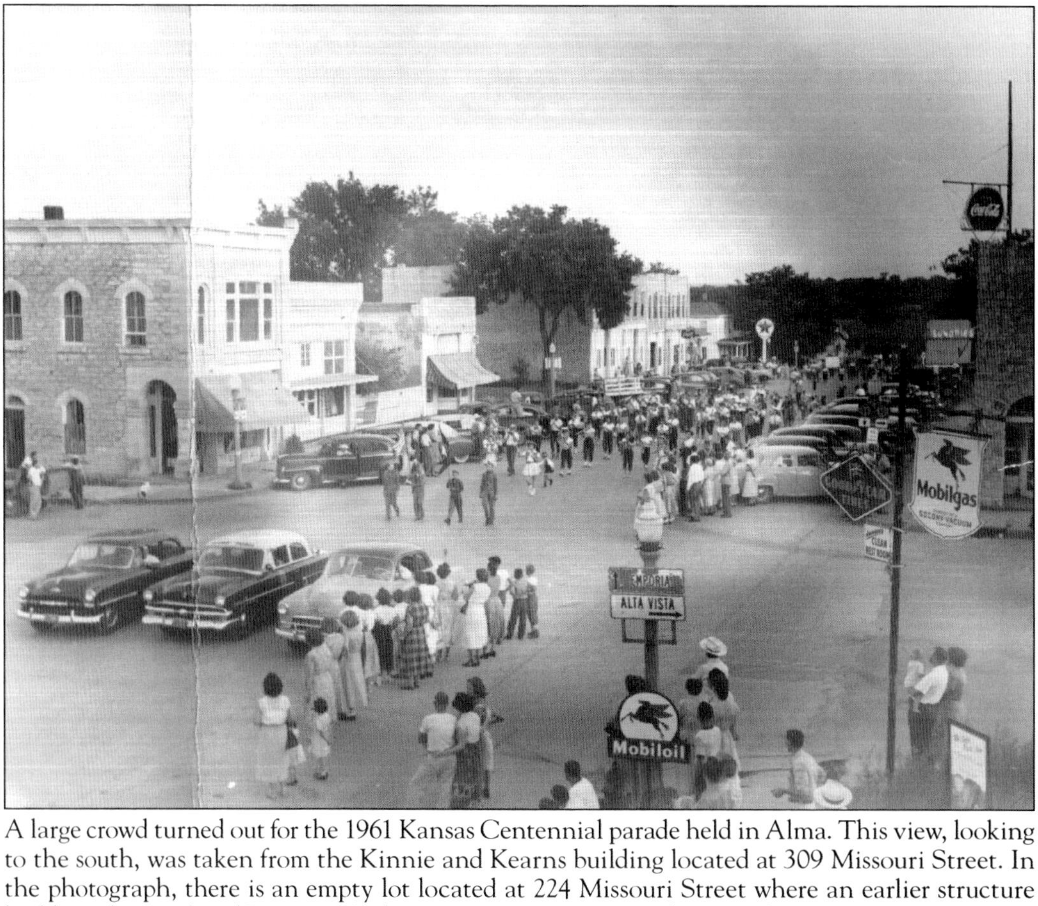

A large crowd turned out for the 1961 Kansas Centennial parade held in Alma. This view, looking to the south, was taken from the Kinnie and Kearns building located at 309 Missouri Street. In the photograph, there is an empty lot located at 224 Missouri Street where an earlier structure had been lost to fire. (Courtesy Wabaunsee County Historical Society.)

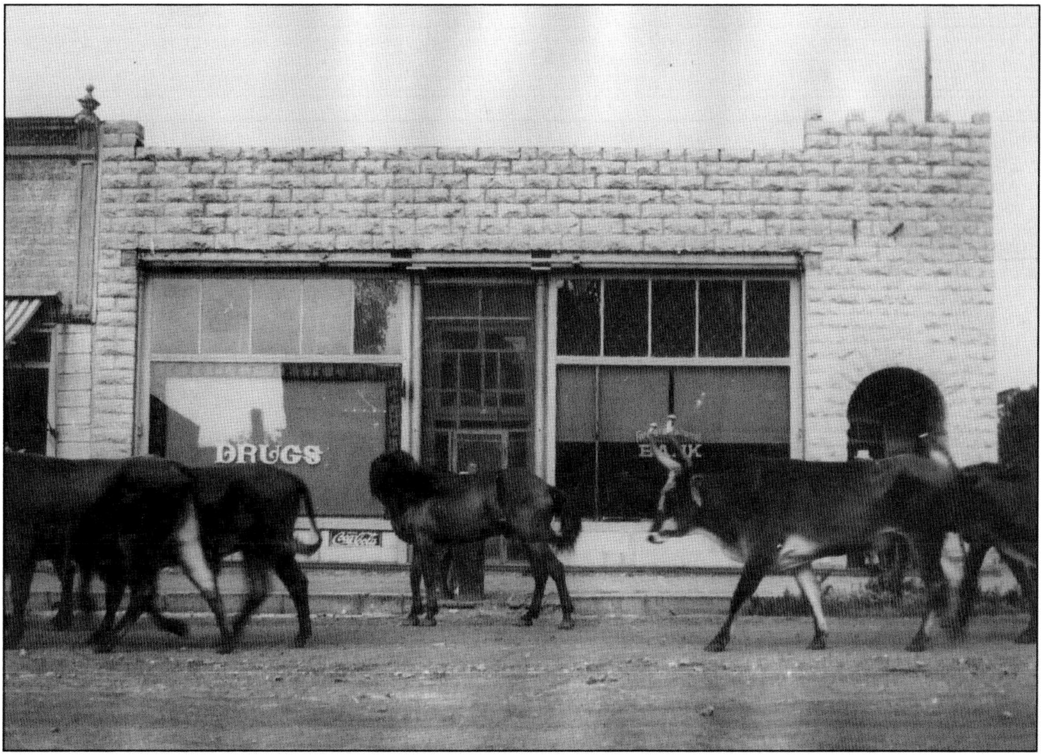

This view of Johnson's Drug Store and the Farmer's National Bank dates to the early 1920s. It was not uncommon for cattle, and in this case a horse, to be driven down K-99 Highway through the center of town. Today, this building is occupied by the Wabaunsee County Historical Museum. (Courtesy Janet Wertzberger.)

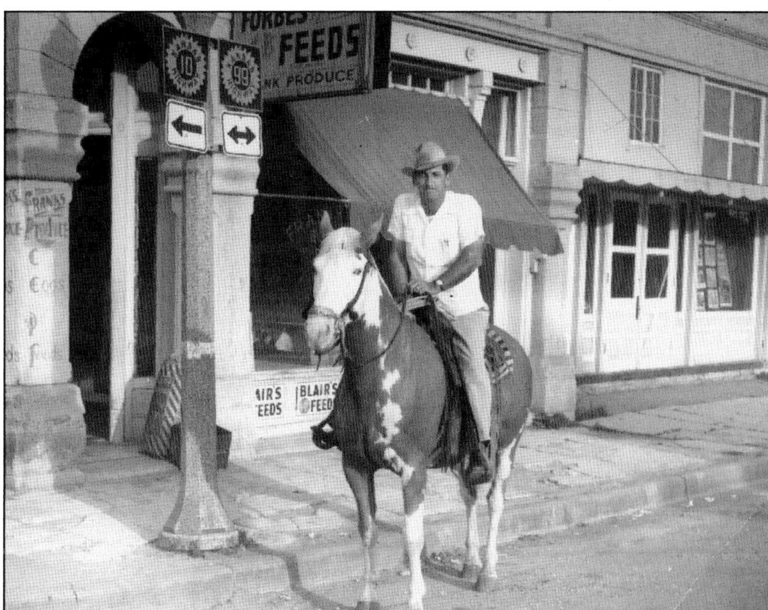

Clarence "Buffalo" Frank is seen on his horse, Checkers, in front of Frank's Produce, located at 226 Missouri Street in Alma. Frank and his wife, Roberta, opened the produce business in 1945, operating in what is now commonly known as the Palenske Hall building until his death in 1964. Frank was also elected to four terms as Wabaunsee County Sheriff. (Courtesy Dorothy Kemble.)

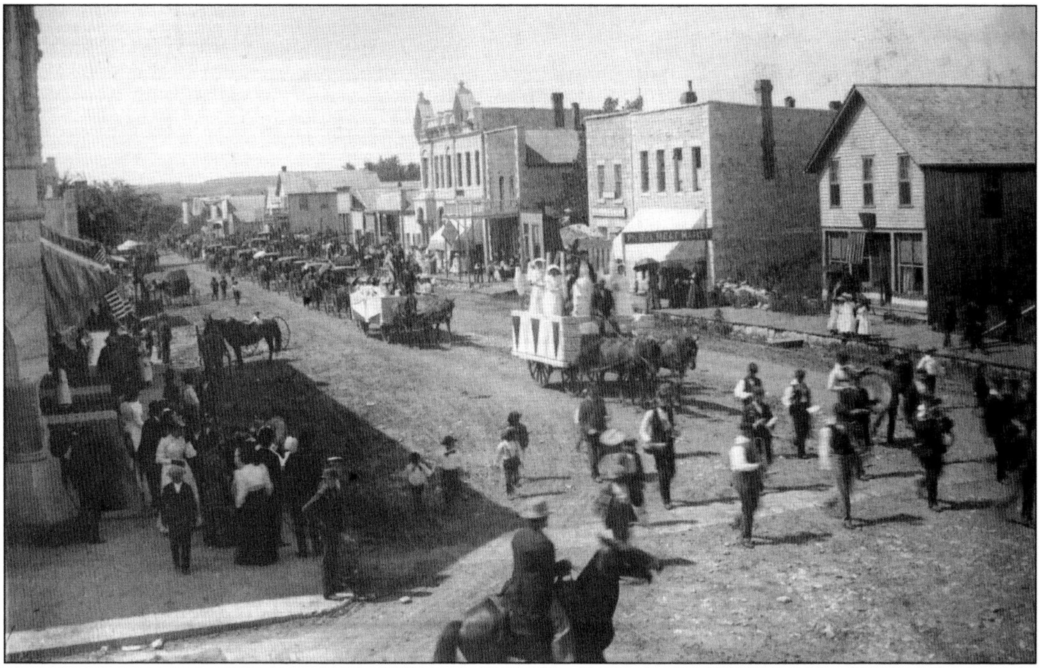

This parade photograph was taken from the balcony of the Brandt Hotel, looking to the south down Missouri Street. A frame structure stands at the far right of the image where the Hochhans Building would be erected in 1910. Also, one can see that the building at 315 Missouri Street had yet to succumb to fire before being reconstructed by Hal Weaver in 1906. (Courtesy Wabaunsee County Historical Society.)

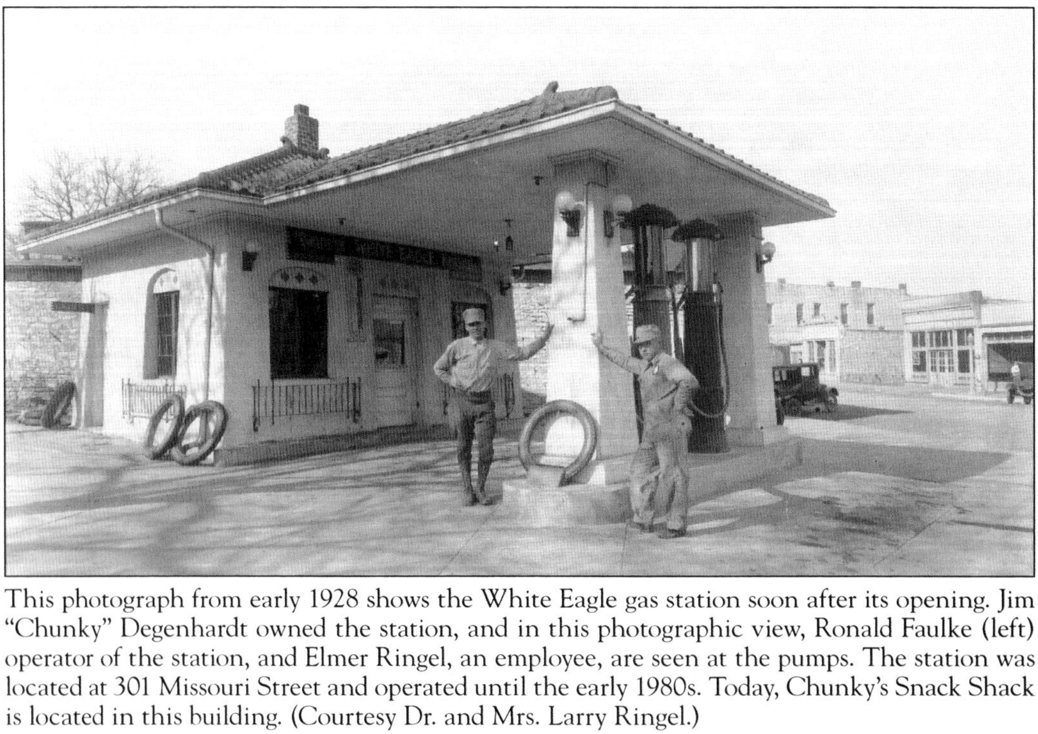

This photograph from early 1928 shows the White Eagle gas station soon after its opening. Jim "Chunky" Degenhardt owned the station, and in this photographic view, Ronald Faulke (left) operator of the station, and Elmer Ringel, an employee, are seen at the pumps. The station was located at 301 Missouri Street and operated until the early 1980s. Today, Chunky's Snack Shack is located in this building. (Courtesy Dr. and Mrs. Larry Ringel.)

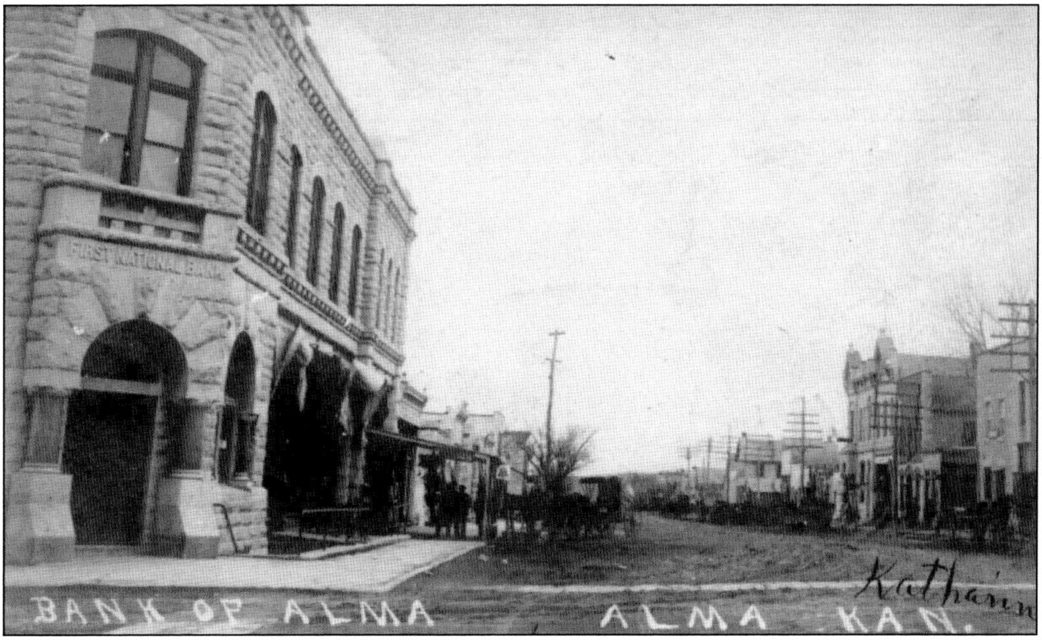

This view of Missouri Street in Alma looks south from Fourth Street. One can see the entrances to the basement "underground" below the bank building at 326 Missouri Street. The streets were still dirt, although limestone crosswalks appear to have been installed at the intersections in this c. 1905 view. The first Wabaunsee County Courthouse, at 227 Missouri Street, is still standing. (Courtesy Dr. and Mrs. Larry Ringel.)

These buildings at 303–305 Missouri Street, rarely photographed, are seen as they are being destroyed by fire in 1977. Meseke's Plumbing, left, and the Fast Wash Laundromat were destroyed by a fire that erupted in a machine at the laundry. Miraculously, the neighboring Kinne and Kearns Building was undamaged. These structures were a total loss and razed after the fire. (Courtesy Maurice Meseke.)

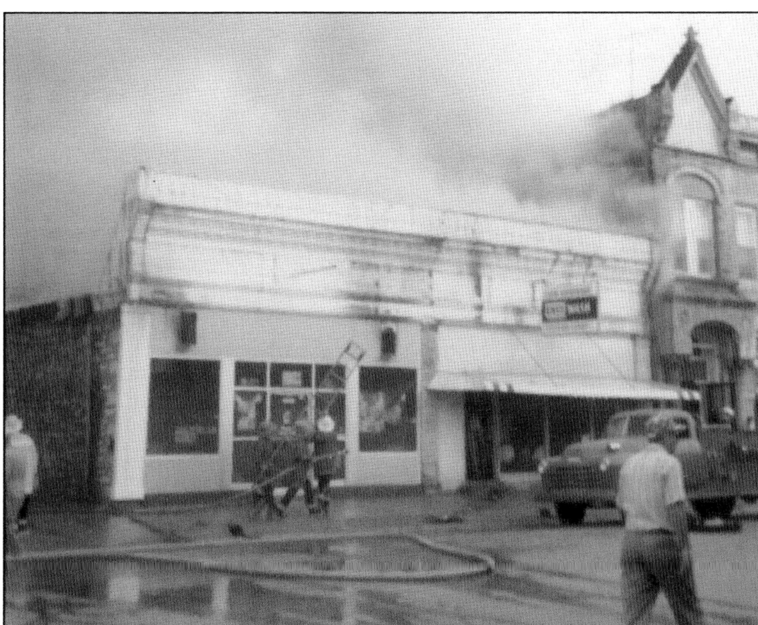

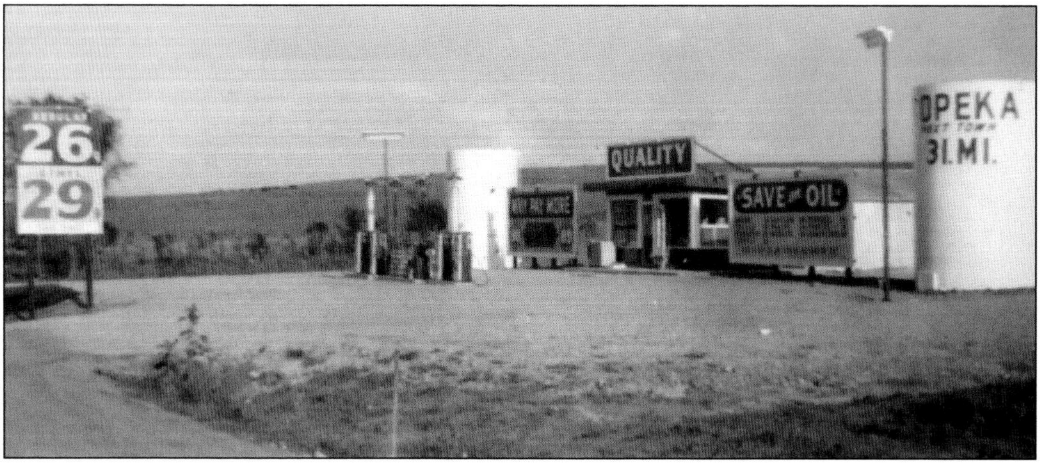

Jack Ginder built this gas station three miles north of Alma on old Highway 40 in the late 1940s. One of the many Quality gas stations that Ginder owned in northeast Kansas, this business was razed and replaced with a new Quality station on Highway 99 when Interstate 70 was constructed in the 1950s. Jim Lewis operated both stations for over 30 years. (Courtesy Linda Coon.)

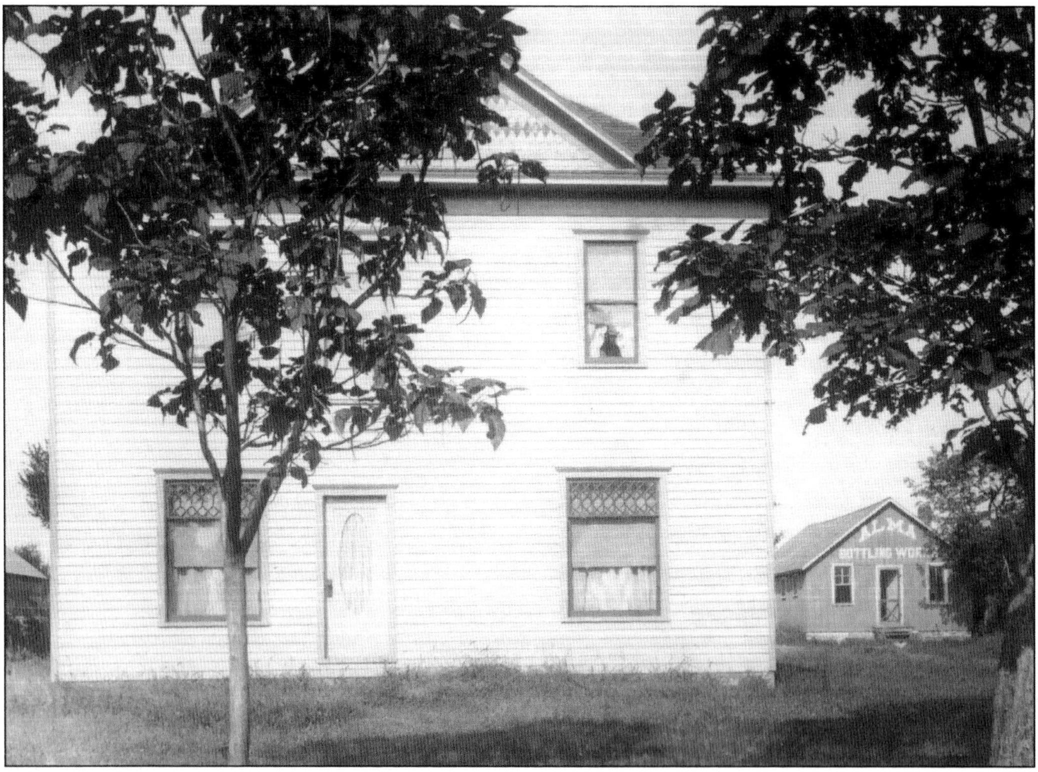

The home of James and Dorthea Barger, located at 1021 Ohio Street in Alma, is seen in this 1900s photograph. The Alma Bottling Works building was located in the backyard. The Bargers operated the bottling works for many years prior to World War II. After the war, the bottling works building was demolished and a chicken house shed constructed on the site. (Courtesy Wabaunsee County Historical Society.)

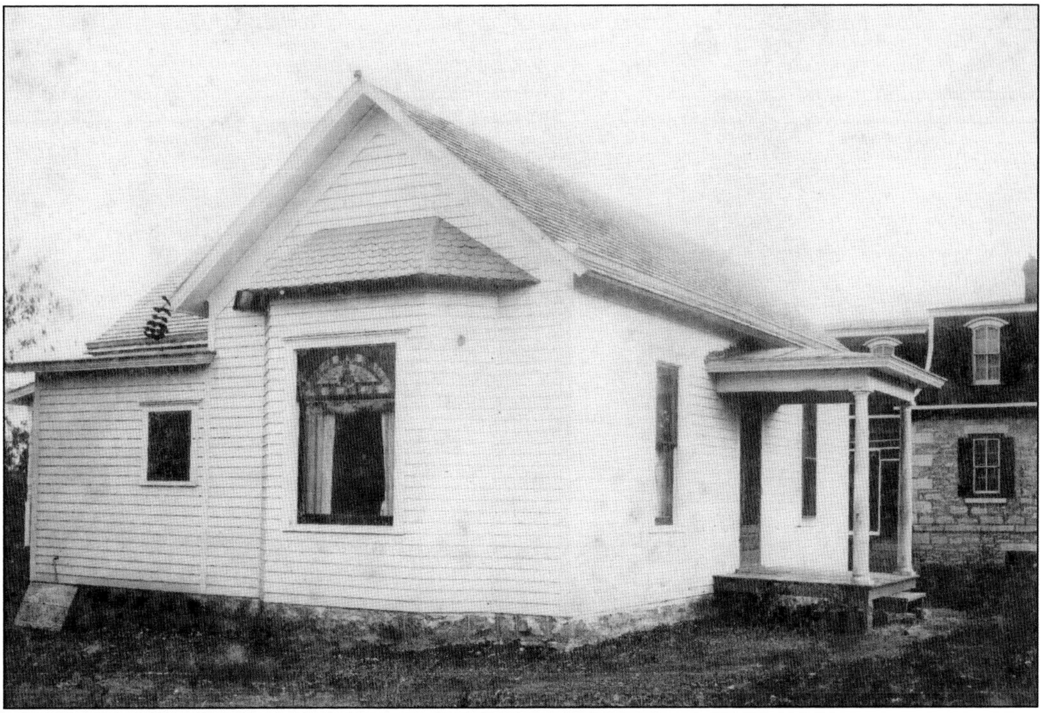

Above, this house is located at the southeast corner of Kansas Avenue and First Street in Alma and east of Holy Family Church; the home faces the west. Despite its small size, the house featured a stained glass window on the north side. Below, this residence is located at 222 West First Street just to the west of the Holy Family Church. Barbara Schubert and her two children are seen at the front of the house. For many years, Schubert's grandson Charles Herman lived here. (Above, courtesy Wabaunsee County Historical Society; below, courtesy Charles Herman.)

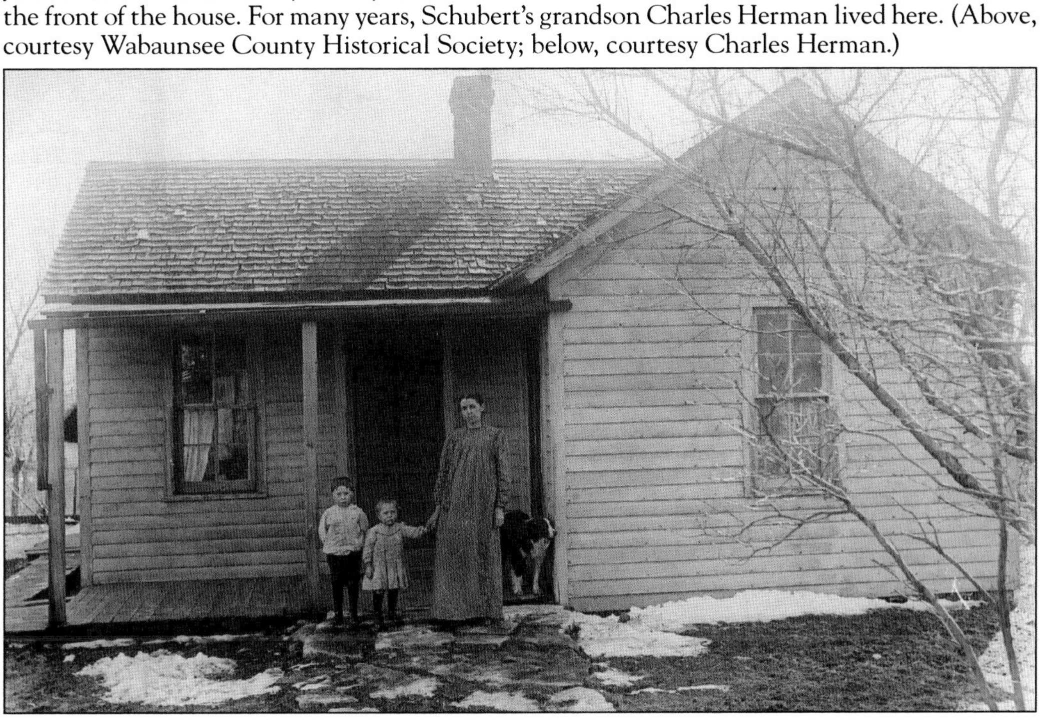

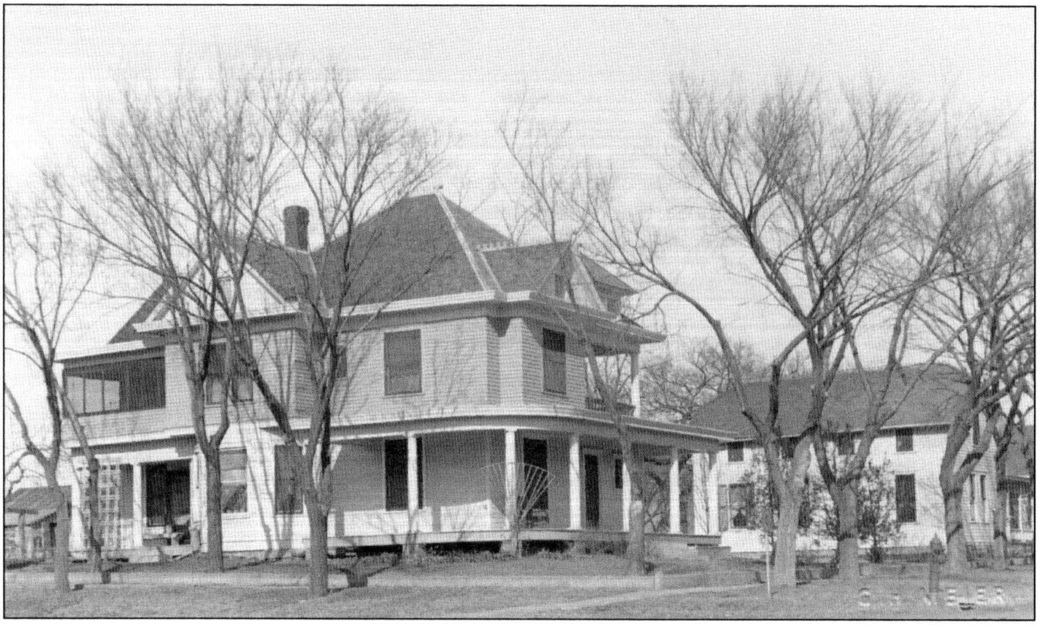

This spacious house is located at the northwest corner of Third Street and Kansas Avenue. The residence had four bedrooms on the second floor with additional rooms in the third-floor attic. For many years, this was the home of Alma attorney Bill Baldock and his family. This Gus Meier photograph dates from about 1920. (Courtesy Paul Gronquist.)

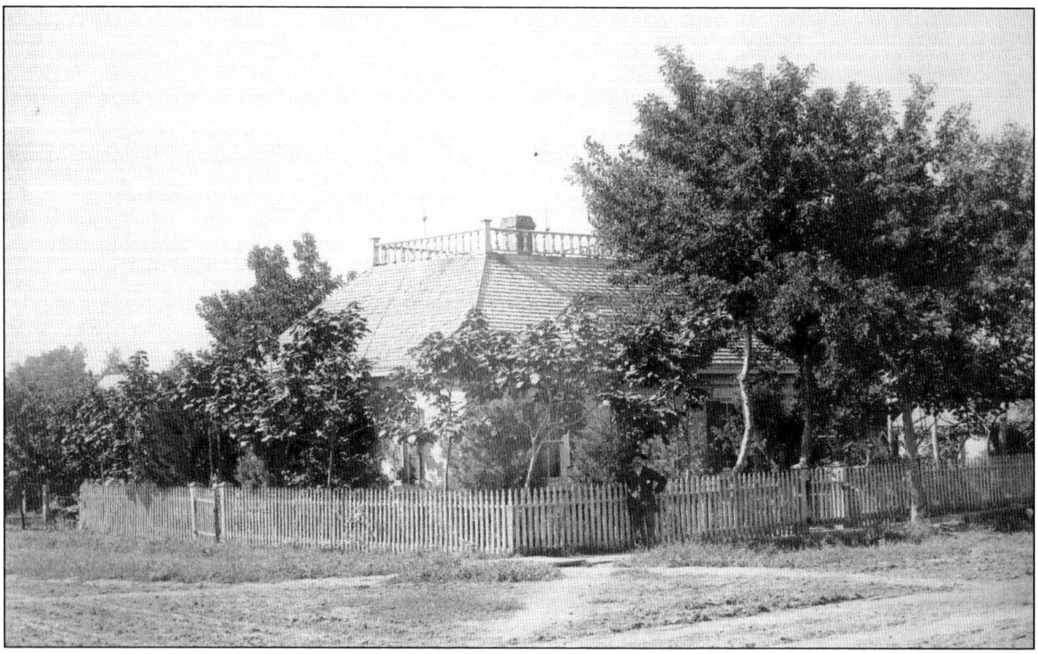

Herman Richter, right center, came to Alma in 1880 and constructed this stone house in what is now the city park. Richter owned a furniture store at 312 Missouri Street and was an undertaker in Alma. In the mid-1890s, Richter sold the home to Alma pioneer Ed Krapp and the furniture and undertaking business to Louis Schrader before moving to a farm west of town. (Courtesy Wabaunsee County Historical Society.)

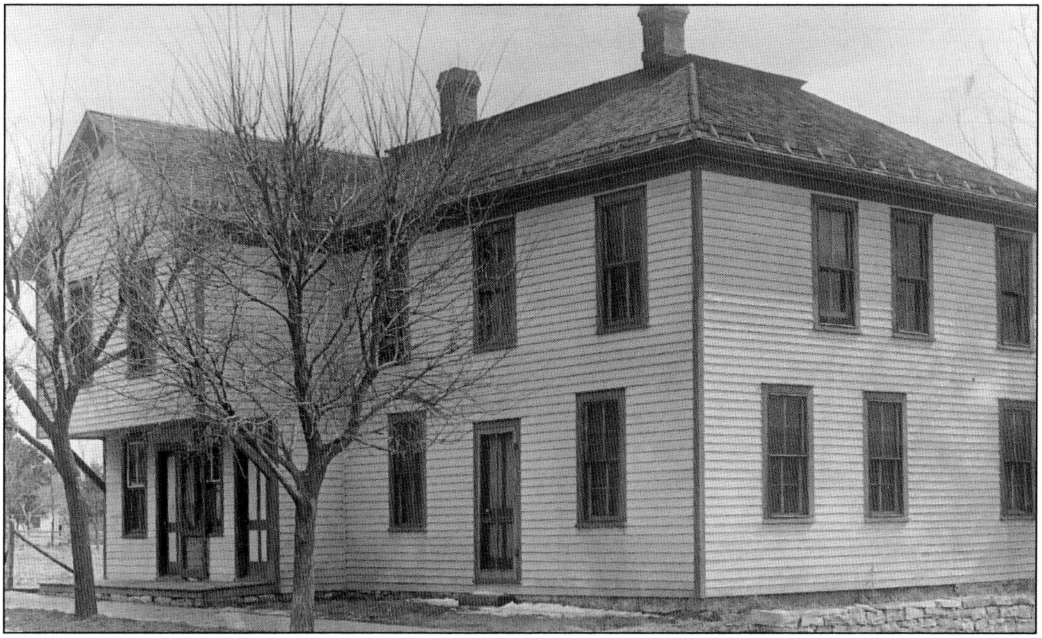

Louis Undorf, owner of the Undorf's Meat Market at 317 Missouri Street, owned this house located at 214 East Third Street. Undorf's brother-in-law August Utermann, owner of Central Livery Stable in Alma, lived in the home seen below, just a half a block down East Third Street at 306 Grand Avenue. Members of the Utermann family can be seen on the porch. While the Undorf house looks virtually unchanged a century later, the Utermann house, below, is barely recognizable today. (Above, courtesy Paul Gronquist; below, courtesy Wabaunsee County Historical Society.)

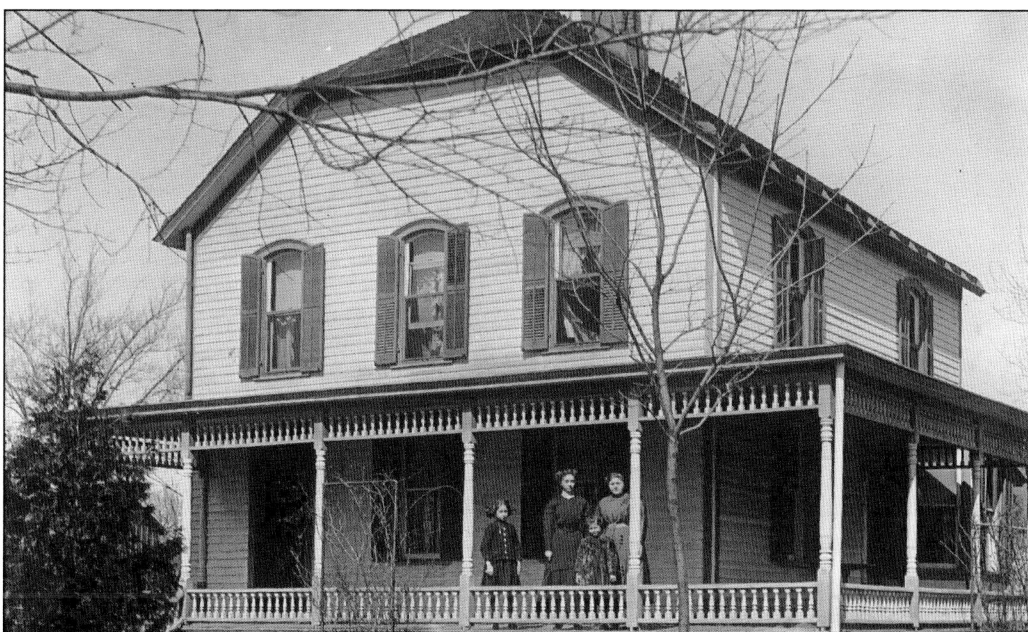

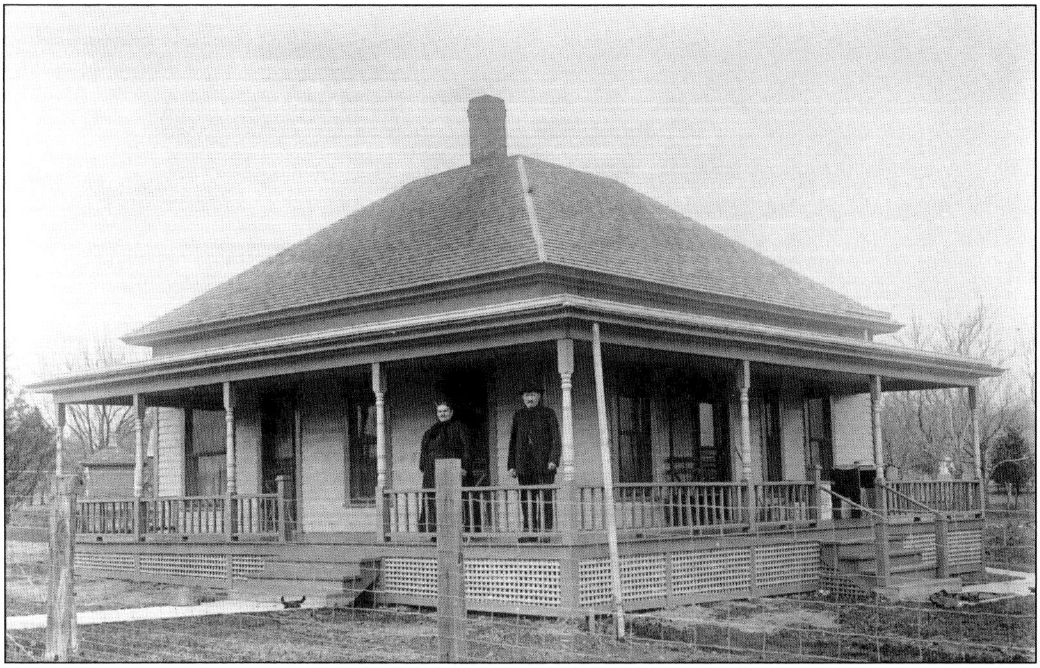

Mr. and Mrs. Moritz Kraus are seen standing on the porch of their home located at 305 Illinois Street. This house is one of the oldest standing in Alma; the photograph dates from the late 1870s. This home would have an addition and garage added to the rear of the structure in later years. (Courtesy Wabaunsee County Historical Society.)

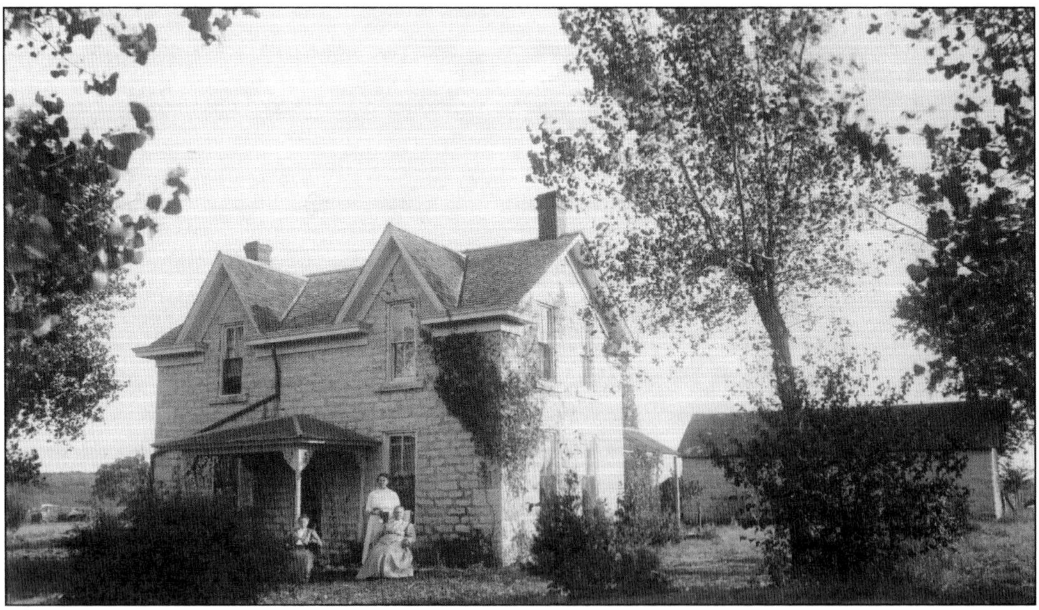

Members of the McComb family are seen in the front yard of their home located at 404 East Fourth Street. The residence is very recognizable today, with a front addition and an enclosed back porch being the primary changes from this view. The outbuilding seen to the right of the house stands today; however, about half of the building's length has been removed. (Courtesy Wabaunsee County Historical Society.)

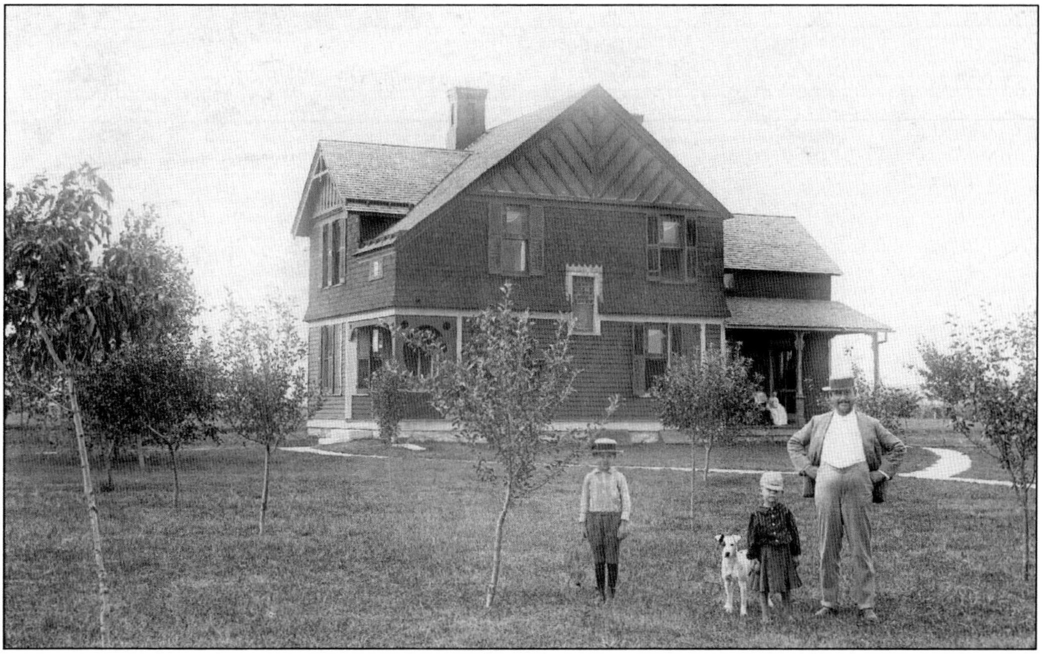

A man identified as Mr. Pfeifer and his children pose in front of their new home located at 28029 Park Valley Road. In the 1890s, the house was sold to Chet Davis and was, for many years, the home of Davis and his wife, Emma. Today, it still contains the original stained glass windows that can be seen in this view. (Courtesy Wabaunsee County Historical Society.)

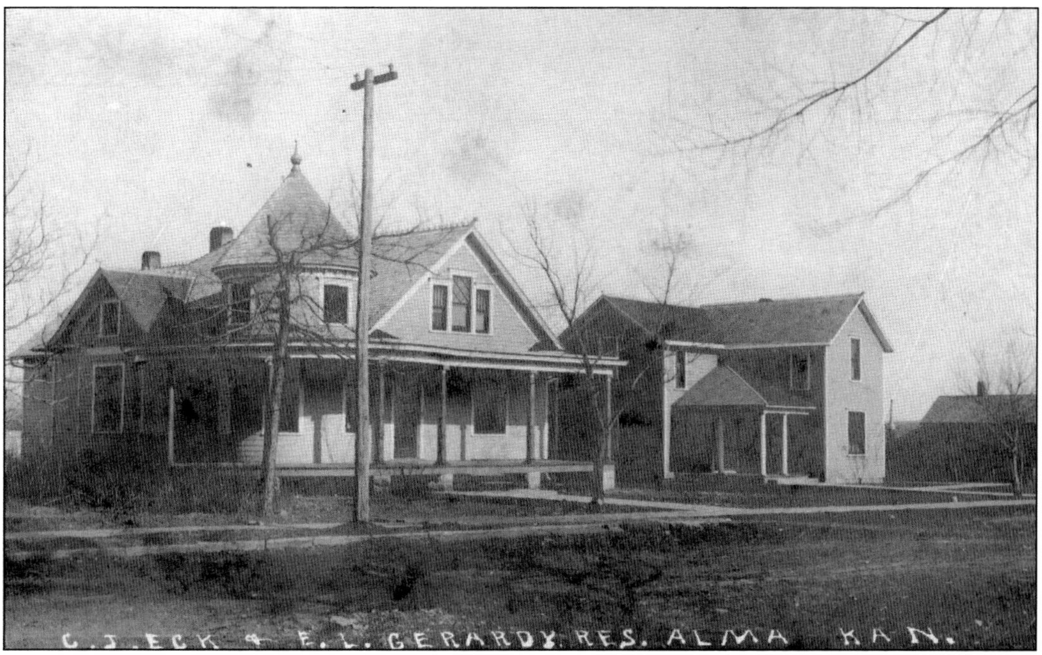

The residences of C.J. Eck, owner of Eck's Lumber Company in Alma, and E.L Gerady are seen in this c. 1910 real-photo postcard view. Eck's house (left), located at 215 East Seventh Street, has been meticulously restored, and both homes are structurally unchanged today. (Courtesy Wabaunsee County Historical Society.)

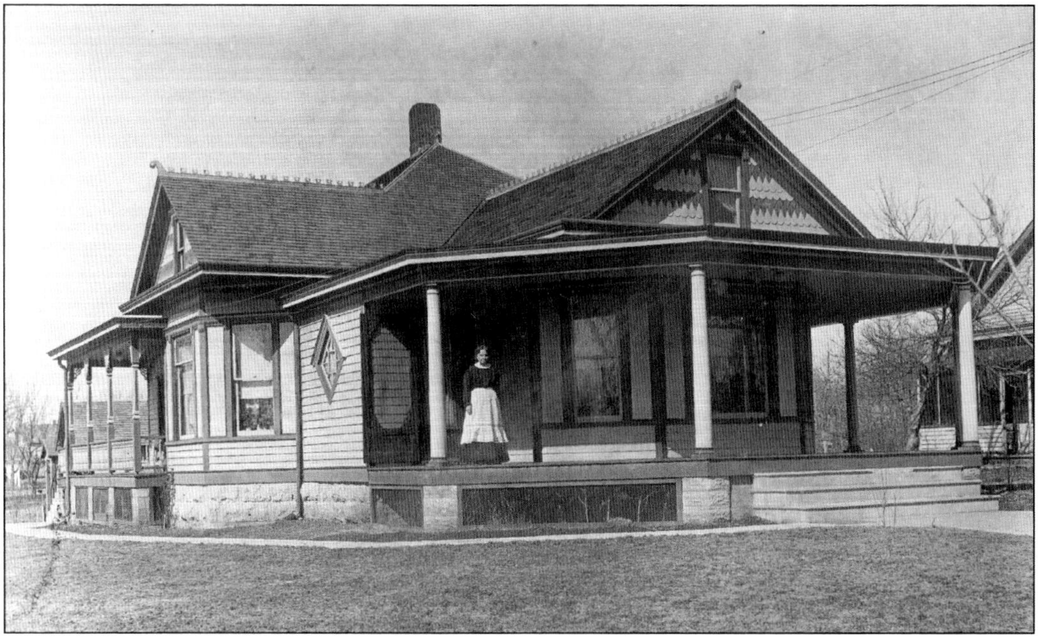

Similarities in the L.J. McCrumb and the William Speer residences, which are located side by side at 715 and 719 Missouri Street in Alma, respectively, lead one to believe they were constructed by the same builder. Today, the McCrumb house remains structurally unchanged and is quite recognizable; however, the Speer home's roofline has been altered, and the turret over the porch has been removed. Both views of these houses date from around 1900. (Both, courtesy Wabaunsee County Historical Society.)

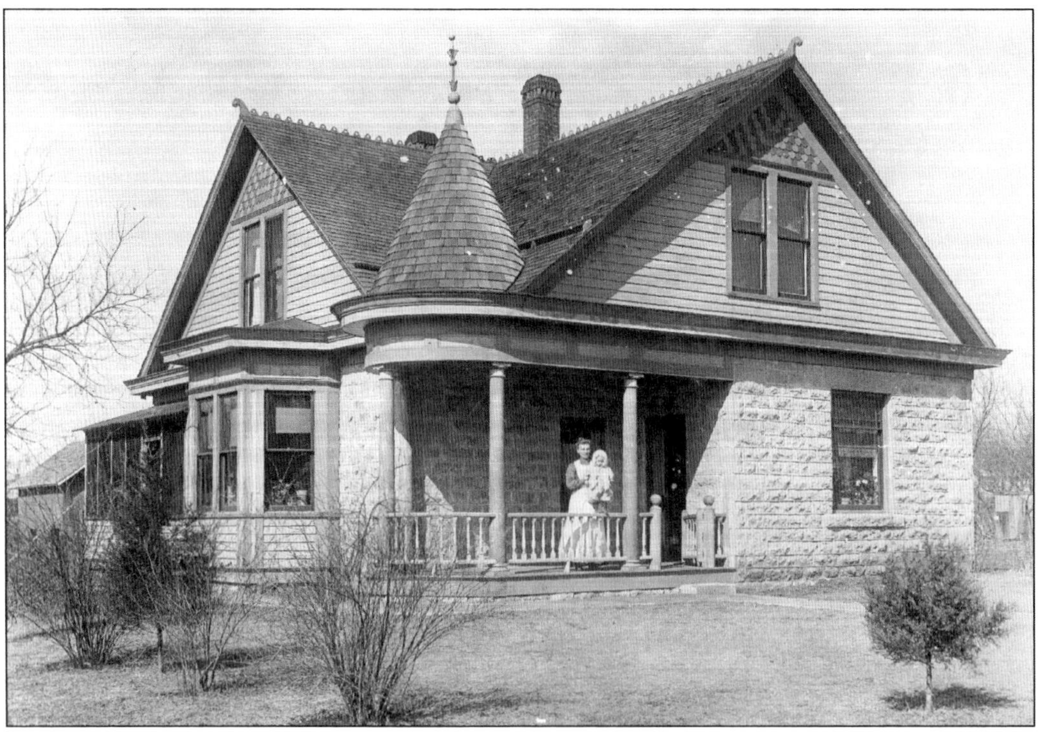

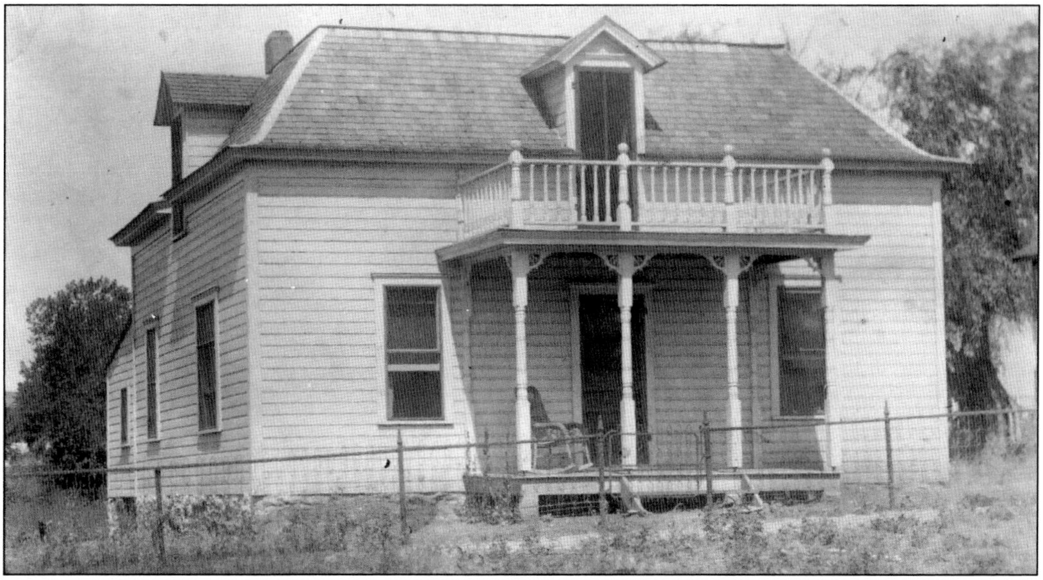

Above, this house located at 723 Kansas Avenue sports a second-floor balcony located over the front porch. Such balconies were common in the early 20th century, as no homes were equipped with air-conditioning and residents often sat on the balcony to enjoy the cool morning and evening air. Below, the sprawling home at 811 Missouri Street stands much unchanged today, with the exception of an addition and porch at the rear of the house. At left, on the horizon, the first Alma city school can be seen. (Above, courtesy Wabaunsee County Historical Society; below, courtesy Paul Gronquist.)

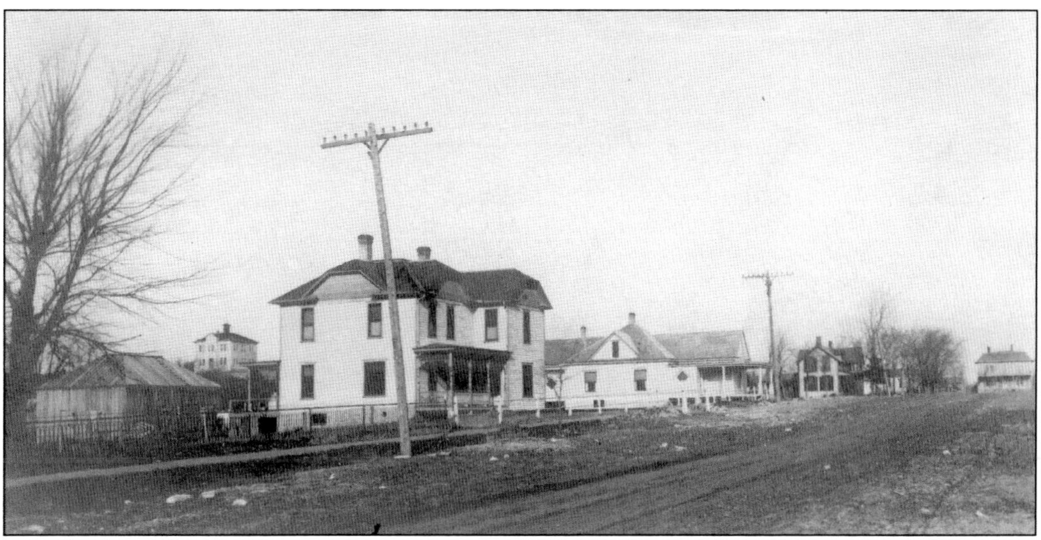

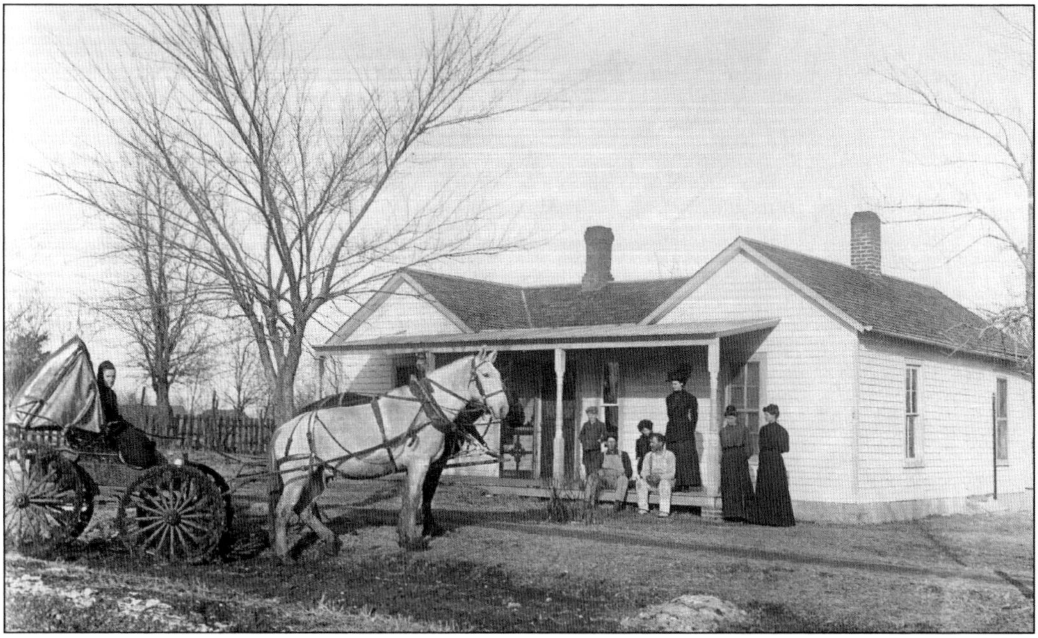

Unidentified members of the Barger and Davis families are gathered at this house, located at 910 Kansas Avenue. Although some changes have been made, the home is quite recognizable today. The north end of Alma was far less inhabited when this 1890s photograph was taken. The street itself was a mud path with grass growing in the center. (Courtesy Wabaunsee County Historical Society.)

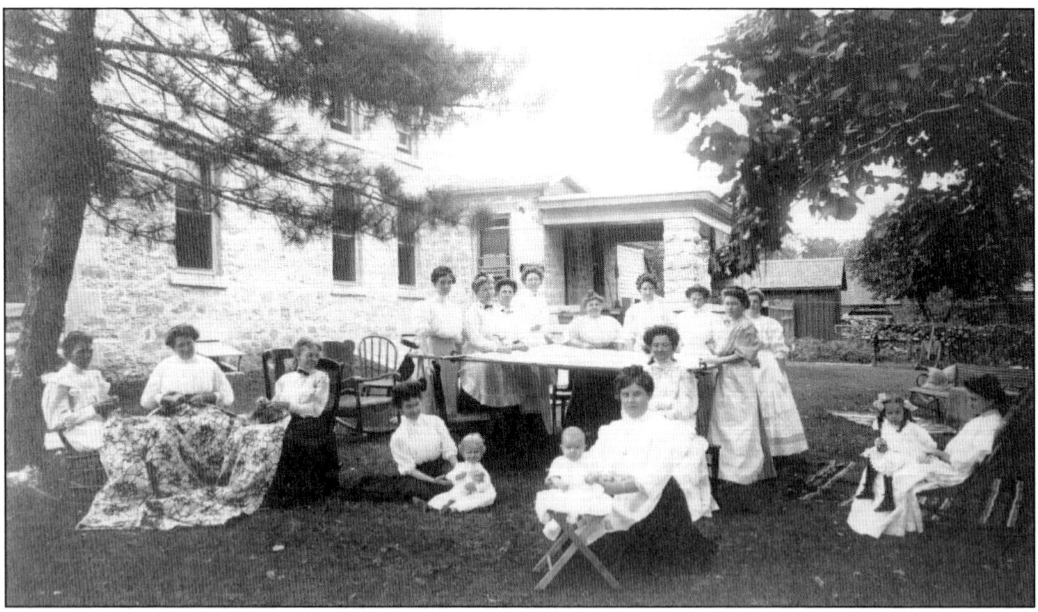

A group of ladies is having a quilting party in the yard at the A.S. Allendorph residence in Alma, located at 205 West Seventh Street. Allendorph came to Wabaunsee County in 1888, and although he was trained as a civil engineer, he chose instead to become a cattleman. In addition to this fine home, Allendorph owned a 5,080-acre ranch northwest of Alma. (Courtesy Wabaunsee County Museum.)

Two

Council Grove

The history of Council Grove, Kansas, dates much earlier than even Kansas Territorial days, to the very beginning of the westward movement in America. A ford across the Neosho River brought early explorers and then travelers across ground that would become Council Grove. In 1825, the US government and the Osage Indians signed a treaty under the "Council Oak" tree, giving a right-of-way to travelers along what would be called the Santa Fe Trail. Caravans and wagon trains of travelers often gathered for the journey westward at the same location. In 1847, Albert G. Boone and James G. Hamilton, licensed to trade with the Kaw Indians, established a trading post on the Kaw Reservation at Council Grove and placed young Seth Hays in charge. Hays constructed the first house and store, and he was the first white settler in what would become Morris County.

Hays, a grandson of Daniel Boone, opened the Hays House Tavern and Restaurant in 1857, and although it has passed through several owners, it is the oldest continuously operated restaurant west of the Mississippi River.

In 1851, the Methodist Episcopal Church South constructed a mission in Council Grove that was located within the Kaw Reservation. The mission was constructed to provide a school for Kaw children at which Thomas S. Huffaker was the teacher. The Kaw were suspicious of the white men, and rather than send all of their children to the school, 30 orphan boys were sent instead. The cost of maintaining the school was prohibitive, and in 1854 it was closed. The school building was sold to Huffaker, who owned it for 14 years. The structure passed through several owners until Huffaker's son Carl Huffaker returned to Council Grove in 1926 with his wife, Bertha, and daughter Marjorie and purchased the mission property that his father had owned. Reportedly, Huffaker spent $37,000 to remodel the interior of the building and replace the heating system. The family lived in the structure for a number of years. In 1951, Huffaker sold the Kaw Mission to the Kansas State Historical Society for $23,500. It is now home to the Kaw Mission State Historic Site and Museum.

On February 26, 1855, the first post office was opened at Council Grove in what was then Wise County. A post office has operated continuously in the town since that date.

A much earlier type of post office operated at Council Grove from 1825 to 1847, known as the Post Office Oak. Travelers on the Santa Fe Trail would leave messages in a hollow spot in the base of a large oak tree for travelers who came behind them. There might be messages about the location of water, safe passage, or specific notes for individuals scheduled to pass that point on the trail. The Post Office Oak, a National Historic Landmark, was cut down on September 9, 2008, as the tree had become completely hollow and was in danger of falling on nearby buildings. The stump of the 300-year-old bur oak remains preserved at the landmark site.

In 1858, the Town Company of Council Grove incorporation was accepted by the Kansas Territorial Legislature. Thomas Huffaker, Seth Hays, Christopher Columbia, and Hiram Northrup were named officers of the town company and the town site was surveyed. On April 31, 1869, Council Grove became a third-class city and in 1870 elected its first city officers, including R.B. Lockwood in the office of mayor, A.J. Hughes as city attorney, and S.M. Strieby as city clerk.

In 1868, the Missouri-Kansas-Texas (MKT or Katy) Railroad arrived in Council Grove, bringing with it growth and prosperity. In the 1860s, numerous railroad companies sought rights-of-way throughout Kansas. The right-of-way was valuable to the railroad because, in addition to the right to lay tracks, the railroads were given a land grant to all of the odd-numbered sections of land along the passage. The railroads, in return, could sell the land to individuals and could also establish and plat towns at locations that were convenient for the servicing and fueling of trains. At the time, every growing community wanted and needed the railroad to pass through it. Many towns in the state were relocated when the railways passed them by just a few miles.

In 1871, the question of the location of the county seat became contested upon the incorporation of Parkerville, a dozen miles to the northwest of Council Grove. An election was held that year to settle the question, and Council Grove prevailed by more than a 2-to-1 margin.

The first public school recorded in the history of Morris County was established in 1857 in Council Grove, with Sarah Stevenson as teacher. In 1882, the number of pupils enrolled in the Morris County's 63 school districts had grown to 2,509, an impressive number by today's standards.

Council Grove is the site of two reservoirs, the Council Grove City Lake Park and Council Grove Lake, operated by the US Army Corps of Engineers. The City Lake, as it is often called, was constructed in 1942 by the City of Council Grove as a public water supply. The 434-acre lake contains 348 waterfront lots that were developed first into cabins and recreational housing, and many are now year-round lakefront homes. The Council Grove Lake, constructed as part of the Flood Control Act of 1950, was one of many lakes built in the 1950s and 1960s by the Corps of Engineers to prevent the repeated flooding that towns along tributaries to the Kansas River experienced during the first half of the 20th century. Construction began in 1960 on the lake, and it was placed into flood-control operation in October 1964. The lake, 3,310 acres in size, offers a variety of recreational opportunities for visitors.

Today, Council Grove is home to 2,265 citizens. In the last 50 years, the city has seen a decline in population of 15 percent. However, that number is consistent with population trends for small towns throughout Kansas. Council Grove's economy has long benefited from its position as the county seat, and government plays a significant role in the local economy. Increasingly, Council Grove is becoming a tourist destination, drawing on its rich history, 13 sites that are currently listed on the National Register of Historic Places, as well as its location as the beginning point of the Flint Hills Scenic Byway. And, as it has been for a century and a half, ranching and farming play the most significant roles in Morris County's economy and in that of Council Grove.

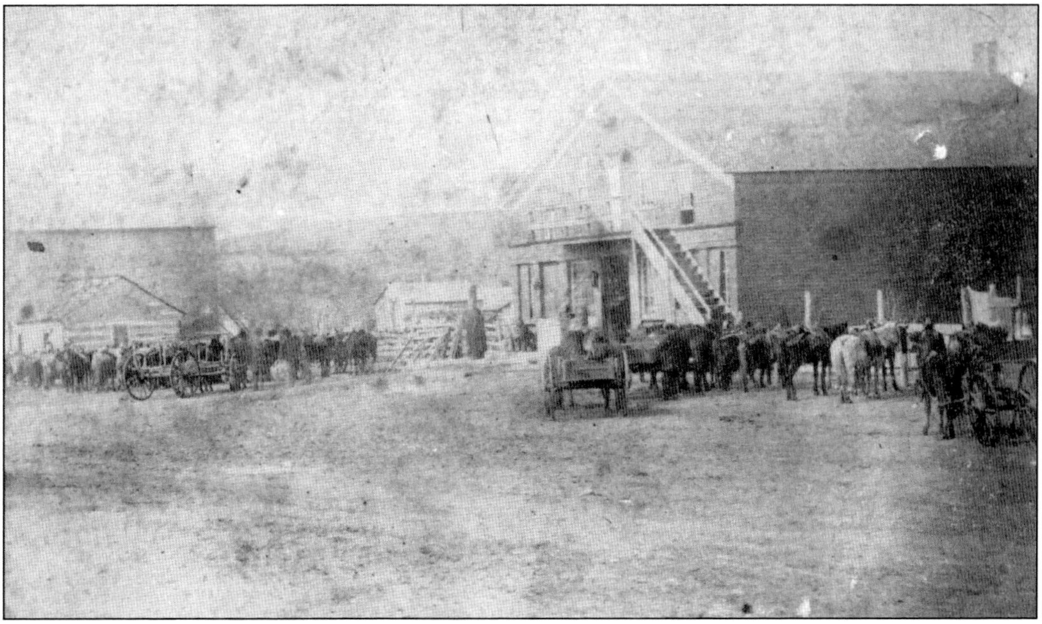

Seth Hays came to what is now Council Grove in 1847 to establish a trading post to conduct business with the Kaw Indians. Hays operated out of a log house until 1859 when he built the Frame Store, seen here in 1868. Hays outfitted many travelers on the Santa Fe Trail, as this was the last place to buy supplies before arriving in Santa Fe, New Mexico. (Courtesy Morris County Historical Society.)

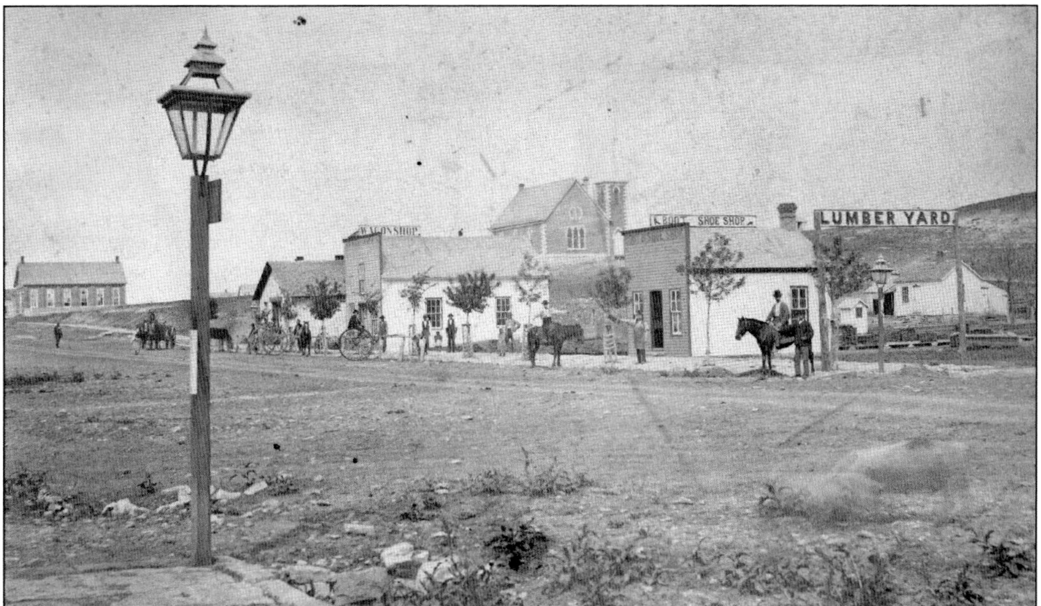

This early street scene from Council Grove dates from the 1870s. Council Grove was incorporated in 1858, three years before Kansas statehood. It is said that Council Grove received its name from the location of an 1827 treaty signing with the Osage Indians under a large oak tree. The treaty gave a right-of-way through Indian Territory for the Santa Fe Trail. (Courtesy Morris County Historical Society.)

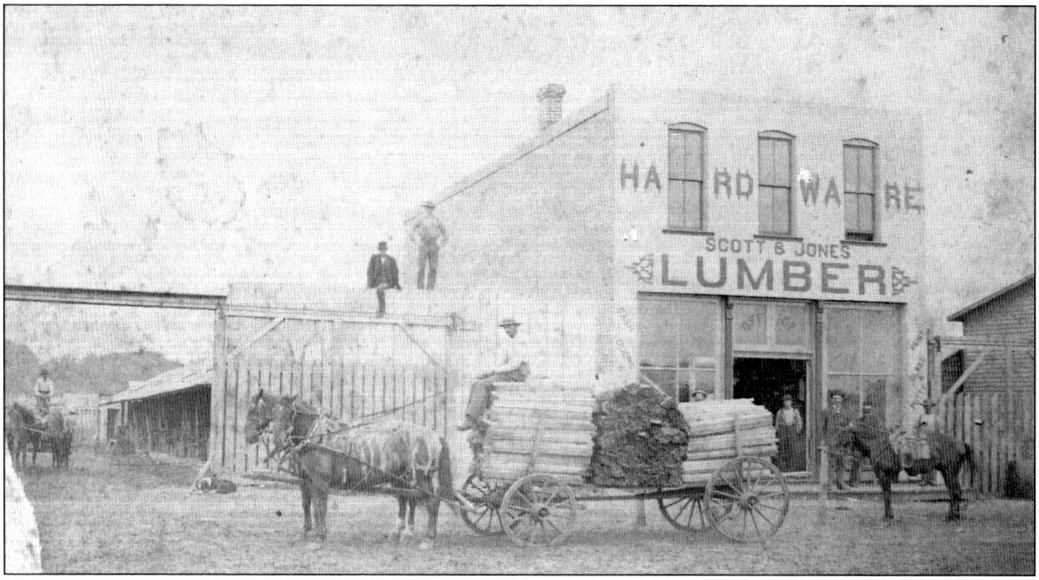

Scott and Jones Lumber was located at the intersection of South Sixth and East Main Streets. This photograph dates from the 1880s. Around 1900, this company was sold, becoming Burgner Bowman Lumber Co. Lumber companies were a vital part of every expanding community. In much of the Flint Hills, lumber was a valuable commodity, making such businesses essential for growth. (Courtesy Morris County Historical Society.)

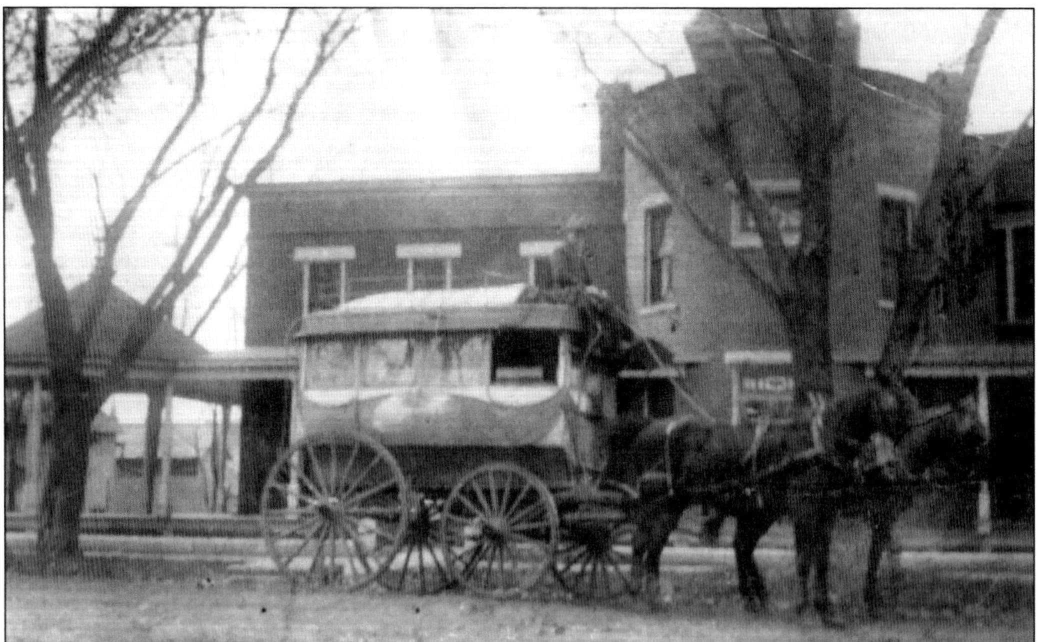

The Cottage House Hotel began in 1867 as a small, three-room cottage that also housed a blacksmith shop. After the arrival of the railroad, demands for hotel rooms grew, and the structure was expanded to a 5,000-square-foot hotel. Here, a stagecoach is stopped in front of the Cottage House Hotel. Today, the lodging is operated as a bed-and-breakfast, located at 25 North Neosho Street. (Courtesy Morris County Historical Society.)

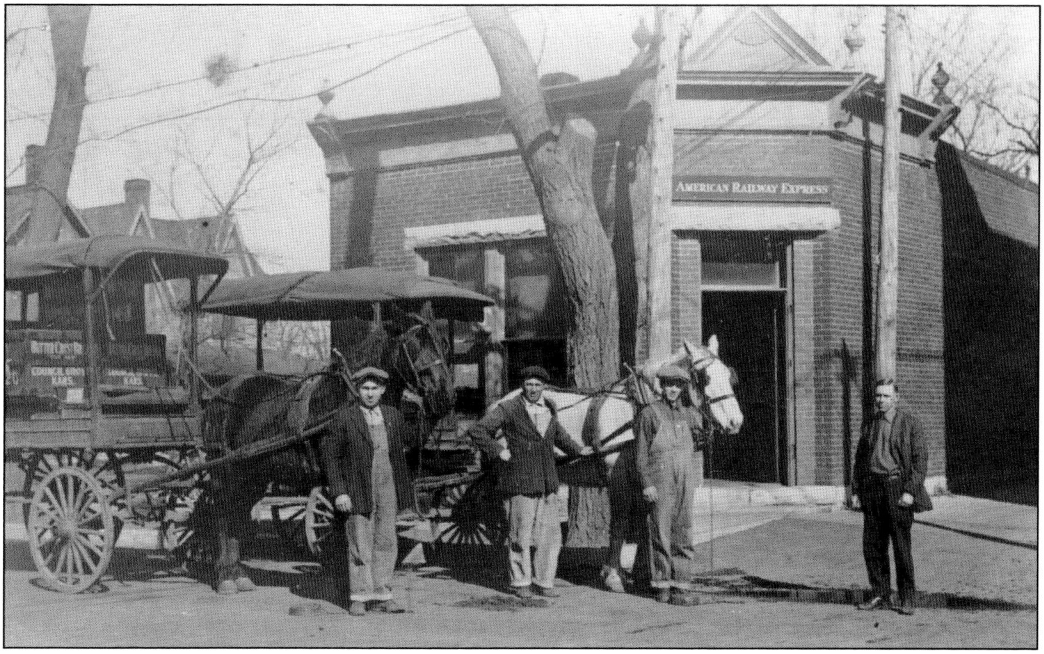

Employees of the American Railway Express Agency in Council Grove pose with delivery wagons in front of their building located at 24 North Neosho Street. Pictured, from left to right, are Estil Allen, Harry Rees, Guy Kirkpatrick, and Harry Prather. The company was founded in 1839 and became the largest freight delivery company in the United States before declaring bankruptcy in 1975. (Courtesy Morris County Historical Society.)

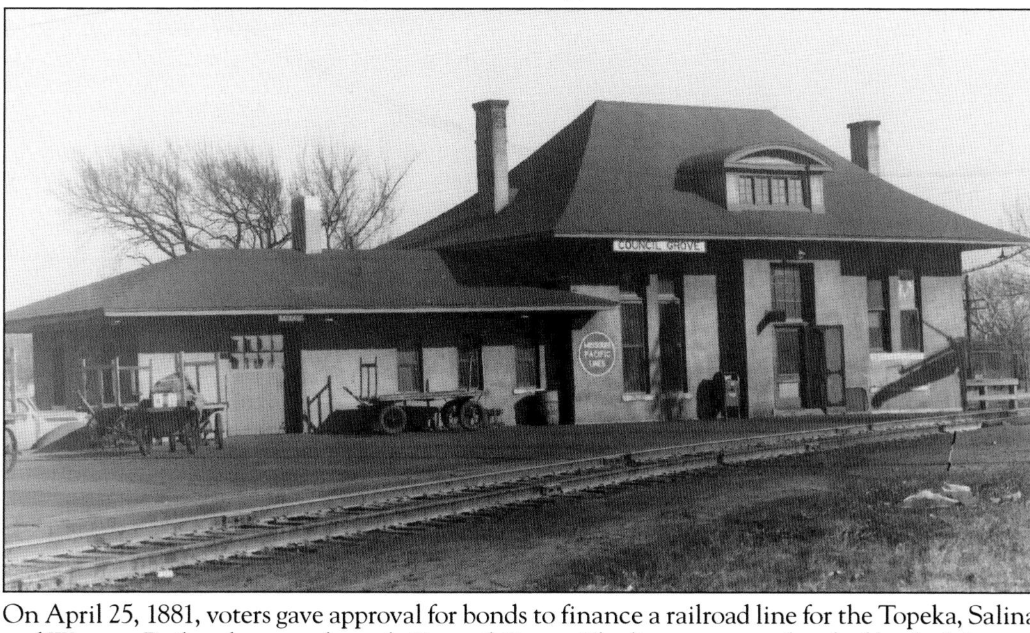

On April 25, 1881, voters gave approval for bonds to finance a railroad line for the Topeka, Salina and Western Railroad to pass through Council Grove. The line was soon absorbed by the Missouri Pacific Railroad. Its depot at Council Grove is seen here. In 1982, the Union Pacific purchased the Missouri Pacific, whose logo and corporate name were discontinued in 1997. (Courtesy Morris County Historical Society.)

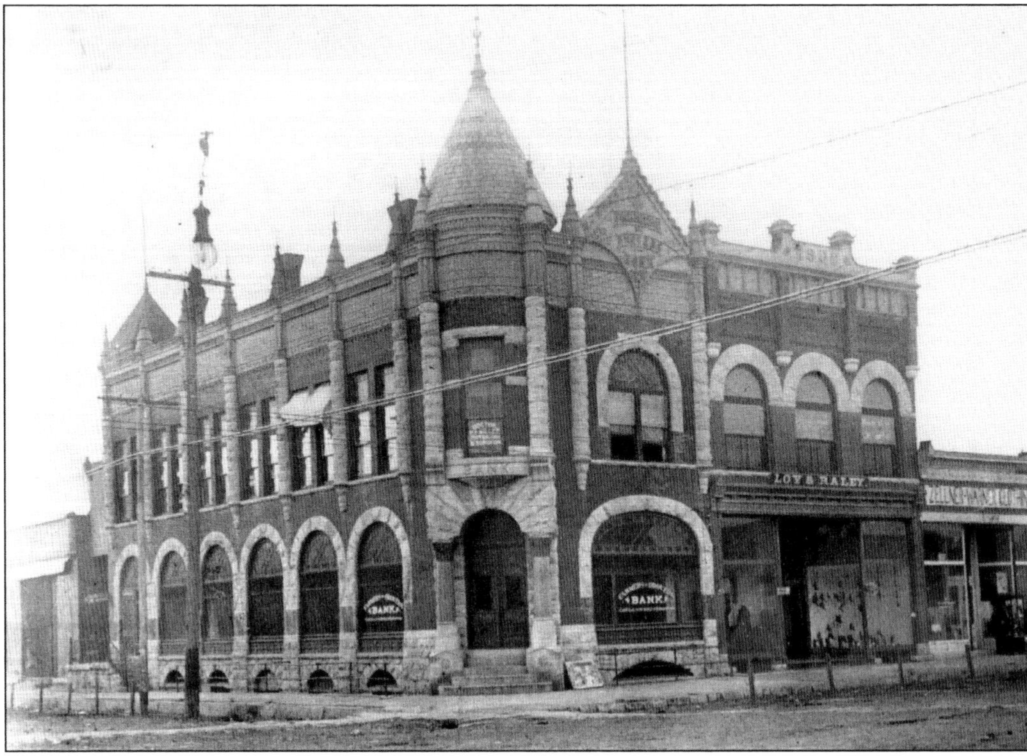

The Farmers and Drovers Bank of Council Grove was founded by W.H. White in 1882 and moved into a new bank building, seen here, on March 3, 1893. In 1902, the bank added a second structure attached to the west side of the first. The second floor of the new building was a large hall used for lodge meetings, dances, and other gatherings. (Courtesy Farmers and Drovers Bank of Council Grove.)

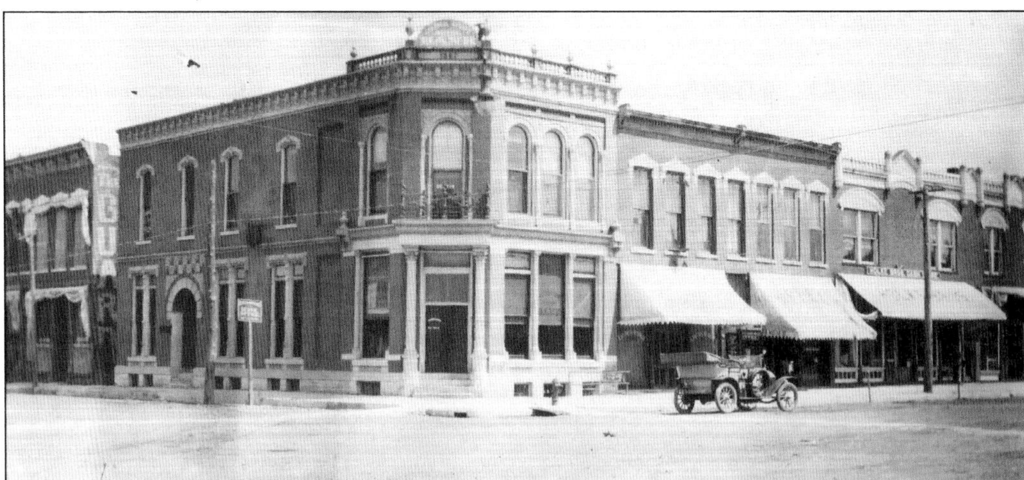
Originally known as the Morris County State Bank, the Council Grove National Bank organized in 1882 and built this structure, located at 130 West Main Street, in 1887, operating there until 1978. That year, the bank building suffered damage from fire; however, restoration was completed after that blaze to return the interior to its original appearance. This photograph is dated 1913. (Courtesy Morris County Historical Society.)

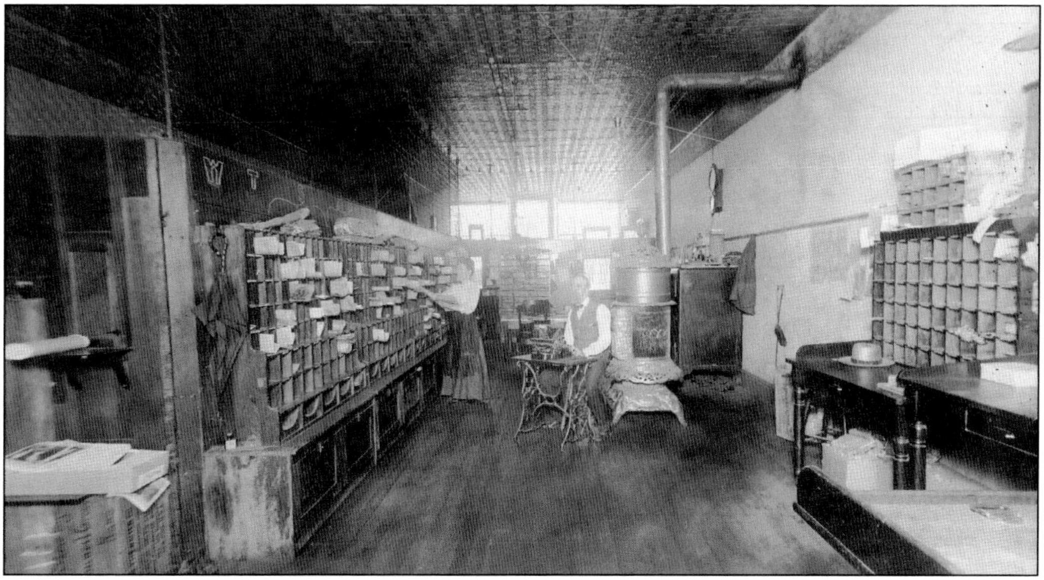

A US post office was established in Council Grove, Kansas Territory, on February 26, 1855, when Morris County was still known as Wise County. Council Grove is the oldest post office in Morris County, having operated continuously for 155 years. This view is a very early, undated interior view of the Council Grove Post Office. (Courtesy Morris County Historical Society.)

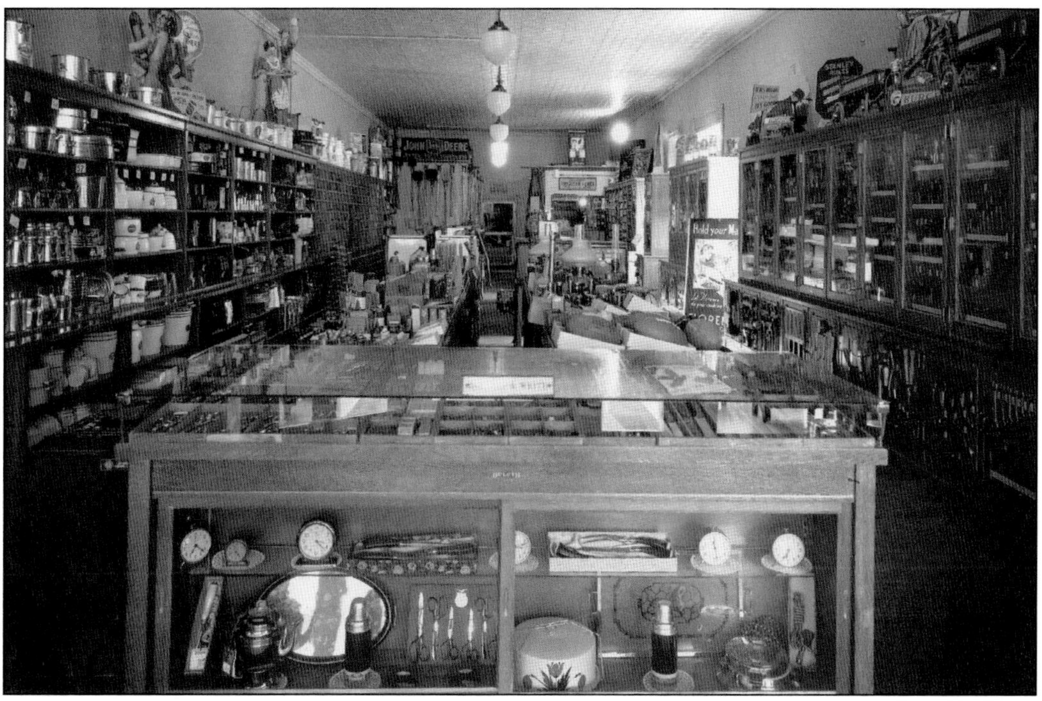

Durland and White operated a hardware store many years in Council Grove. In this interior view from the around 1940, it appears that the store offered a wide variety of merchandise, including garden tools, toys, kitchenware, and farm implements and equipment. An exterior view of Durland and White Hardware from 1920 can be seen on the bottom of page 55. (Courtesy Morris County Historical Society.)

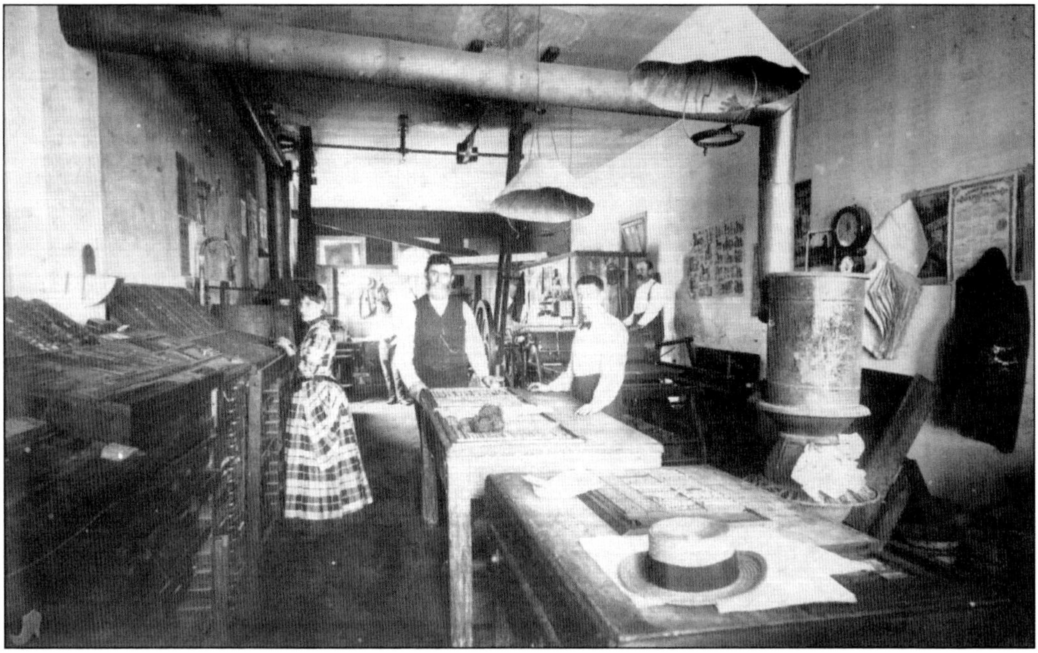

This view of an early printing company located upstairs at 116 West Main Street dates from the early 1880s. Seen in the office are, from left to right, Lily Munsell-Ritchie, Oliver Munsell, Ernest Munsell, and Frank Munsell. This building burned in a September 19, 1886, fire that destroyed over a half-dozen businesses downtown. (Courtesy Morris County Historical Society.)

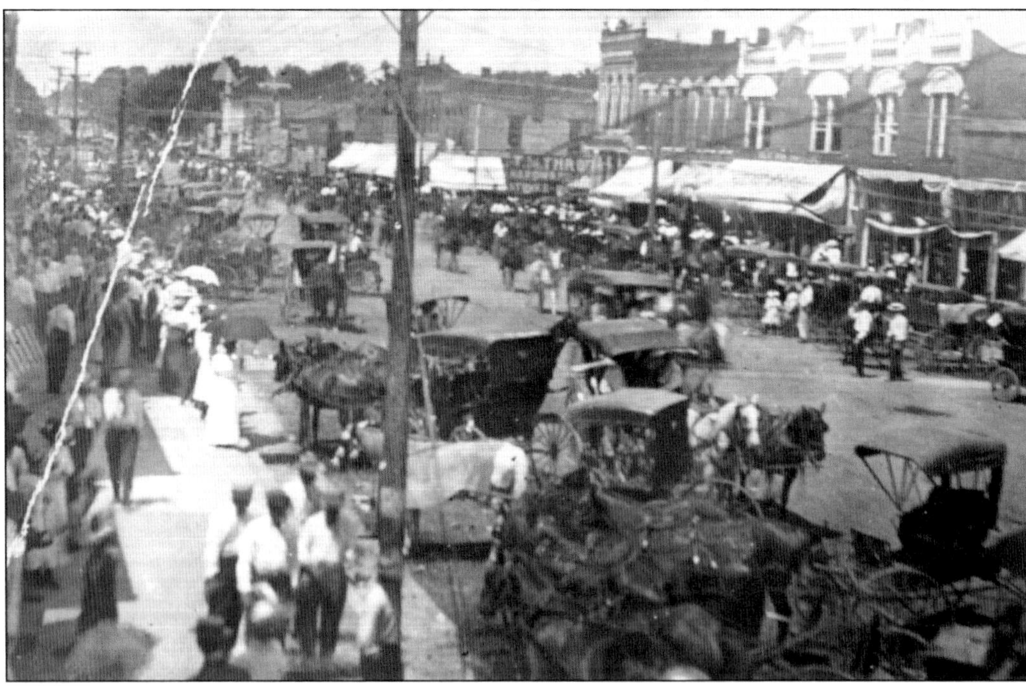

This view of the business district in Council Grove dates from the mid-1910s. Council Grove was the largest city and seat of county government in Morris County. Holidays, parades, and even Saturday nights brought out a crowd. (Courtesy Morris County Historical Society.)

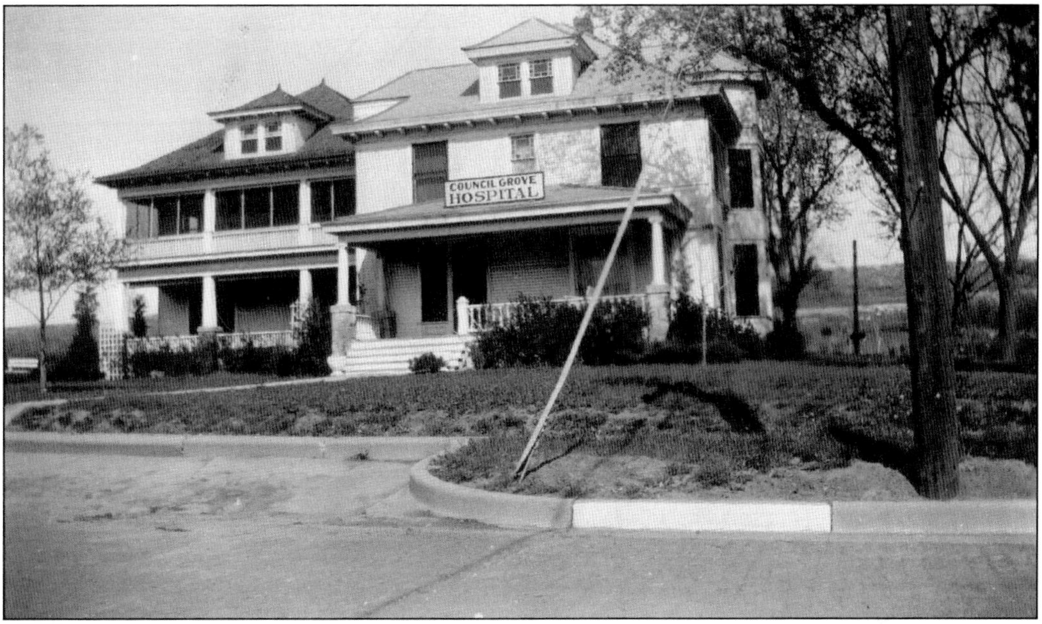

This view of the first Council Grove Hospital dates from the 1920s. This hospital was razed and a new facility constructed in 1965. The new hospital in Council Grove is now known as Morris County Medical Center. (Courtesy Morris County Historical Society.)

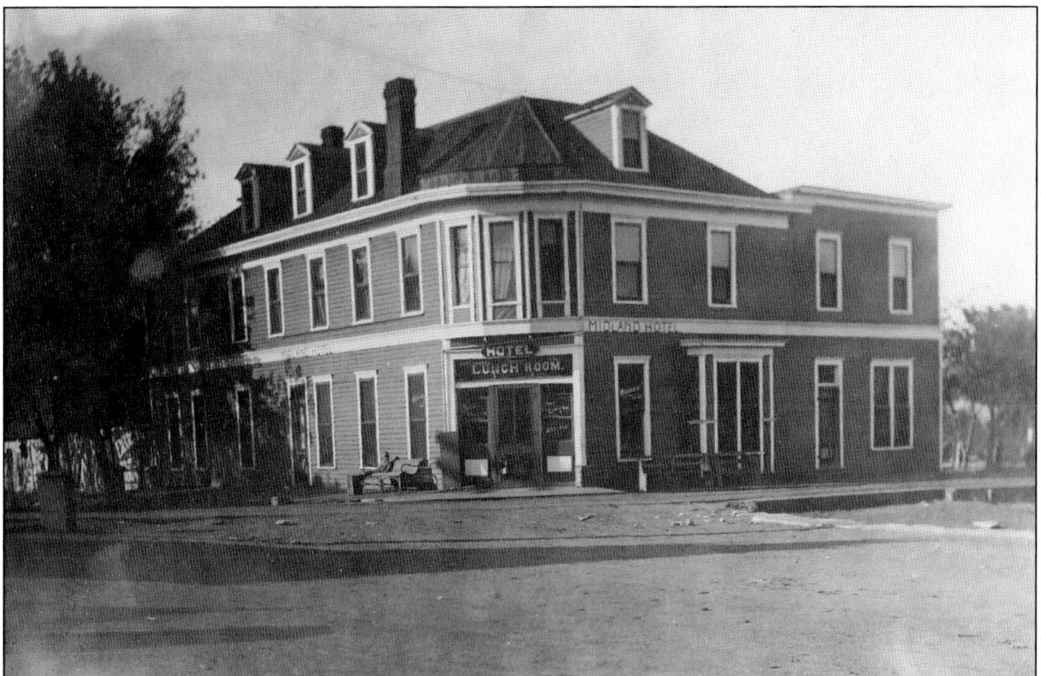

The Midland Hotel in Council Grove is seen in this 1910s photograph. Council Grove boasted numerous hotels due to the demand for rooms created as a result of its location on the Santa Fe Trail. The first hotel was constructed in Council Grove in 1856. (Courtesy Morris County Historical Society.)

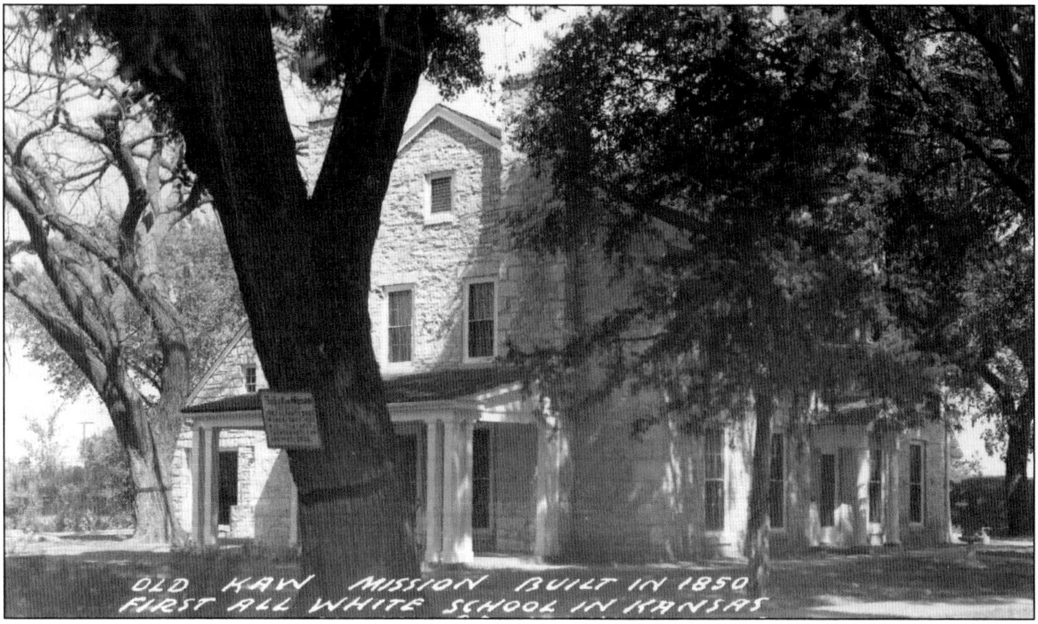

The old Kaw Mission was built in 1851 by the Methodist Episcopal Church South to educate Kaw Indian youth. Distrustful of the white men, the Kaw only sent orphan boys to the school. The school operated from 1851 through 1854, when the Kaw reservation was reduced in size by the US government. The mission is now a State of Kansas Historic Site, located at 500 North Mission Street. (Courtesy Greg Hoots.)

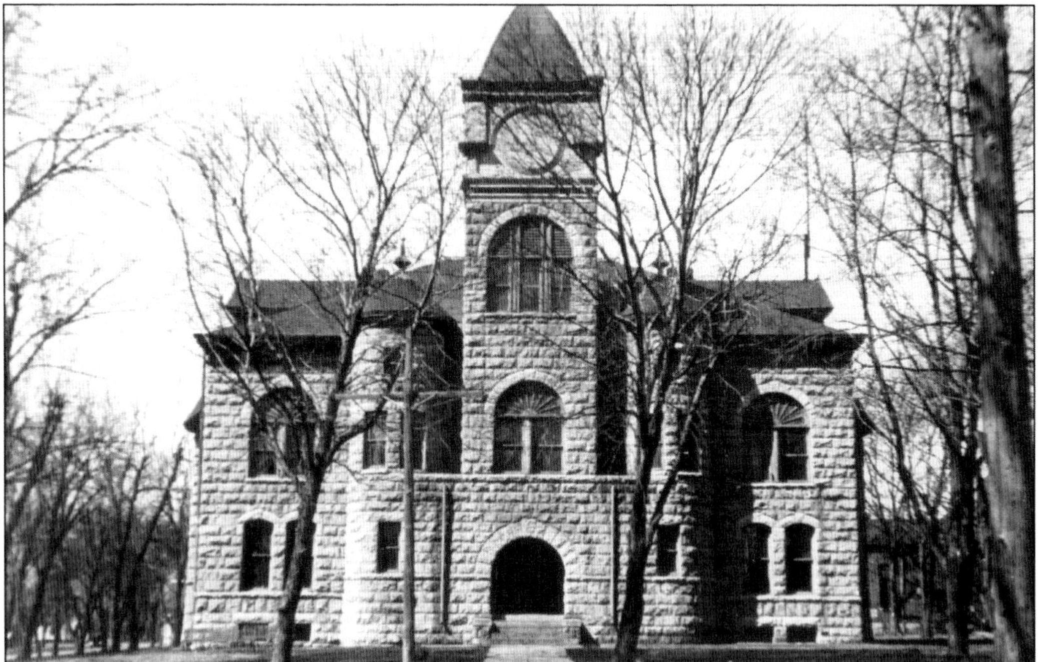

The Morris County Courthouse is seen here soon after its construction in 1904. The courthouse and jail, located in Council Grove, operated in these facilities until 2004, when a new Morris County Courthouse was constructed. (Courtesy Morris County Historical Society.)

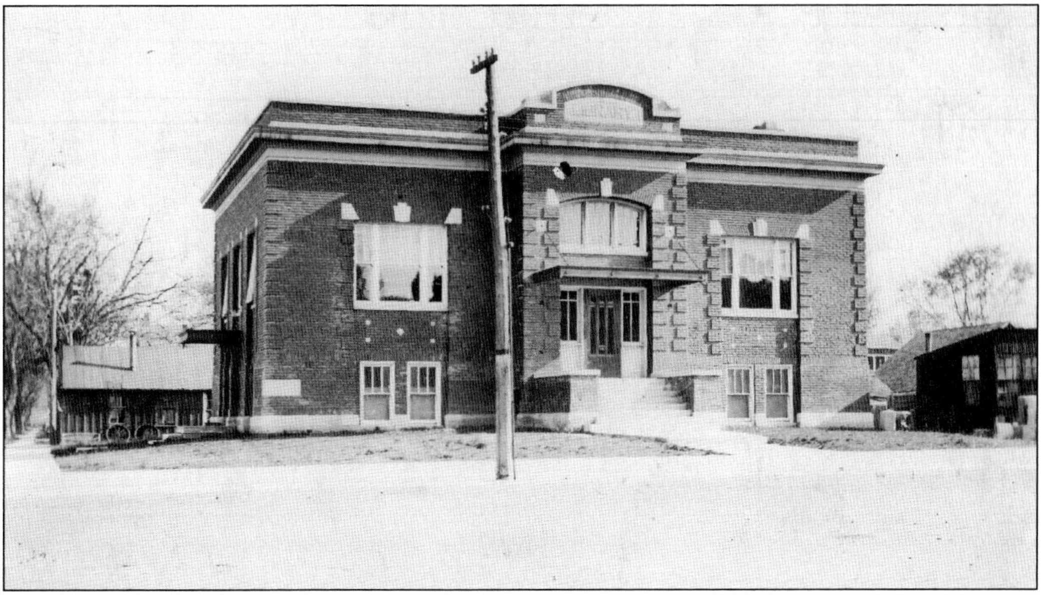

The Carnegie Corporation of New York gave grants to cities and towns across the United States to build libraries between 1898 and 1919. In Kansas, 59 public libraries were built with Carnegie funds, including the Council Grove Library, constructed with a $10,000 grant and located at 303 West Main Street. This building is now home to the Morris County Historical Society. (Courtesy Morris County Historical Society.)

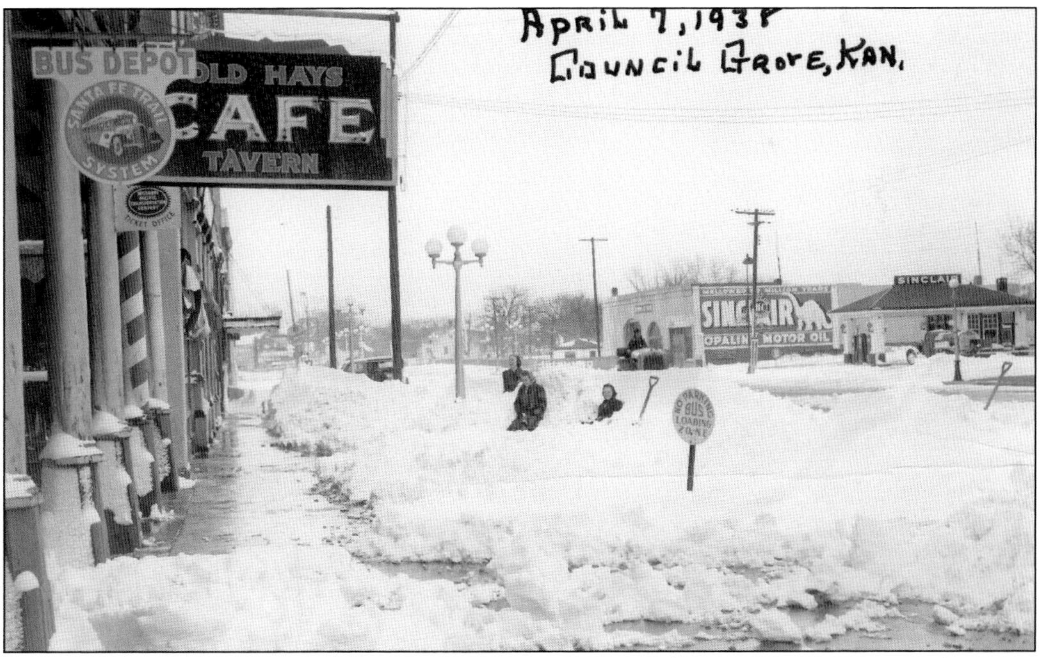

Seven to ten inches of wet snow covered Council Grove in this spring storm on April 7, 1938. Here, three ladies seem to be enjoying shoveling the sidewalk in front of the Old Hays House Café. Seth Hays opened an eating establishment on the site in 1857, making it the longest continuously operating eatery west of the Mississippi River. (Courtesy Morris County Historical Society.)

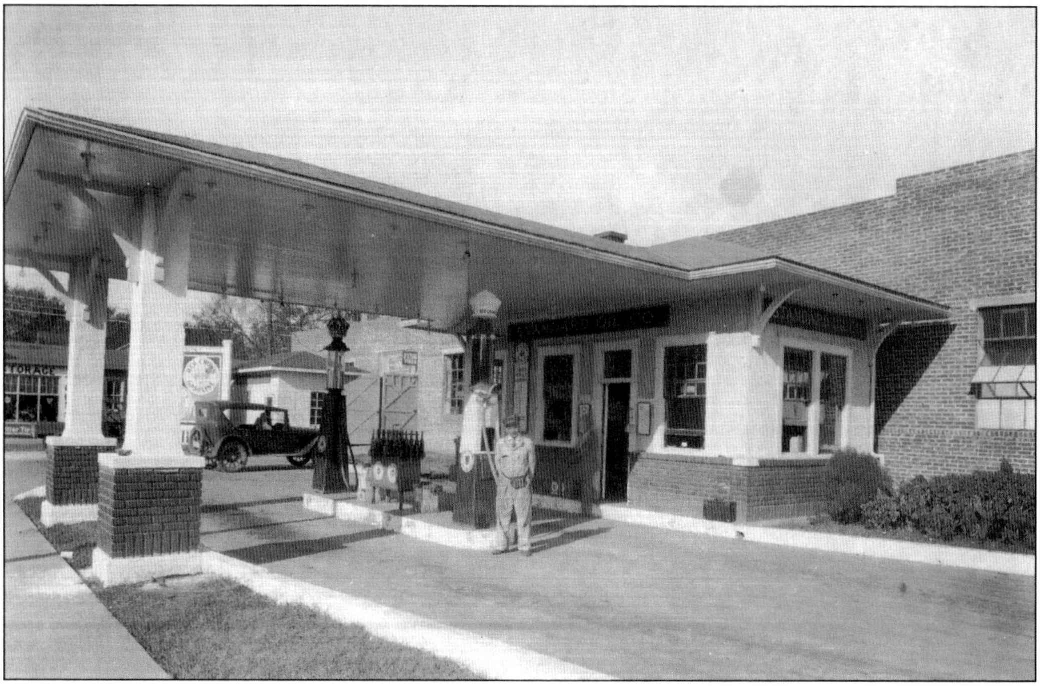

Above, Sam Houdenshill is seen standing in front of the Standard Oil station located at the northeast corner of Main and Missouri Streets in Council Grove. For many years, Standard Oil owned all of its stations and hired local operators to manage them. This photograph dates from the mid-1920s. Below, the Standard Oil station is seen inundated with floodwater during the 1929 deluge. Downtown Council Grove experienced repeated flooding throughout the first half of the 20th century, including severe floods in 1903, 1904, 1908, 1929, 1935, and 1951. (Both, courtesy Morris County Historical Society.)

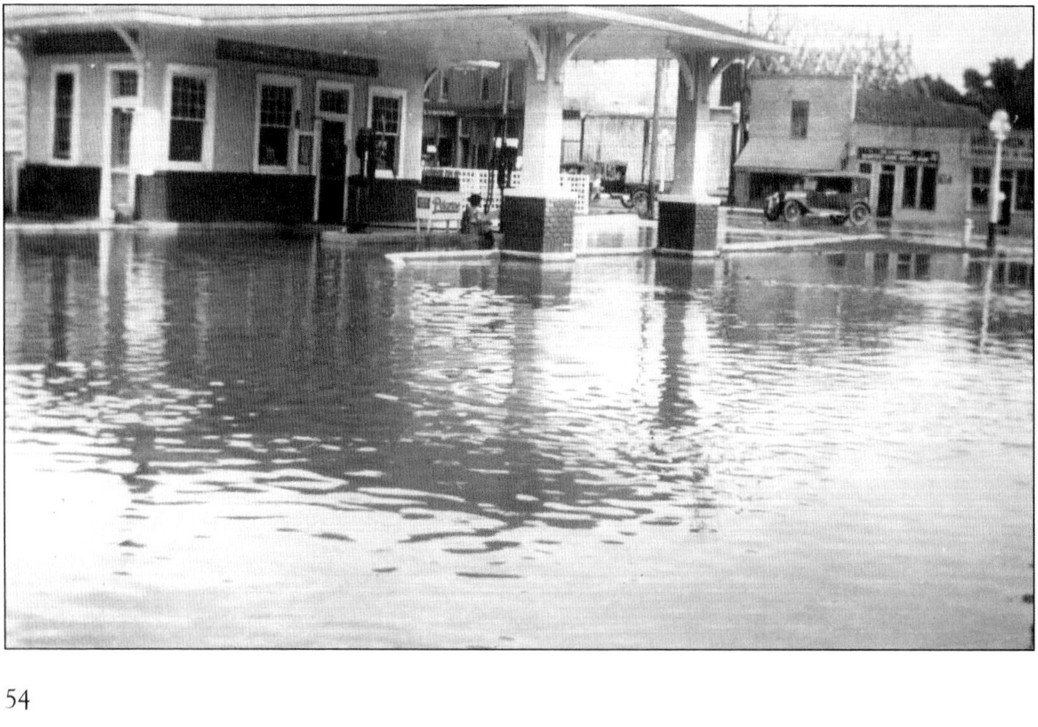

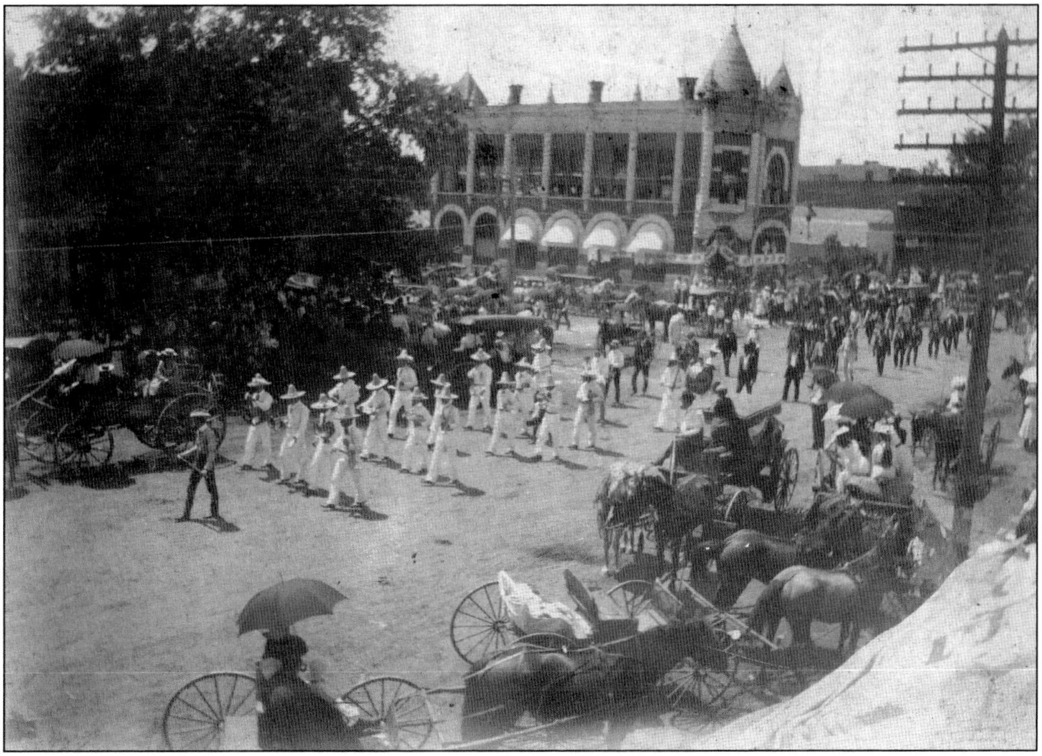

Above, the Farmers and Drovers Bank located at 201 West Main Street can be seen in this parade view dated 1901. In 1902, the bank purchased the lot to its west and added a second building (see page 48), noticeably absent in this view. Below, Ku Klux Klan members can be seen in a parade down Main Street in Council Grove dated 1920. The Klan was very active in Kansas in the early 1920s before its marked decline by the beginning of the Great Depression. (Both, courtesy Morris County Historical Society.)

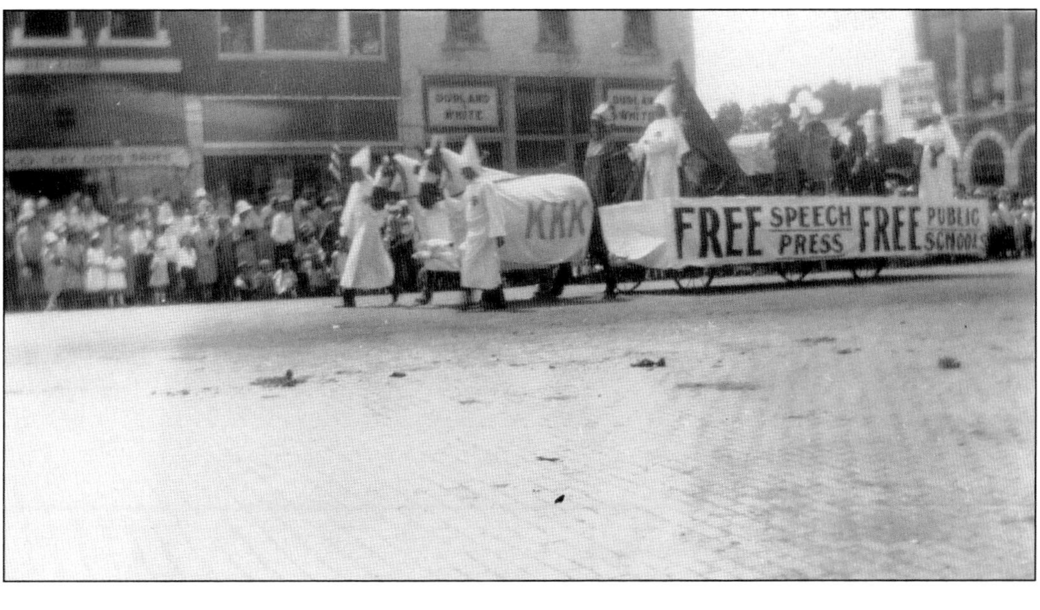

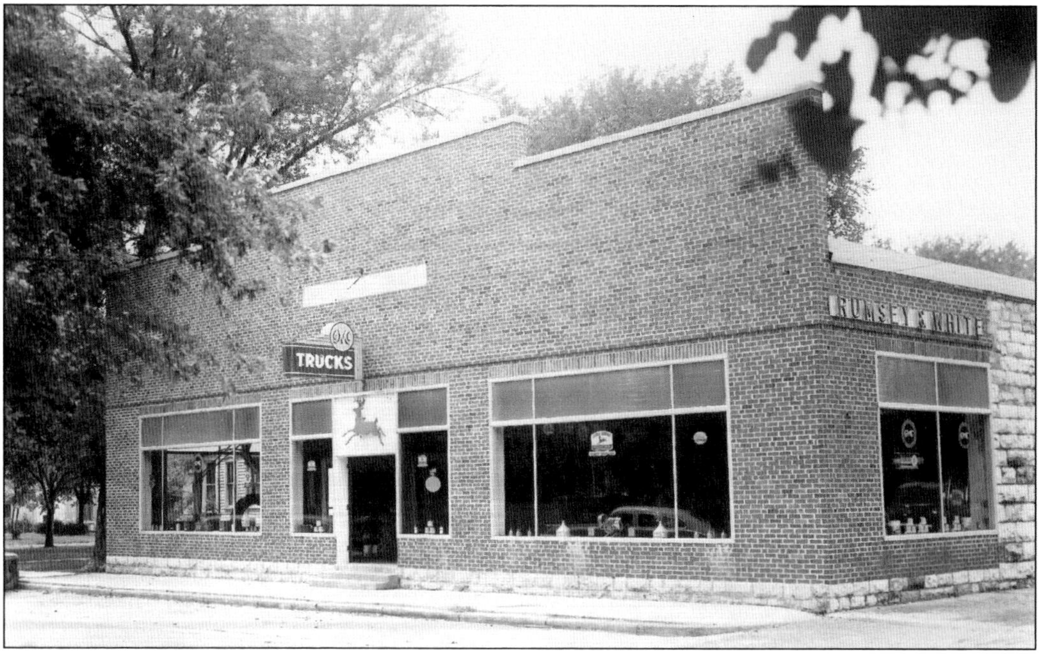

Rumsey and White offered a variety of services and products for Council Grove shoppers. These 1948 photographs demonstrate how early-20th-century businesses in small towns wore many hats to meet the needs of their customers. Above, the Rumsey and White building sports dealership signs for GMC trucks and John Deere tractors. Below, Rumsey and White's John Deere service and parts department offers full service for its customers. (Both, courtesy Morris County Historical Society.)

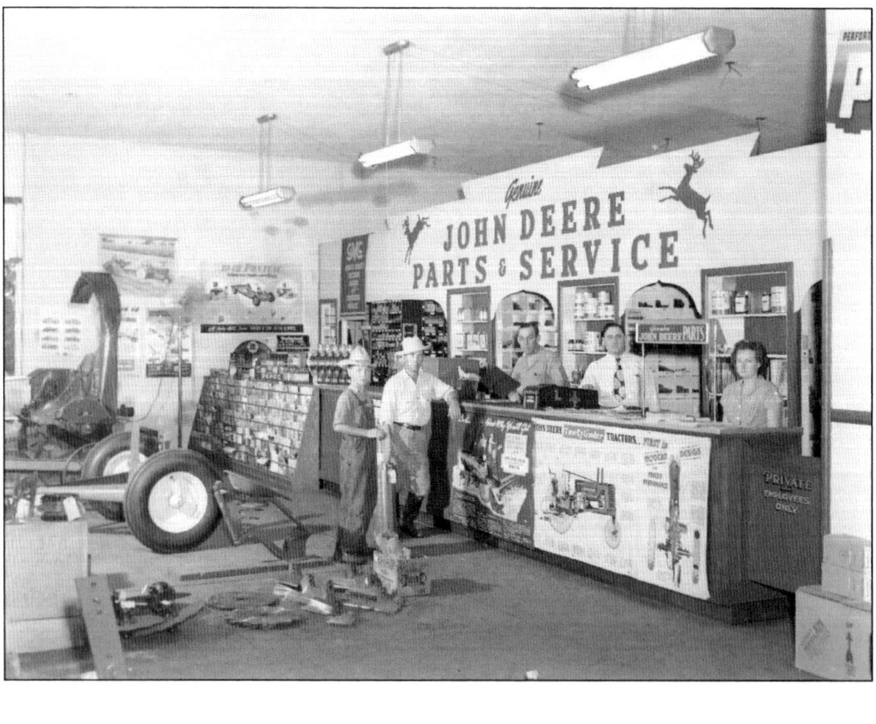

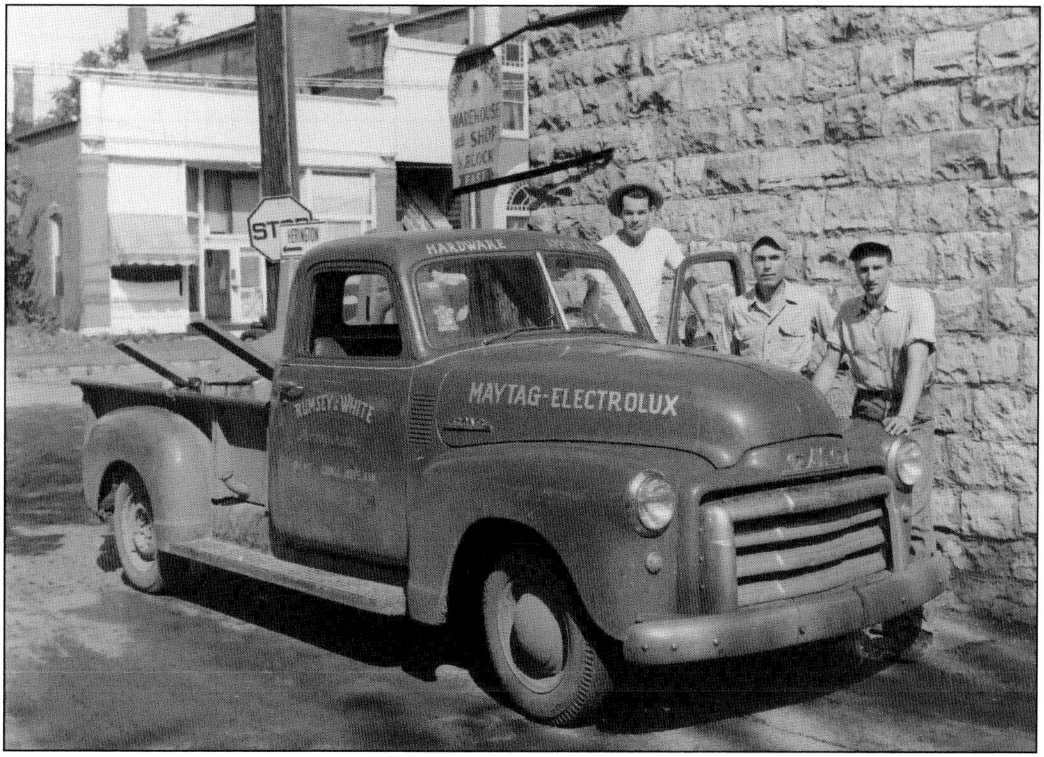

Above, Rumsey and White also provided heating and plumbing services in Council Grove at the time of this 1948 view. Three unidentified members of the service department are seen outside the building with a service truck. Below, Rumsey and White offers a wide variety of goods from hardware items to household goods and, in the foreground, even an outboard motor. (Both, courtesy Morris County Historical Society.)

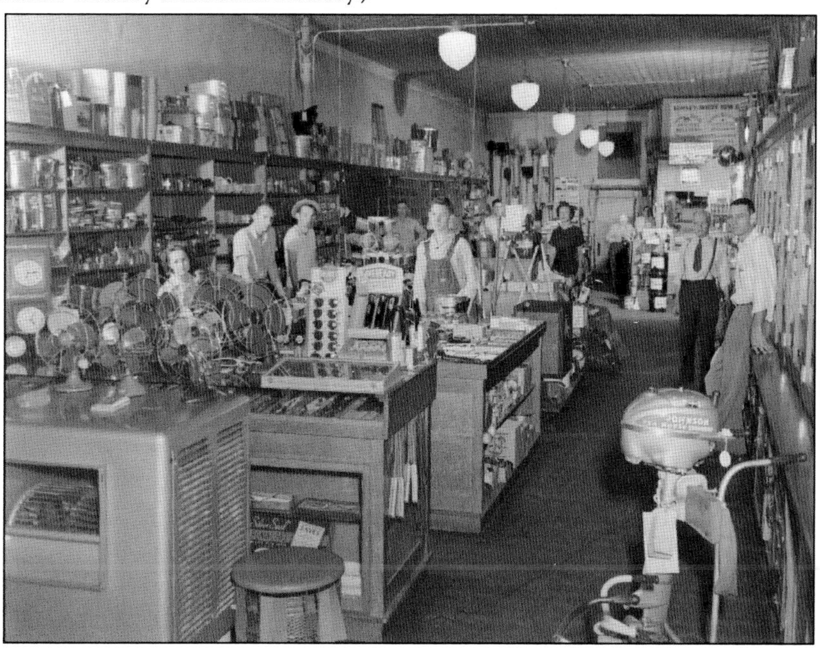

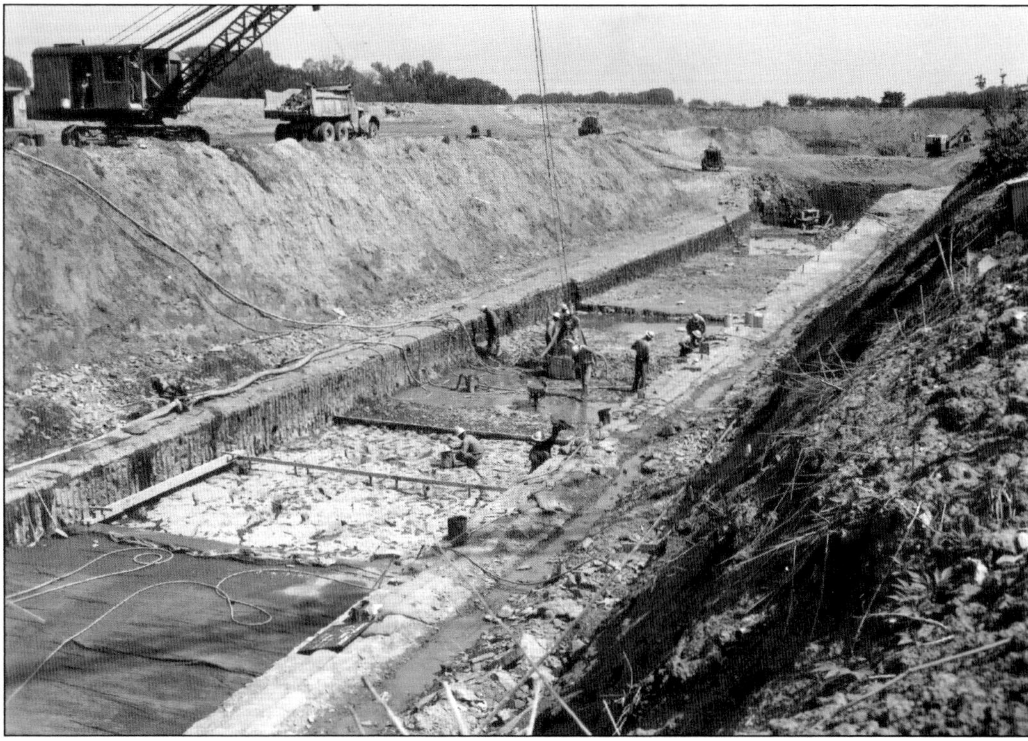

Above, Army Corps of Engineers workers can be seen preparing the embankment for the dam at Council Grove Lake in this photograph taken September 27, 1963. Below, in this view of the lake outlet, heavy machinery can be seen compacting the spillway. This image, dated May 9, 1962, looks to the south. Construction began on the lake in 1960, and it was officially placed into operation in October 1964 at a cost of $11.5 million. (Both, courtesy Morris County Historical Society.)

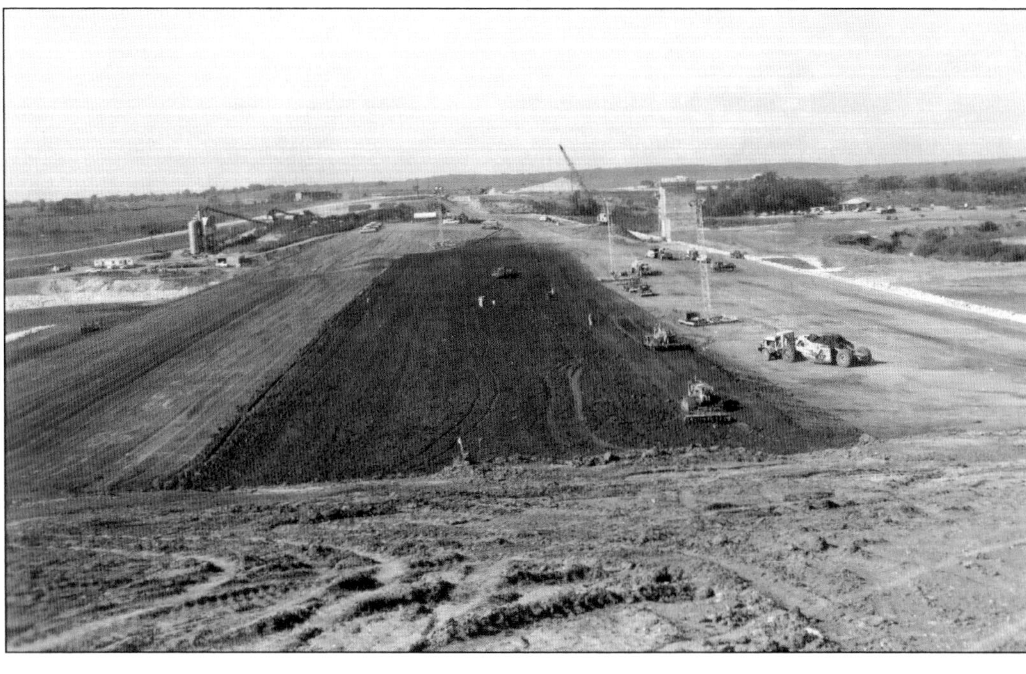

Three

Flint Hills Scenic Byway

The Flint Hills Scenic Byway winds 48 miles through the enormous pastures of southern Morris County, following K-177 Highway to the south into the heart of Chase County. The byway received official designation as a Kansas State Scenic Byway in 1995. On September 22, 2005, the byway received an official designation as a National Scenic Byway from the Federal Highway Administration.

A traveler motors south of Council Grove seeing expansive pastures on both sides of the highway. While the distances seem vast, they only appear larger and more panoramic the further one travels. Seventeen miles south of Council Grove, one arrives at the Tallgrass Prairie Preserve in Chase County. On the west side of the road stands the Stephen F. Jones Spring Hill Farm and Stock Ranch. Jones amassed 7,000 acres of land in Chase County, on which he built a picturesque limestone mansion completed in 1881, costing $25,000. To the south of the house is a three-story limestone barn and stable, 60-feet-by-110-feet in size, constructed at a cost of $15,000. Jones and his wife, Louisa, had five children, but only their youngest, Louisa "Loutie," was living with her parents while they were in Strong City.

Three miles south of the Jones house, the traveler crosses US Highway 50, and to the left one sees the home and barns of Barney Lantry's Deer Park Farm. Constructed in 1878, the Lantry ranch's name came from the small herd of pet deer he kept on the property. When Stephen Jones decided to leave Chase County in February 1888, he sold his Spring Hill Farm to his neighbor and partner in the Strong City Bank, Barney Lantry. The stone Jones mansion became quarters for hired men working for Lantry.

Barney Lantry operated stone quarries around Chase County, the most notable referred to as Crusher Hill. Soon, the railroads became a primary customer of Lantry's. Chase County limestone from his quarries built the roadbeds and depots for railroads across the western United States. And Lantry became the wealthiest man in Chase County. In addition to having huge success in business and ranching, Lantry was a major figure in the Democratic Party in Kansas. In 1894, he was the unsuccessful Democratic candidate for state treasurer.

Lantry's holdings amounted to 13,000 acres, including the Spring Hill and Deer Park Farms and the stone quarries. When he died in 1895, the county mourned the passing of the wealthiest man in the state of Kansas. Mourners lined the streets of Strong City as Lantry's body was transported to the depot to be returned to Wisconsin for burial.

Lantry's son Henry continued to successfully operate the stone and ranching business in Strong City until his death in 1904. At that time, Lantry's other son, Charles, liquidated all of the assets in Kansas, selling the ranch and stone quarries, before moving to North Carolina to pursue a railroad construction business.

Lantry's body had been transported to Madison, Wisconsin, for burial, and when his wife, Bridget, died the next year, she too was interred there, beside her husband. In 1896, an elaborate mausoleum was constructed of granite and marble in Resurrection Cemetery with the name Lantry over the door, dated that year. Despite his wealth, there was never any money endowed to maintain the structure, and in 1997 it was crumbling and the cemetery believed the crypt to be empty. The structure was demolished, and when removed, four graves were discovered under three inches of concrete. The stone with the carved Lantry name was placed on new earth, covering the graves.

The traveler passes down Cottonwood Street in Strong City. Buildings of cut stone once lined both sides of the street. Just before crossing the railroad tracks, one sees the Strong City depot, constructed in 1913 by the Atchison, Topeka & Santa Fe Railway. Continuing south on K-177 Highway, the traveler passes along the bottom ground created by years of flooding by the Cottonwood River. Crossing the river on the new bridge, one sees the stone bridge constructed in 1914 just upstream to the west. Just beyond that lies the waterfall over the dam crossing the Cottonwood River. This diversion of the river powered the mill at Cottonwood Falls for years. The stone bridge has recently been restored and is part of a pedestrian walkway between Cottonwood Falls and Strong City. The old road crossed the stone bridge and entered Cottonwood Falls on Broadway Street, went through the business district, and ended at the Chase County Courthouse, built in 1873.

Eleven miles south of Cottonwood Falls, travelers pass the Crocker Ranch on the west side of the highway, homesteaded by Erastus Crocker in 1866. His son Ed Crocker and his wife, Maude Brandley Crocker, lived at the ranch headquarters for many years. Just south of the Crocker Ranch on the east side of the road is the Charles Rogler ranch, homesteaded in 1859. It remained in the Rogler family for 147 years. In 2006, the house and barn were sold to the Pioneer Bluffs Foundation, which operates an interpretive center and community-based organization.

Just a mile and a half south of Pioneer Bluffs, travelers enter Matfield Green. The AT&SF Railway runs along the west side of the highway, while the town of Matfield Green is platted to the east. The stockyards and depot at Matfield Green were a major shipping point for cattle in the Flint Hills from the time the line was established in 1923 until 1960.

Eight and a half miles south of Matfield Green is Bazaar. The first settlement in Bazaar was established in 1856. The AT&SF railroad established a line through Bazaar and a depot in 1887, and the town became a major shipping point for cattle. As many as 2,000 cattle cars were shipped from the depot during the fall season as the town became the busiest railhead in the nation.

Travelers motor 20 more miles south on K-177 Highway to Cassoday through the most spectacular vistas on the byway as the horizon seems to expand forever.

The Flint Hills Scenic Byway is one of the only two National Scenic Byways in the state of Kansas and the only byway in Kansas that contains a National Park Historic Site. Spectacular scenery and a rich history make the Flint Hills Scenic Byway a must-see for everyone.

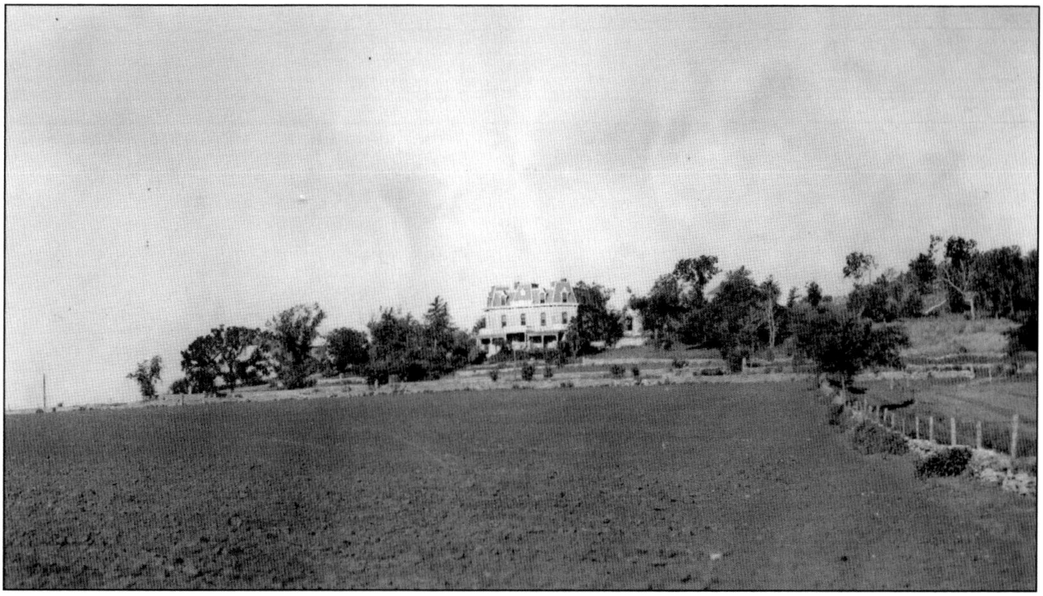

These two views of the Spring Hill ranch were taken in 1930 when the property was owned by Flora Benninghoven, after her husband, Otto, died. The fields in front of the ranch house were cultivated at this time and not in native grass. The state highway claimed much of this area as a right-of-way when K-177 Highway was realigned in the 1950s. Today, the Spring Hill Ranch house and barn are owned by the National Park Service as a part of the Tallgrass Prairie Preserve. (Both, courtesy Phyllis Scherich collection.)

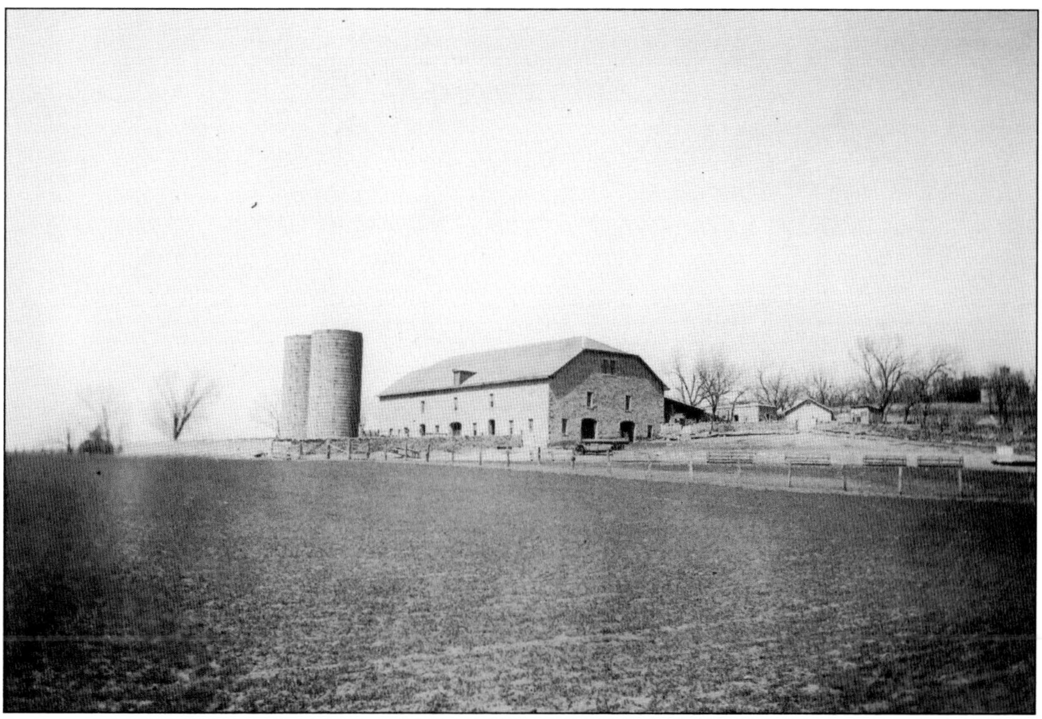

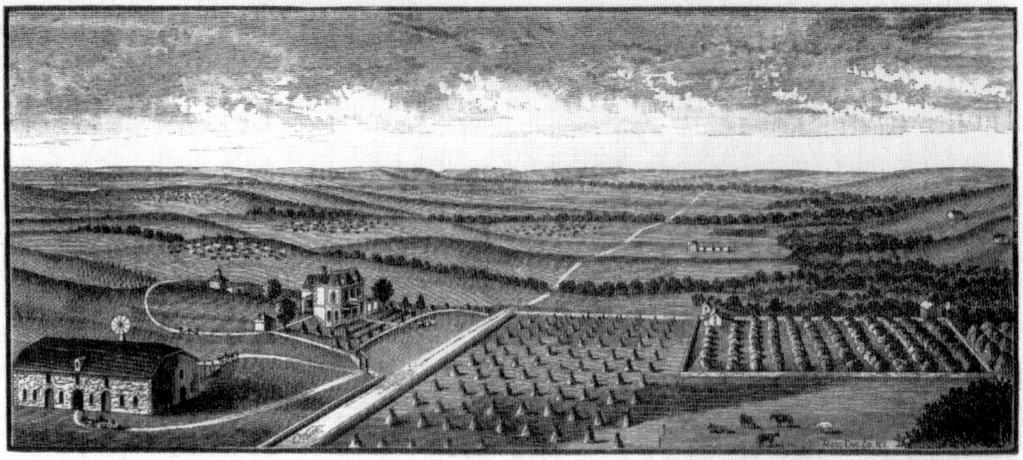

STOCK RANCH OF S. F. JONES, NEAR STRONG CITY, CHASE COUNTY.

This c. 1885 etching was included in a promotional book published by the Missouri, Kansas and Texas (Katy) Railroad. The stone fence along the roadway in front of the barn can also be seen in the photograph on page 2. The fields in front of the house were cultivated. (Courtesy Michael Stubbs.)

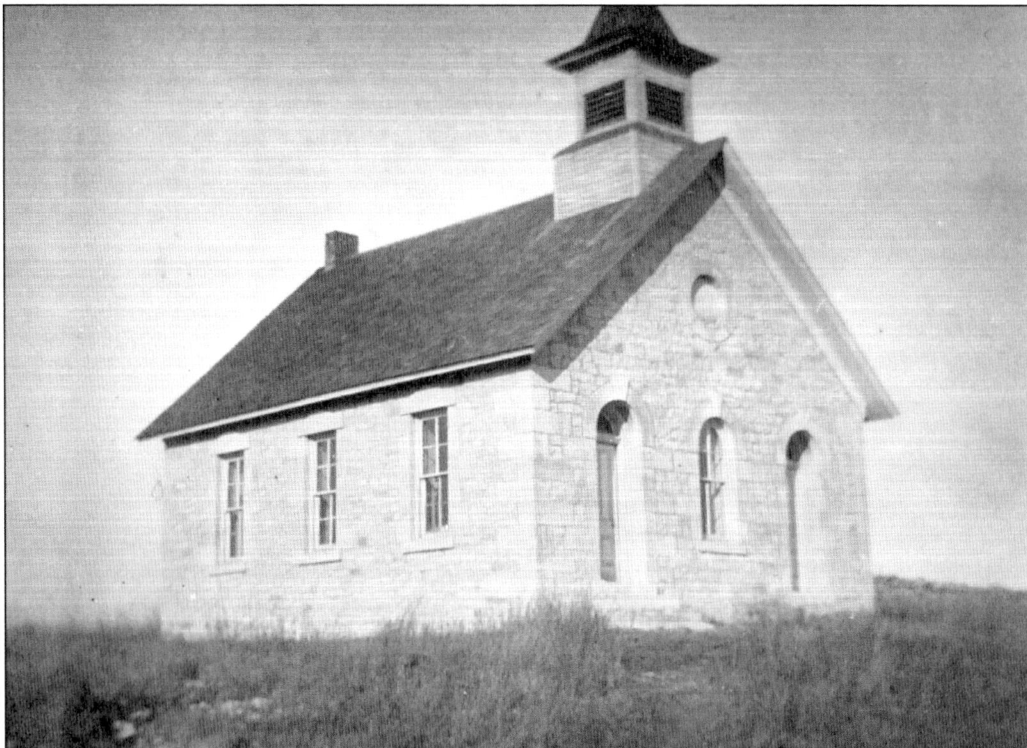

The Lower Fox Creek School, located just north of Stephen Jones's house, was constructed in 1882 by David Rettiger on property donated by Jones using stone from Barney Lantry's quarry. The first day of school was September 1, 1884; the school was closed in 1930. In 1968, fourteen garden clubs in the mideast district of Kansas restored the school. In 1974, it was placed on the National Register of Historic Places. (Courtesy Fred Howard II.)

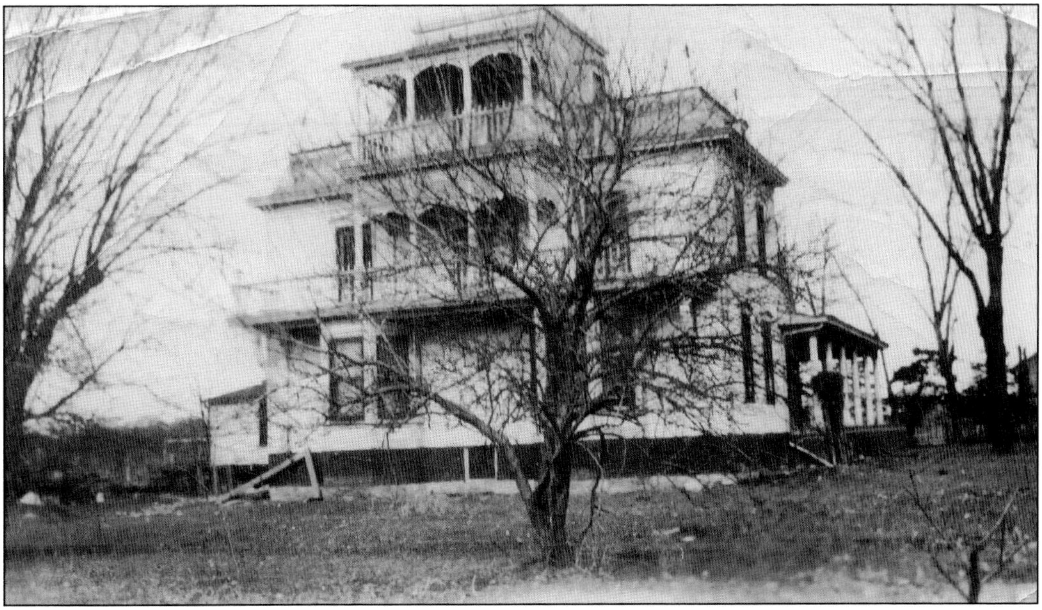

The Barney Lantry mansion, constructed in 1878–1879, was located on the north edge of Strong City. Known as Deer Park Ranch, for Lantry's pet deer, the ranch and quarry holdings included about 13,000 acres. Lantry was also partners with Stephen Jones in the Strong City Bank (see page 66). Lantry amassed a fortune from his limestone quarries as well as his ranching and banking interests. (Courtesy Phyllis Scherich collection.)

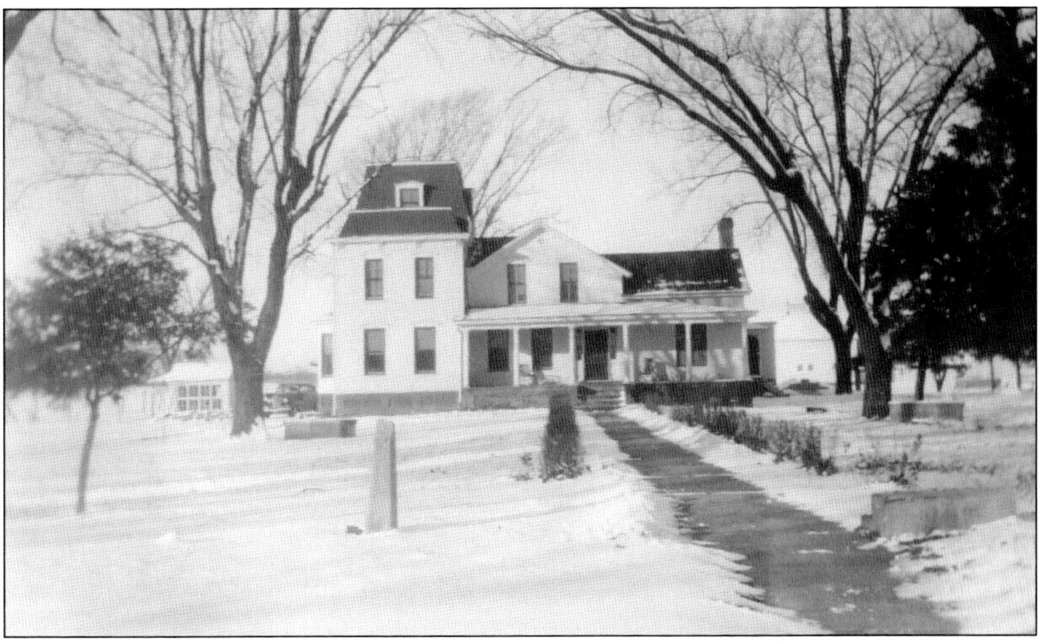

The Lantry mansion, seen here in 1936, became the headquarters of the Davis Ranch in early 1935 when George Davis purchased the property from Lester and Beulah Urschel, along with 10,000 acres. At the same time, Davis purchased the Jones ranch, including 1,080 acres, from Flora Benninghoven. Fred Howard, ranch manager, and his family moved into the Lantry house in the spring of 1935. (Courtesy Phyllis Scherich collection.)

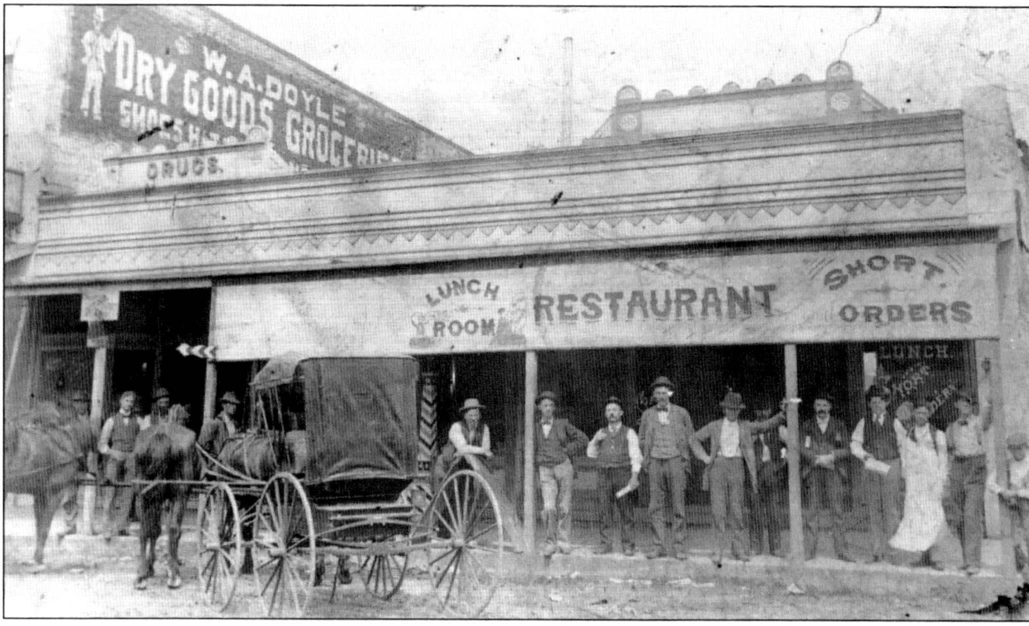

These two views of the east side of the 300 block of Cottonwood Street in Strong City were taken from the same location some 15 years apart. The view above from the late 1880s shows, from left to right, the Rettiger Building with the Doyle dry goods sign, a drugstore, and a lunchroom. In the photograph below, taken during the 1903 flood, the Rettiger Building is identified as Daub Brothers and the hotel and lunchroom on the far right as A.W. Ryan's One Minute Hotel and Café. (Both, courtesy Chase County Historical Society.)

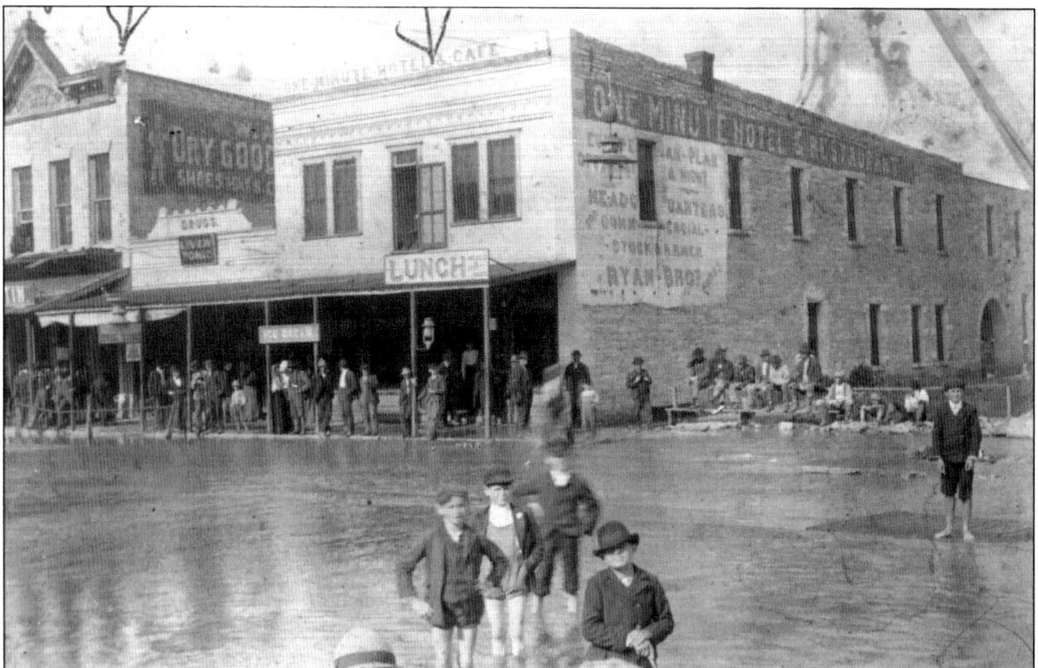

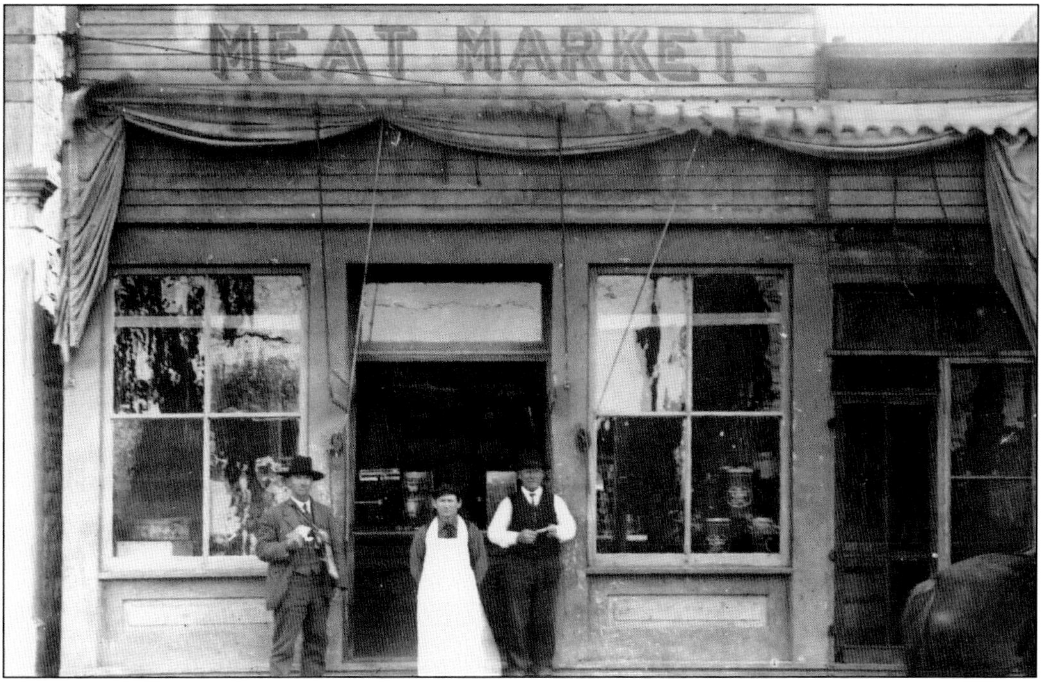

Wally Harvey's Meat Market in Strong City is seen in these two c. 1900 views. In the photograph above are, from left to right, Alvin Stanbrough, Chet Woodring, and Wally Harvey. This building is one of the early frame structures built in Strong City shortly after the town's development in the late 1870s. Below, in this interior view of the Meat Market, an unidentified butcher, left, and Wally Harvey pose for the photographer. Many frame buildings in all of the early Flint Hills towns succumbed to fire before city fire codes were developed. (Both, courtesy Chase County Historical Society.)

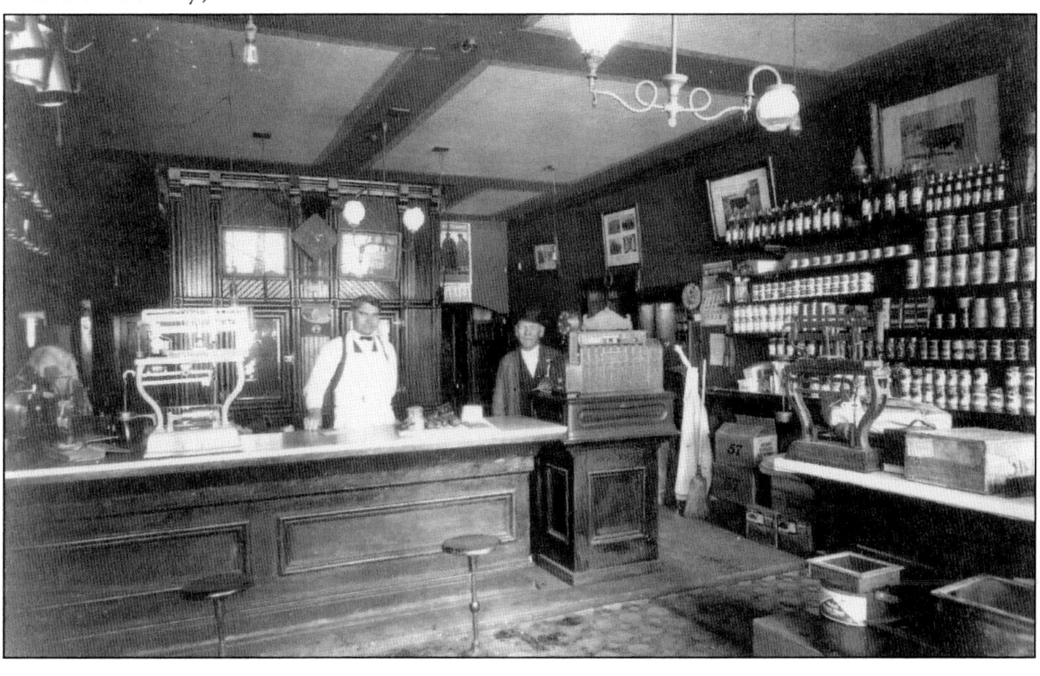

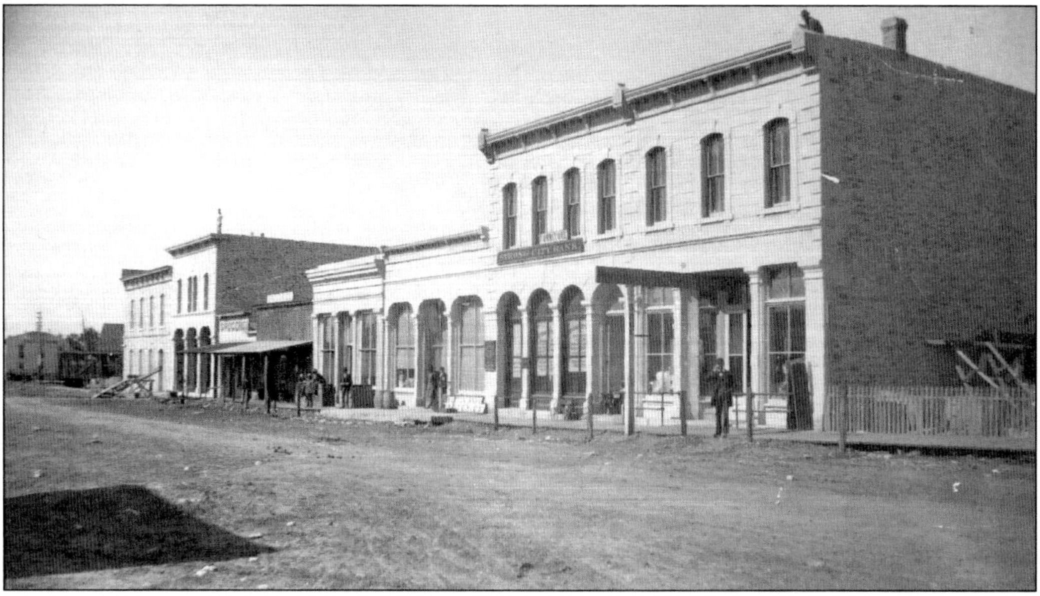

Above, this 1880s view of the west side of the 300 block of Cottonwood Street in Strong City shows, from right to left, an unidentified grocery, the Strong City Bank (owned by Barney Lantry and Stephen Jones), Burton Bro's Groceries, an unidentified stone building, two grocery stores occupying frame buildings, and the Bank Hotel and Café, apparently under construction; there is a man on the roof. Just beyond this block, one can see the roof of the depot. Below, a group of men are seen in front of the Grand Hotel and the Kansas Wagon Depot, located opposite the One Minute Hotel seen on page 64. (Above, courtesy Greg Hoots; below, Chase County Historical Society.)

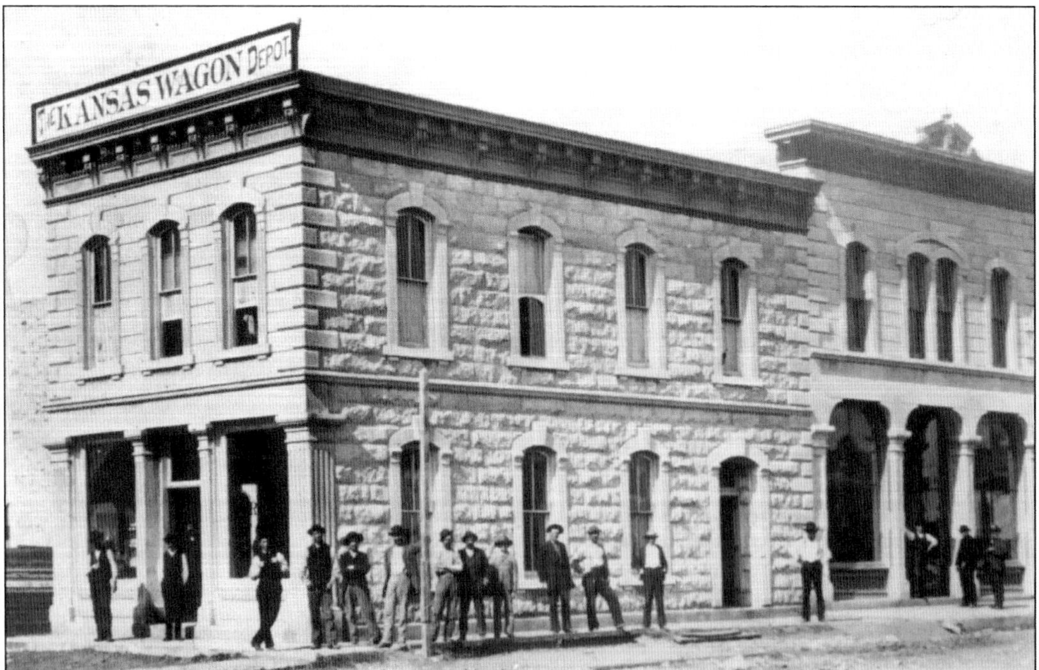

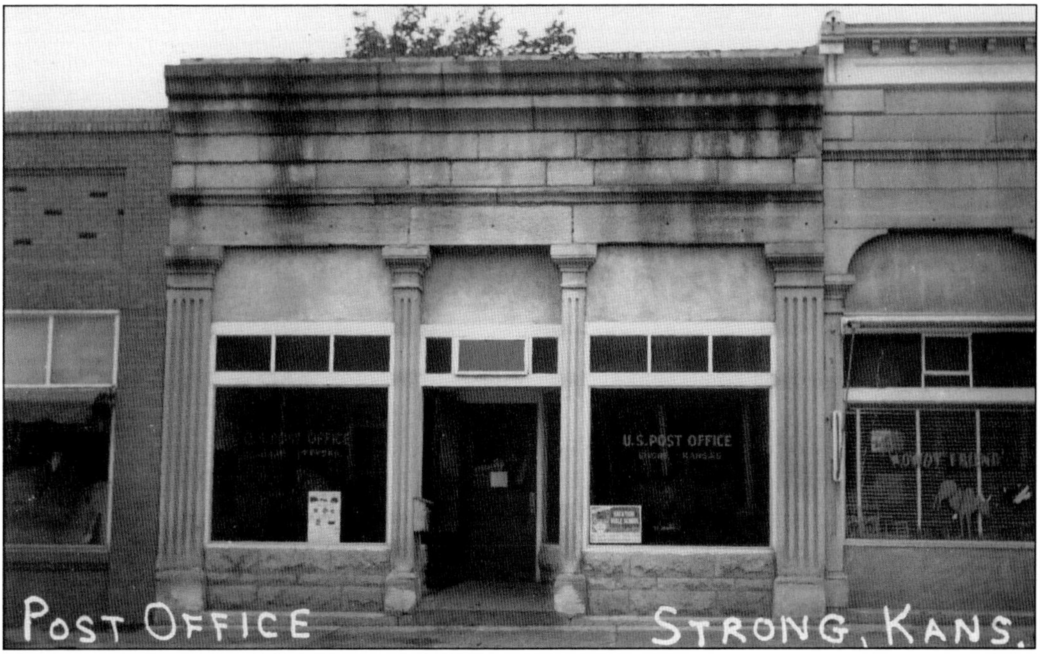

Above, this real-photo postcard view of the US post office located at 309 Cottonwood Street in Strong City dates from around 1920. Strong City was created in 1871 when the Atchison, Topeka & Santa Fe Railway was completed to a point known as Cottonwood Station, as the town was known until 1881. In 1881, in response to a residents' petition, the name was changed to Strong, Kansas. In 1945, the city's name was changed to Strong City. Below, this real-photo postcard looks south on Main Street, now know as Cottonwood Street, into the 400 and 300 block. The trolley and tracks are visible in the center of the street. This card dates from around 1910. (Both, courtesy Greg Hoots.)

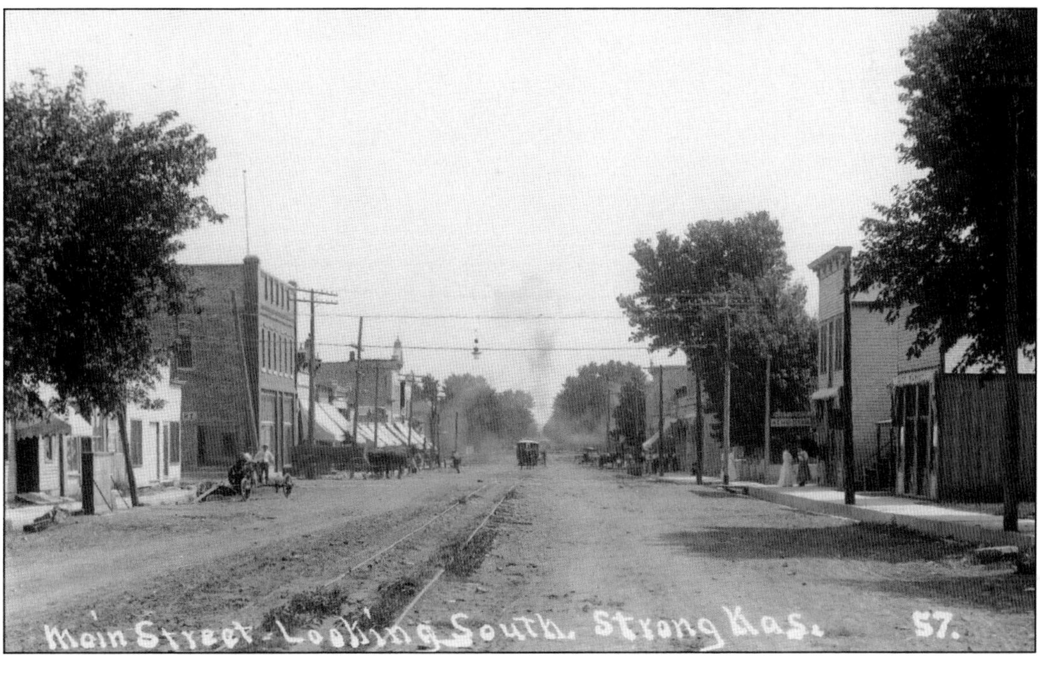

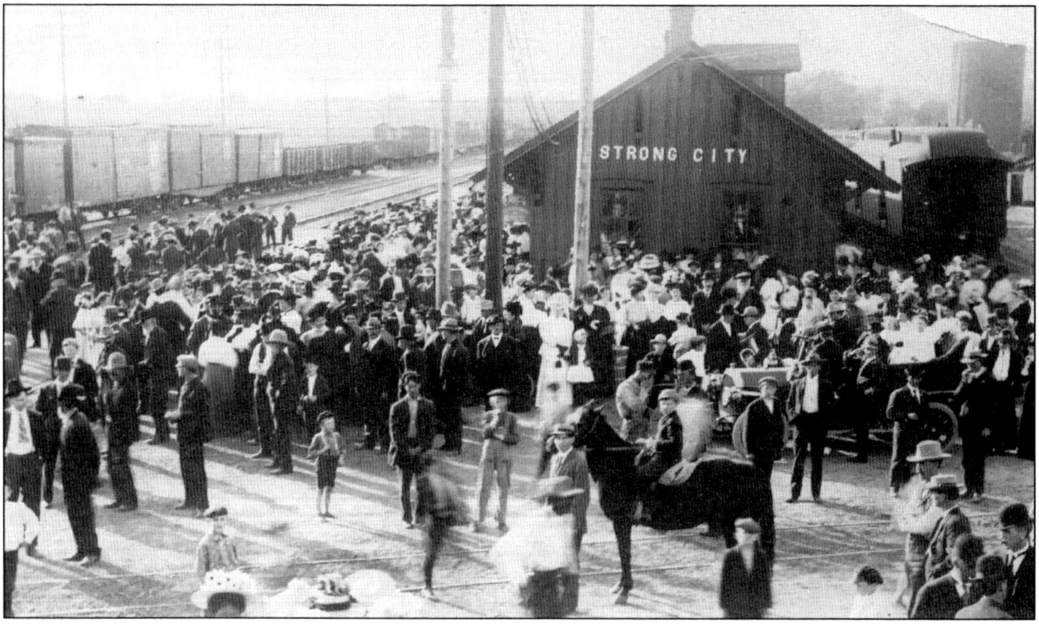

A crowd gathered on October 6, 1908, for the arrival of Pres. William Howard Taft. Taft made a whistle-stop appearance before the large crowd gathered at the old depot in Strong City. It was common for presidential candidates to tour the country from the back of a special car, addressing crowds from the rear of the train. Taft defeated William Jennings Bryan a month later by a comfortable margin. (Courtesy Chase County Historical Society.)

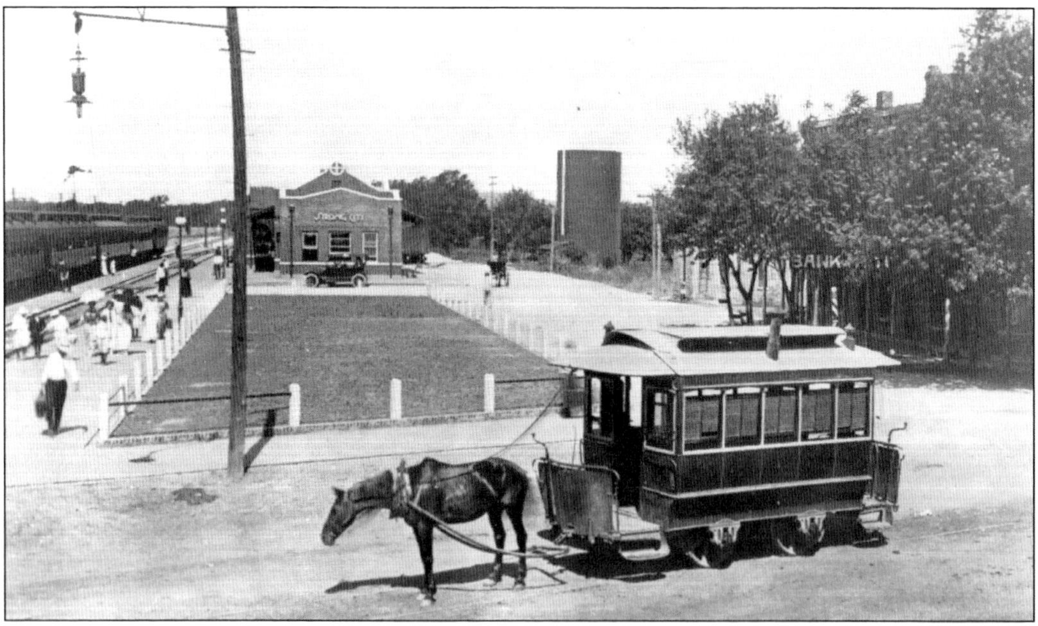

The new Atchison, Topeka & Santa Fe depot at Strong City, seen here, was completed on August 15, 1913, at a cost of $20,000. The old depot (image above) was located about 100 feet to the east of this new depot. Listed on the National Register of Historic Places, the depot was donated in 2006 to the city by the Burlington Northern Santa Fe Railway, and restoration plans are underway. (Courtesy Chase County Historical Society.)

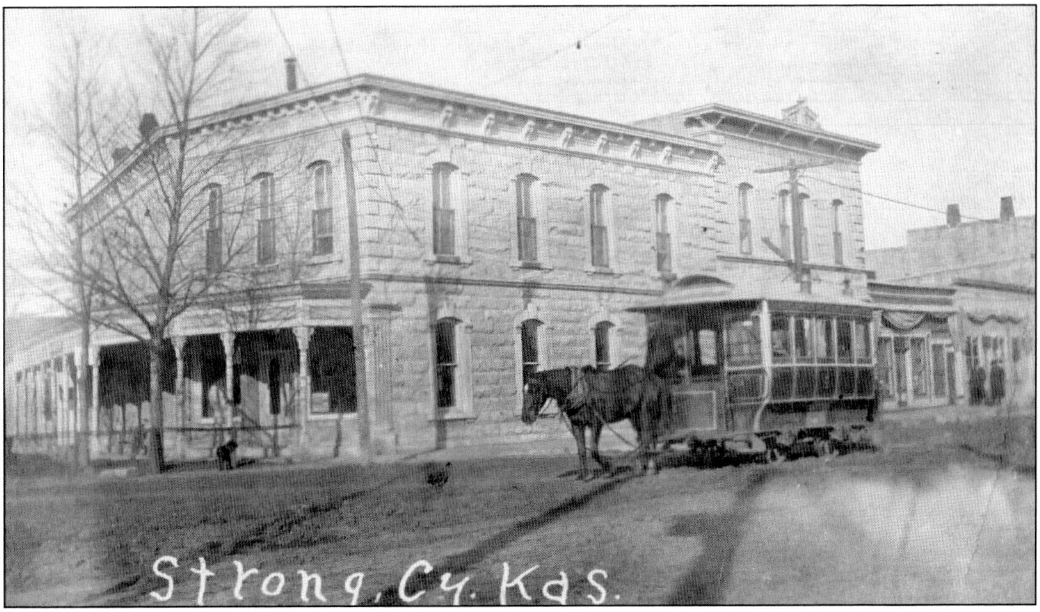

The Bank Hotel and Café were located at 301 Cottonwood Street in Strong City. The Bank Hotel was a landmark in the city. The café was a popular spot for cowboys from area ranches for lunch. The building, constructed in the 1880s, withstood several floods—including ones in 1929, 1935, and 1951—only to succumb to fire in 1970. (Courtesy Chase County Historical Society.)

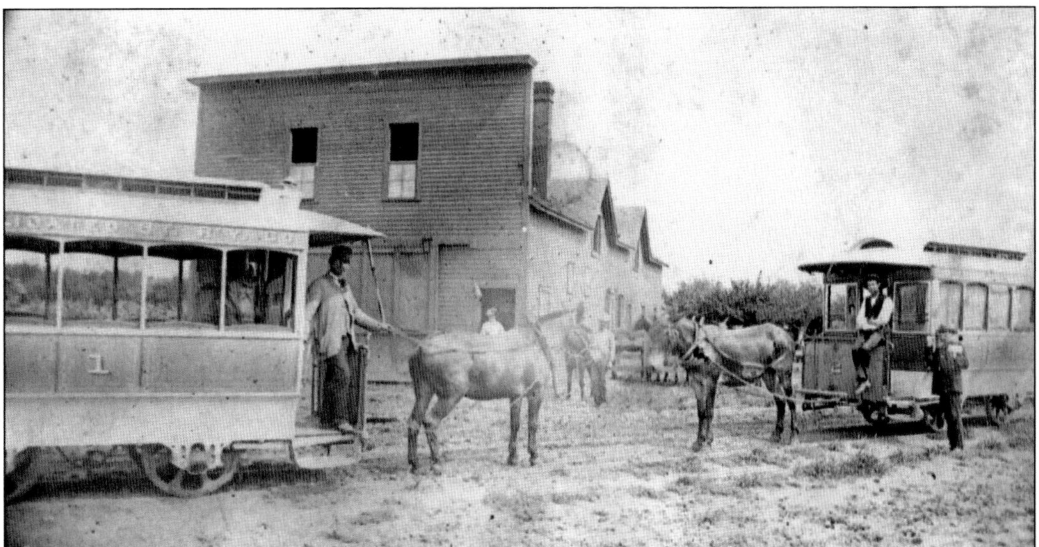

Two horse-drawn trolleys of the interurban line between Strong City and Cottonwood Falls are seen at the horse barn at the south end of Strong City around 1885. Seated in the car at left is Stephen F. Jones of the Spring Hill Ranch, and at the front of the opposite car is his son-in-law Wit Adare. The horse barn in the background burned on March 13, 1901. (Courtesy Chase County Historical Society.)

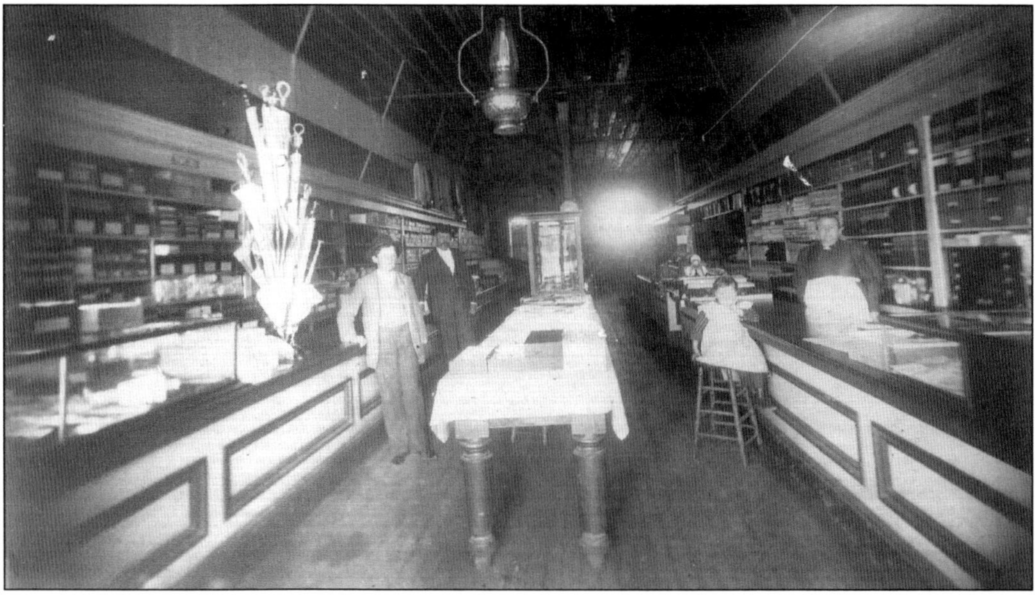

Wit Adare's dry goods store in Strong City is seen in this interior view from the early 1880s. Identified are, from left to right, Peyton Adare, Wit Adare, Annie Jones Adare, and Mildred Hickman. Stephen Jones's daughter Christiana Anna Jones married Calvin "Wit" Adare in Texas in 1867, but the Adares moved to Kansas when Jones settled there in 1878. (Courtesy National Park Service.)

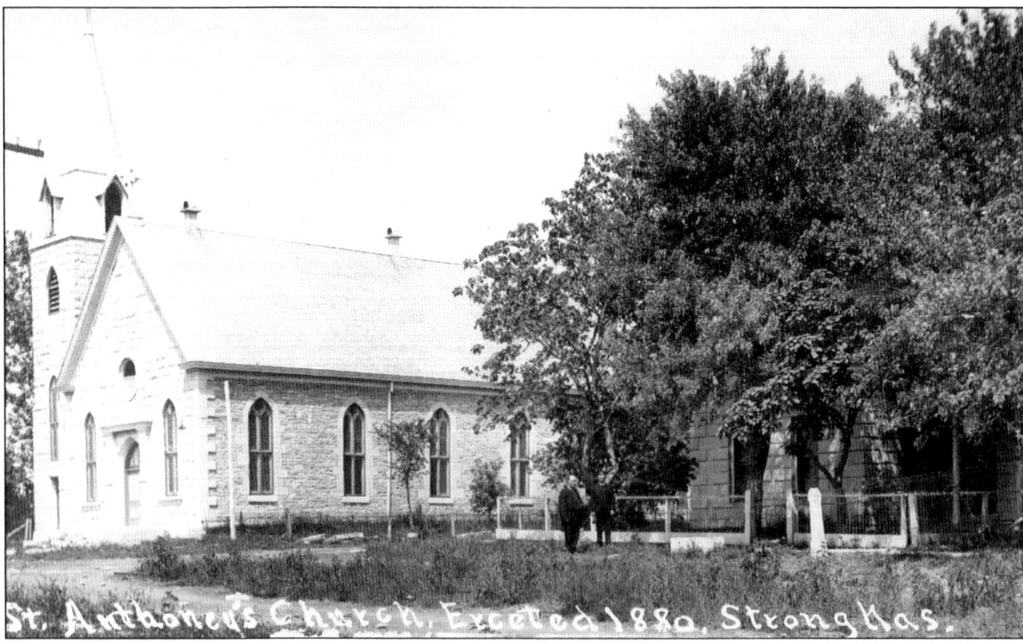

St. Anthony's Catholic Church was erected in 1880 and stands at 602 South Cottonwood Street in Strong City. The interurban trolley that operated in Strong City and Cottonwood Falls had its northern terminal in front of St. Anthony's. The south end of the trolley line was the Chase County Courthouse in Cottonwood Falls. (Courtesy Chase County Historical Society.)

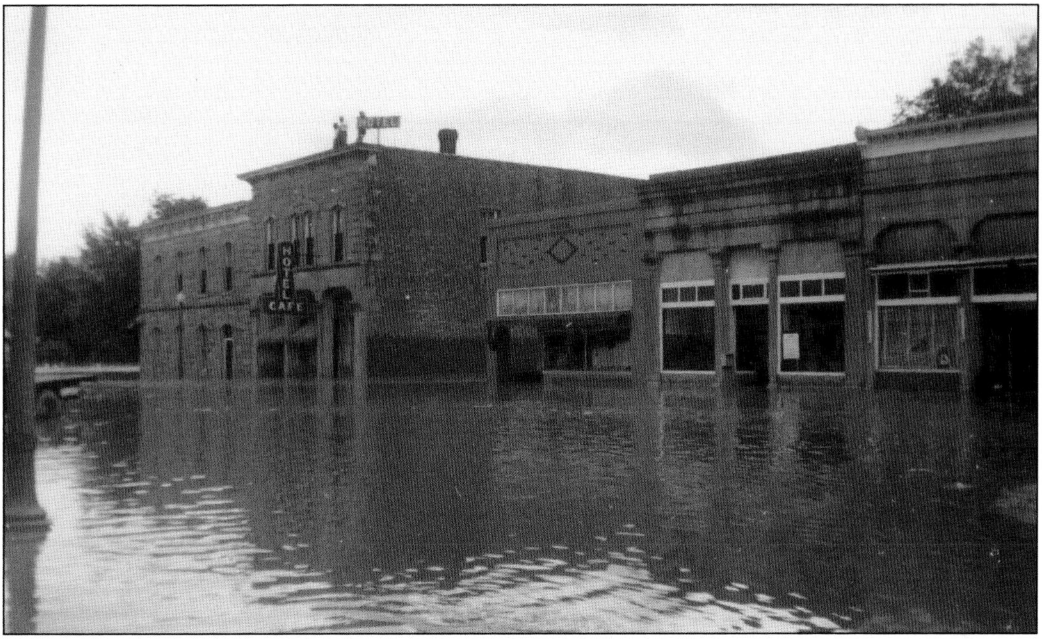

The west side of the 300 block of Cottonwood Street in Strong City is seen here in July 1951 when floodwaters backed up into the business district. Water can be seen four to five feet deep along the Bank Hotel and the Hotel Café. After the 1951 event, a levy was constructed to prevent flooding of this severity. (Courtesy Chase County Historical Society.)

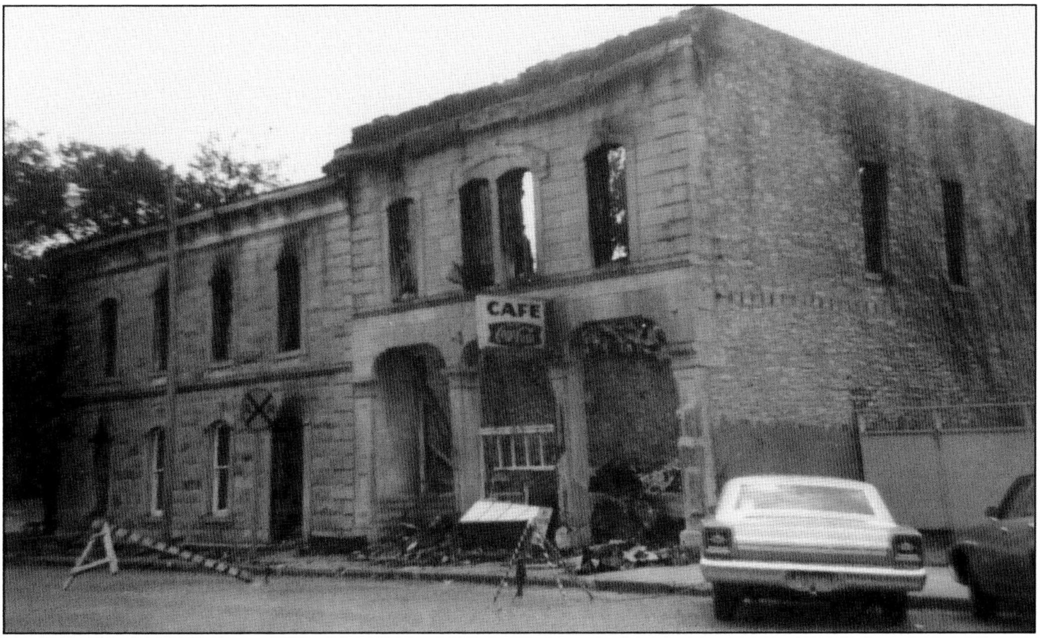

The Bank Hotel and Bank Hotel Café are seen here in 1970 when fire destroyed the buildings. The structures were landmarks in Strong City, dating to the late 1880s. The hotel was located just next door to the Atchison, Topeka & Santa Fe depot, making it a favorite for travelers. The charred remains of the buildings were razed, leaving an empty lot. (Courtesy Chase County Historical Society.)

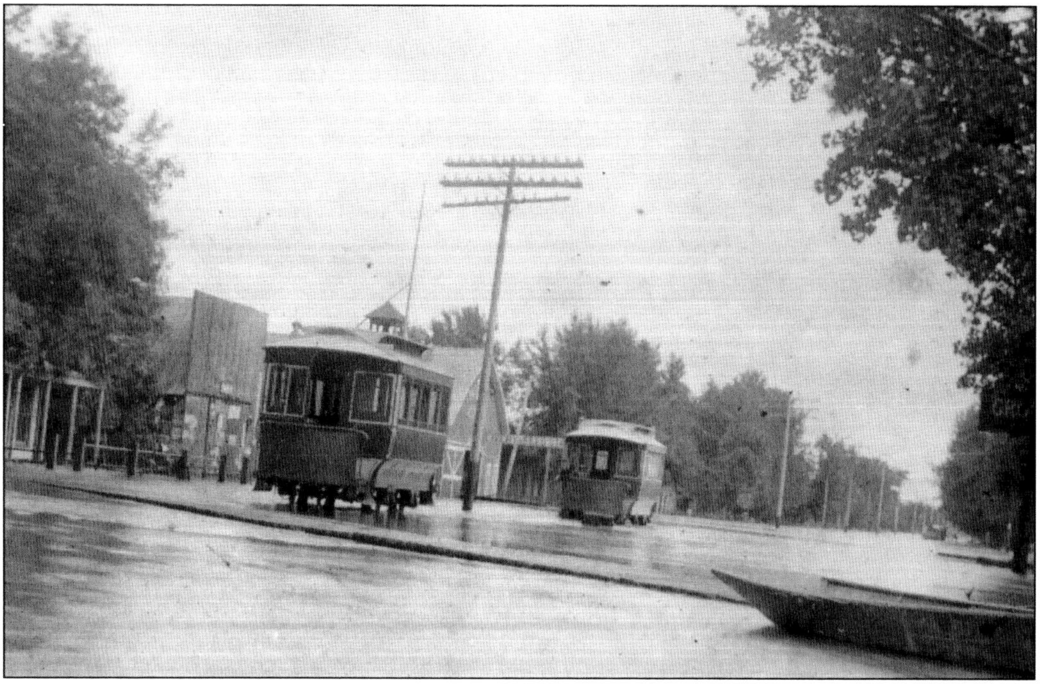

The Consolidated Street Railway Company, financed with capital from both Strong and Cottonwood Falls, was chartered on December 16, 1886, and the first streetcars began running on August 22, 1887. A single horse pulled a 14-foot-long metal streetcar equipped with benches for passengers and small stoves for heat. The driver was exposed to the elements. Here, two cars are stranded during the 1904 flood. (Courtesy Chase County Historical Society.)

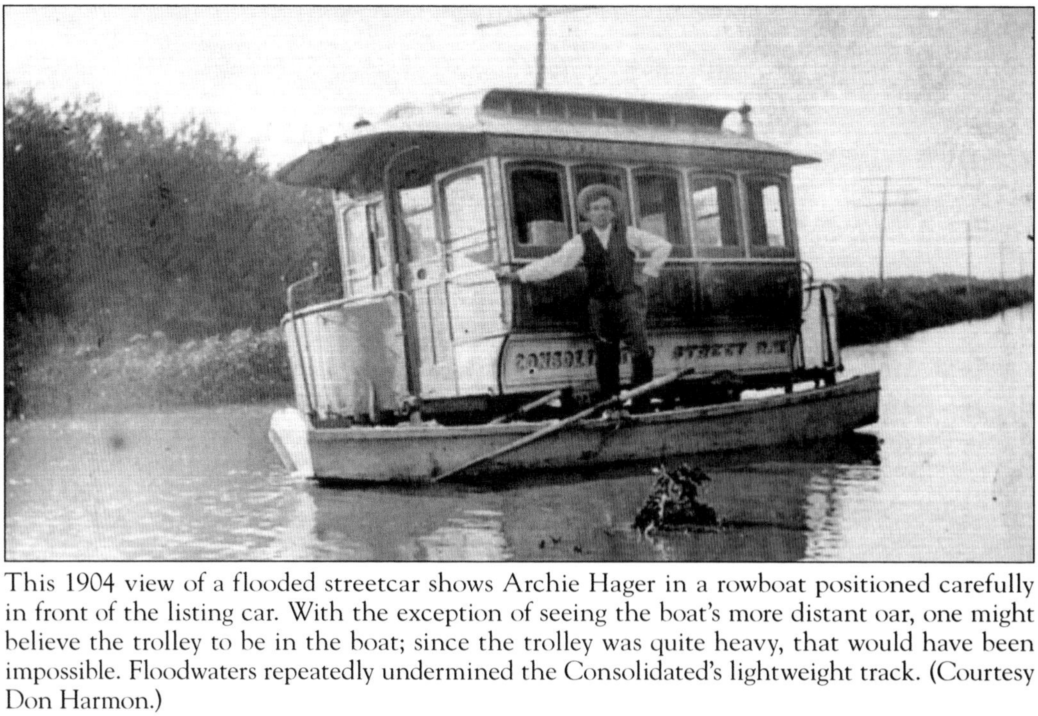

This 1904 view of a flooded streetcar shows Archie Hager in a rowboat positioned carefully in front of the listing car. With the exception of seeing the boat's more distant oar, one might believe the trolley to be in the boat; since the trolley was quite heavy, that would have been impossible. Floodwaters repeatedly undermined the Consolidated's lightweight track. (Courtesy Don Harmon.)

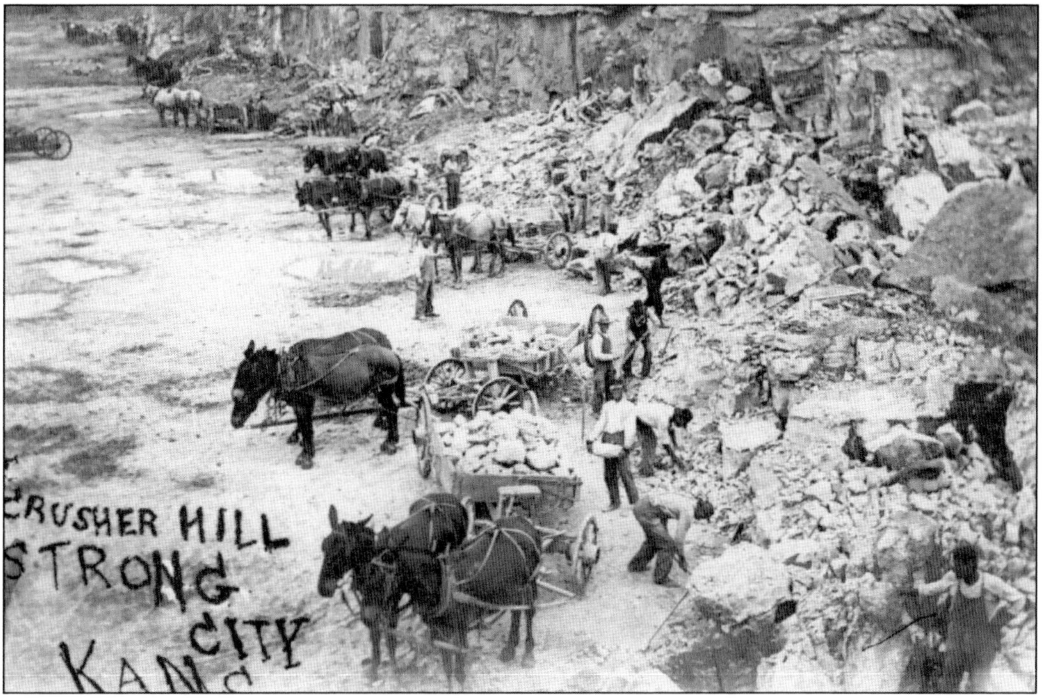

Crusher Hill was the name given to Barney Lantry's quarries located west of Strong City. When Lantry began quarrying limestone in Chase County, there was a shortage of labor, so he brought 300 Quakers to work in his mine. The Quakers had a small community of their own in Strong City. (Courtesy Chase County Historical Society.)

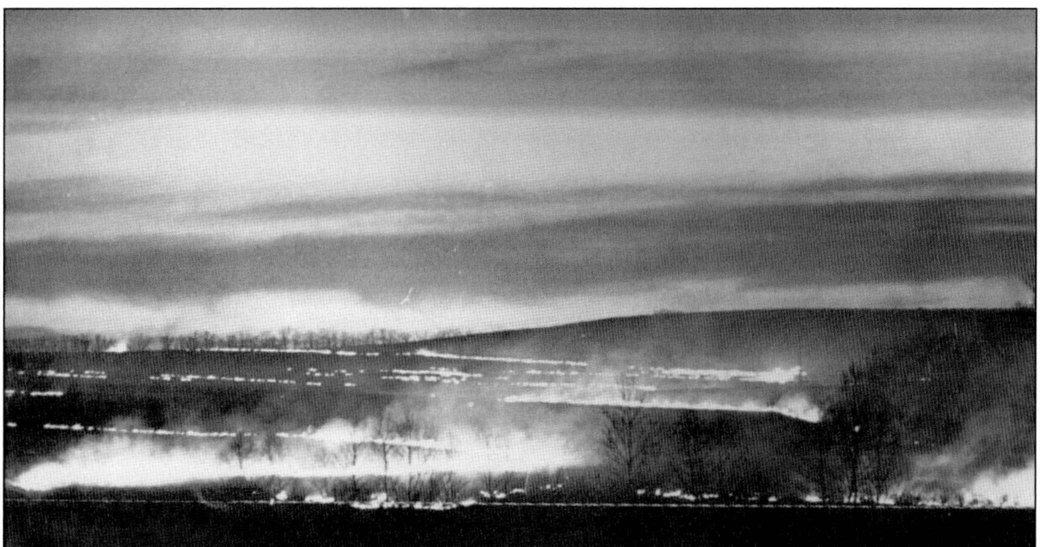

In the 1870s, prairie fires, often started by lightning or trains, endangered livestock, homes, and even towns in Chase County. Ranchers discovered, however, that after an early spring fire, the pastures would rejuvenate, while weeds and woody plants would be destroyed. Controlled burning began in an effort to improve pastures and decrease the likelihood of prairie fire. This night view of a controlled burn is from near Strong City. (Courtesy Greg Hoots.)

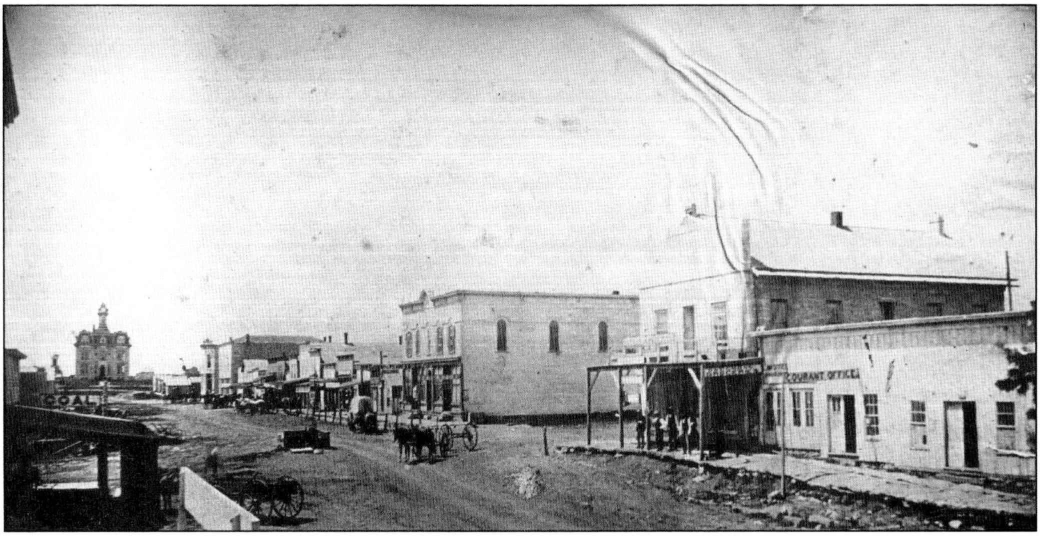

A view of Cottonwood Falls looks south down Broadway Street. This image dates from the late 1870s. The Chase County Courthouse, built in 1873, can be seen at the end of the street. The horse-drawn interurban trolley system would not be not constructed until 1887. This view also predates the disastrous 1883 fire, the effects of which are seen below. (Courtesy Chase County Historical Society.)

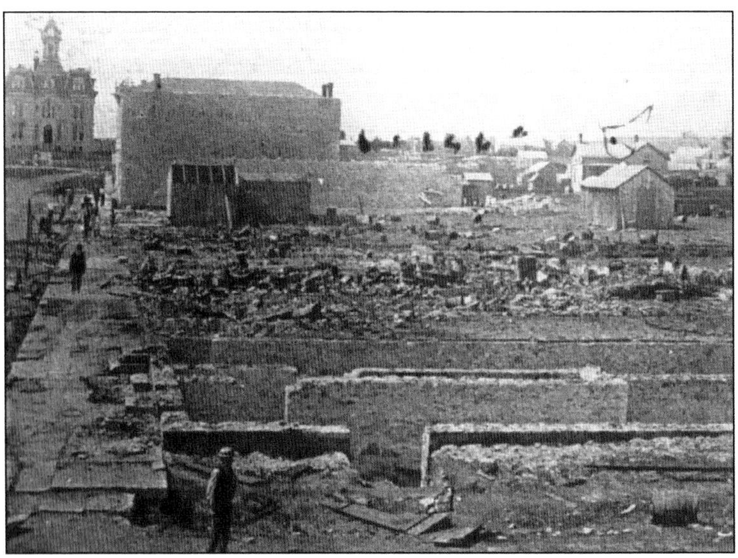

This photograph, from a stereoscope card, was taken the morning after the 1883 fire that destroyed two city blocks on Broadway Street in Cottonwood Falls. Although reported otherwise, according to the news reports of the day, the fire was started by lightning. The fire damage stopped at the Chase County National Bank building. (Courtesy Chase County Historical Society.)

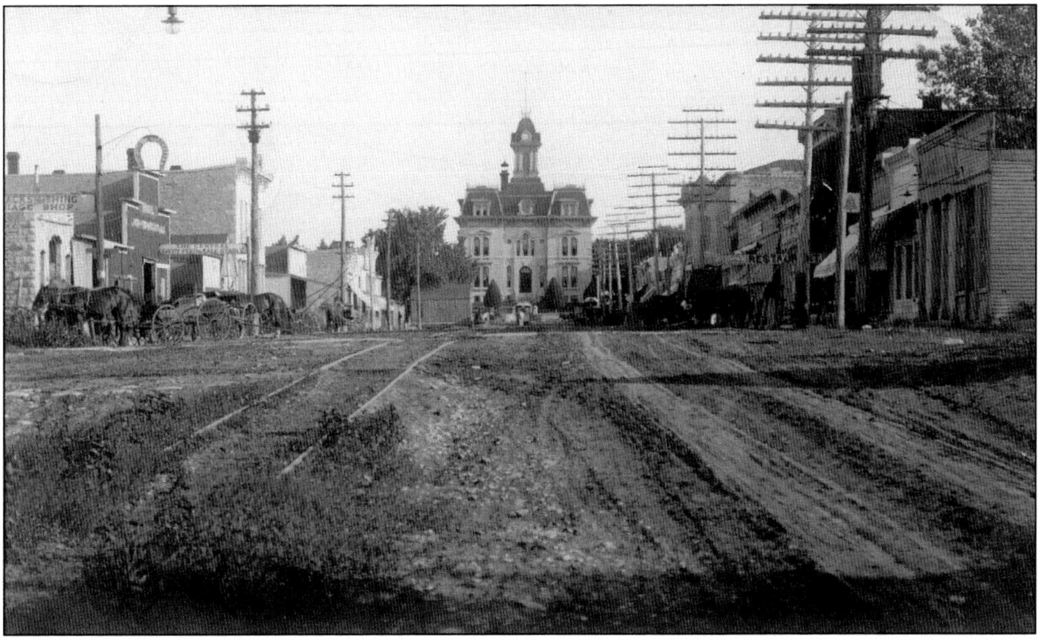

This view of Broadway Street dates from the late 1890s. One can see the interurban trolley tracks that ended at the courthouse. At the far left, with a horseshoe-shaped sign above the building, is H.F. Hoel's Livery and Stable. As there were two trolleys running simultaneously, horses had to maintain a speed of five miles per hour for the system to run on time. (Courtesy Chase County Historical Society.)

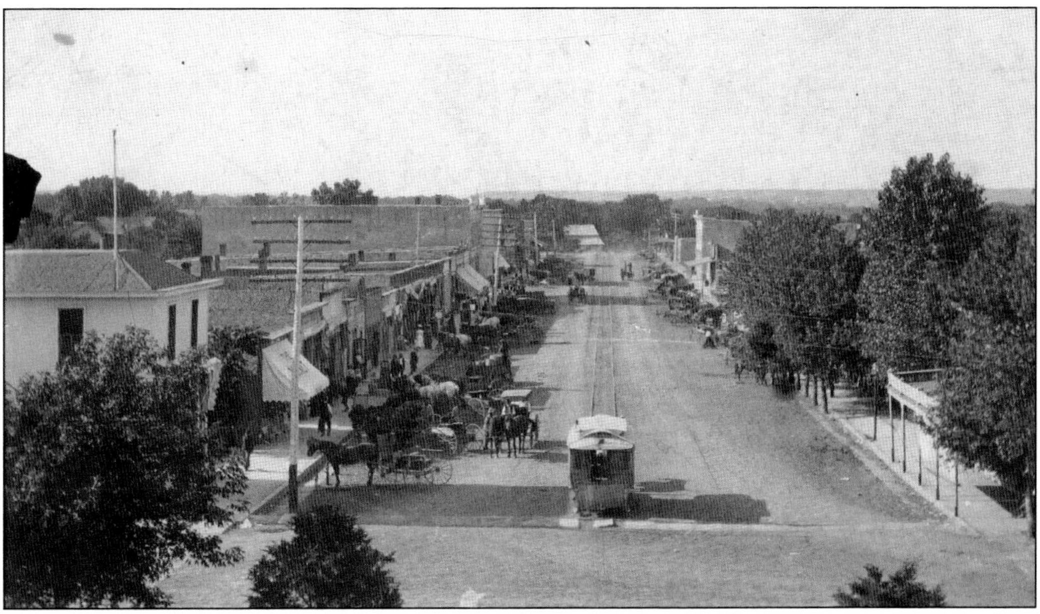

In this view from inside the Chase County Courthouse looking north, one can see the interurban trolley. There were no turnaround tracks at the ends of the line; the horses were simply unhitched from one end of the trolley and rehitched to the other end for the return trip. The trolley system had an excellent safety record despite crossing the AT&SF tracks in Strong almost two dozen times a day. (Courtesy Chase County Historical Society.)

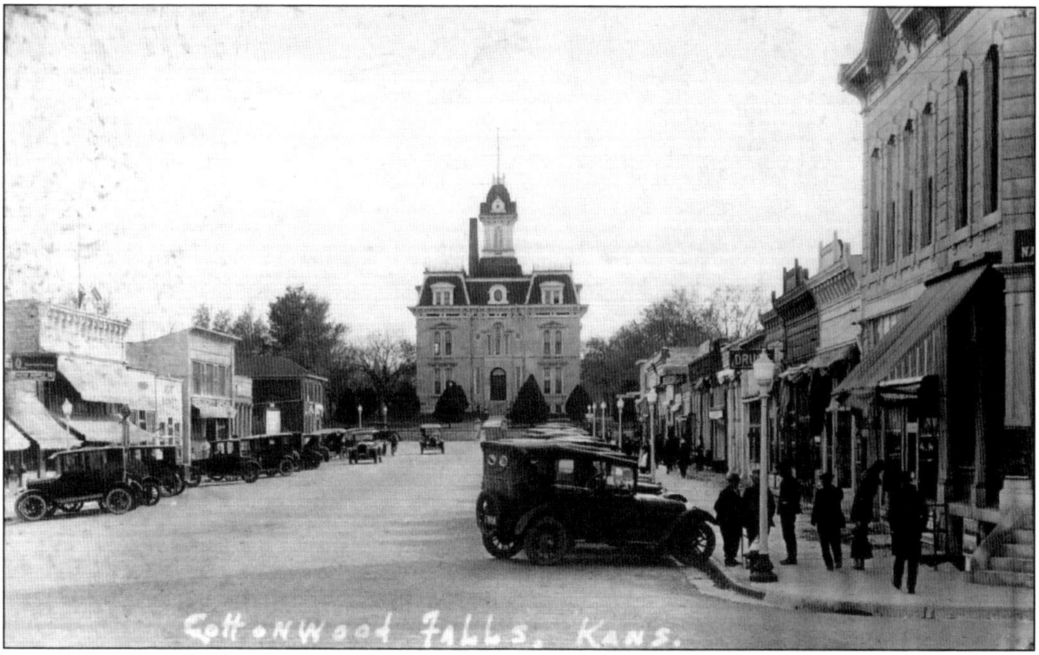

Broadway Street had a modern urban look in this 1920s real-photo postcard. Here, the horse-drawn trolley and its tracks have disappeared, and the street has been paved with cobblestones. The Chase County National Bank can be seen at the far right. Today, that building houses the Chase County Historical Society and museum. (Courtesy Greg Hoots.)

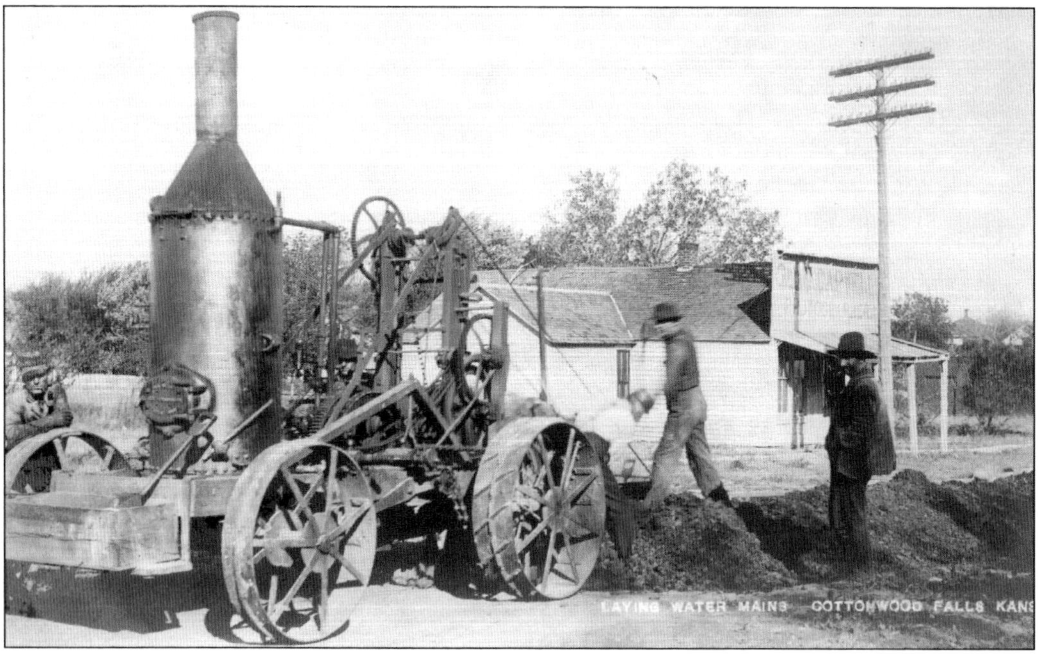

This real-photo postcard captures the laying of a water main in Cottonwood Falls. A steam-powered trenching hoe is seen excavating on East Pearl Street in front of photographer George Capwell's studio, just east of the courthouse. The original water main was wooden, and a section of that pipe is on display at the Chase County Historical Society's museum. (Courtesy Greg Hoots.)

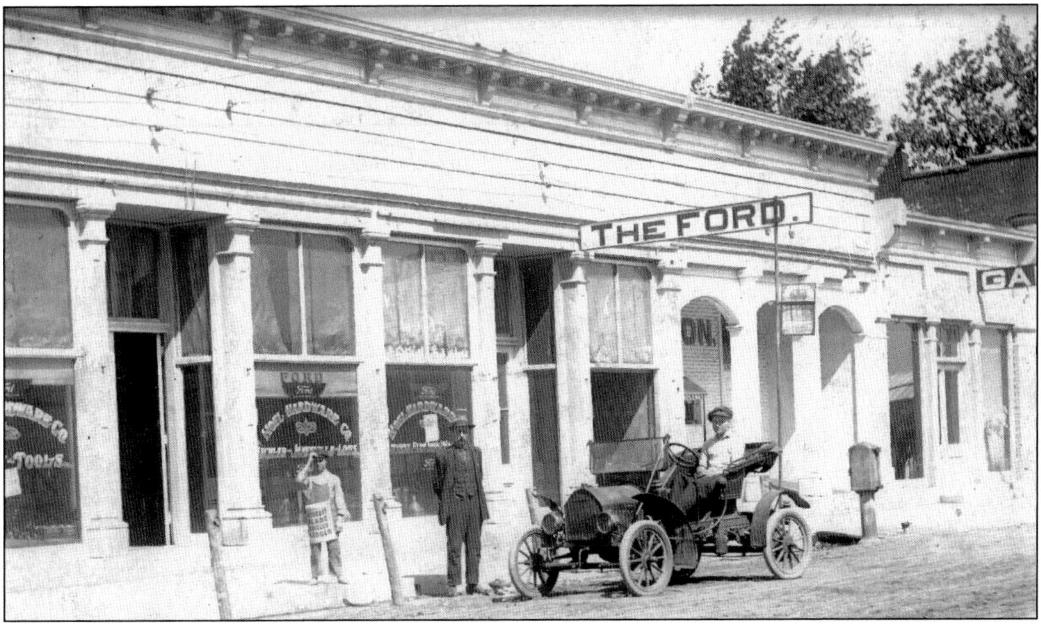

The reverse side of this real-photo postcard contains the handwritten message, "Uncle Billy Wolfrom's garage at Cottonwood Falls Spring of 1915. Clyde Mann in car." Hoel Hardware, the Ford dealer, and Wolfrom's garage are seen in this view of Broadway Street. The only building remaining today is the garage at the far right, located at 303 Broadway Street, now the Unified School District 284 offices. (Courtesy Greg Hoots.)

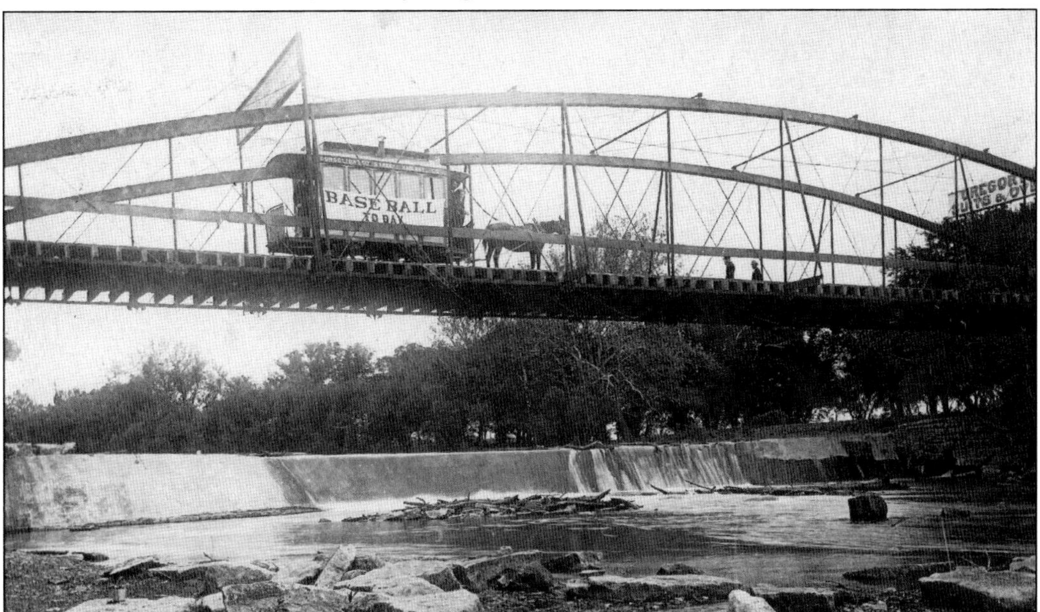

The steel arch bridge over the Cottonwood River was constructed in the early 1870s shortly after the Atchison, Topeka & Santa Fe Railway line arrived in Cottonwood Station, later to become Strong City. The interurban trolley line ran down the center of this bridge and also across the new stone arch bridge that replaced the steel structure in 1914. (Courtesy Chase County Historical Society.)

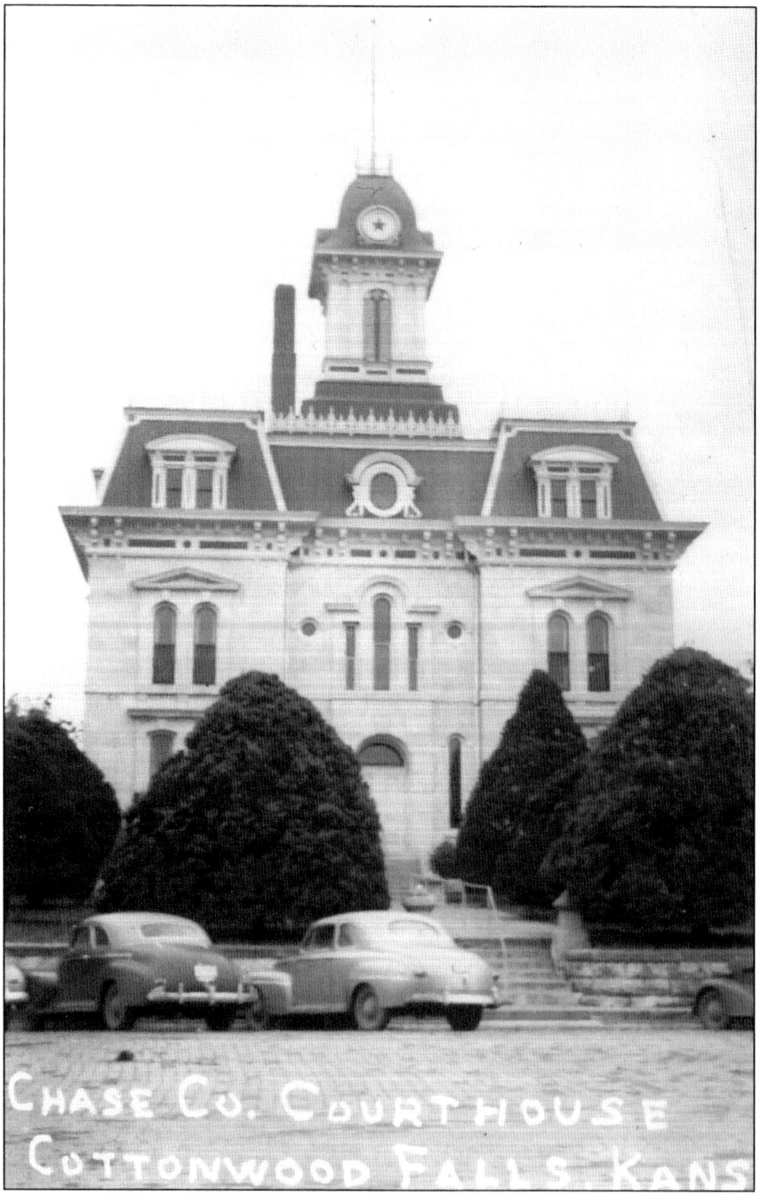

The Chase County Courthouse is located on 2.5 acres of ground donated to the county in 1871 by Isaac Alexander. Lawrence architect John Haskell was superintendent of the job, and more than a dozen stonemasons worked on the project. The building was completed on October 8, 1873, at a cost of $42,599.88. A 500-pound bell was installed in 1886. The courthouse was placed on the National Register of Historic Places in 1971. The facility is the oldest operating courthouse in the state of Kansas. Interestingly, for over a century there were residents living in the courthouse. Over the years, two dozen Chase County sheriffs and their families resided in the building. There was a kitchen in the basement, and the sheriff's family lived on the second floor. The sheriff was allowed 50¢ a day to feed a prisoner. Family members would often take food to the incarcerated. On December 3, 1967, the courthouse caught fire as a Christmas star located on the cupola experienced an electrical short. Only quick and effective action by firefighters saved the building. (Courtesy Greg Hoots.)

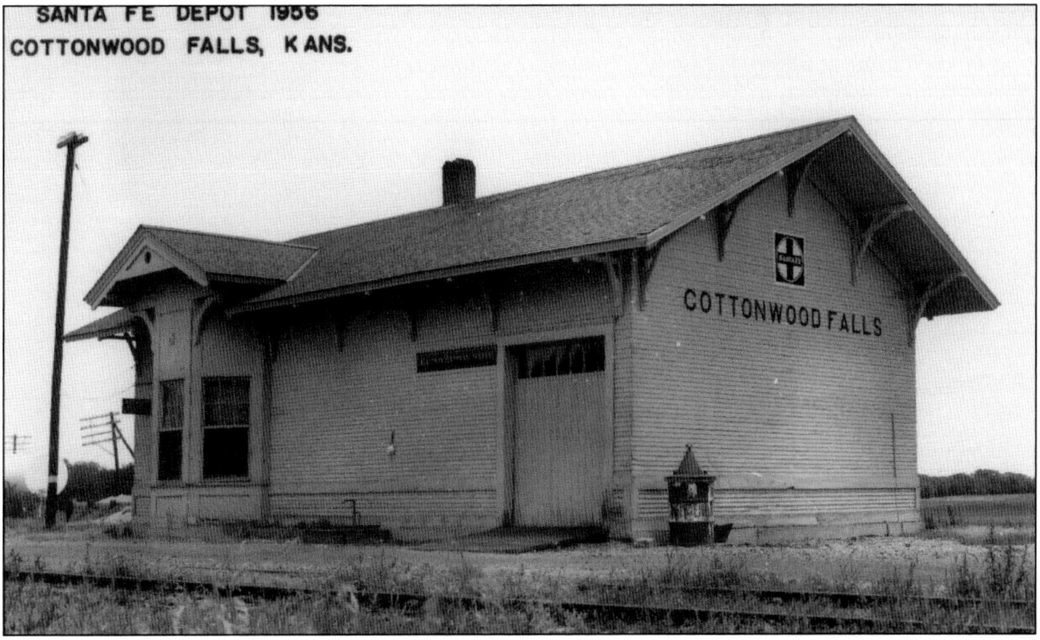

The Cottonwood Falls depot is a curiosity insofar as the Atchison, Topeka & Santa Fe line bypasses the town to the north, passing through Strong City instead. However, a spur line crossed the Cottonwood River into Cottonwood Falls, primarily to provide service to grain elevators located there. (Courtesy Greg Hoots.)

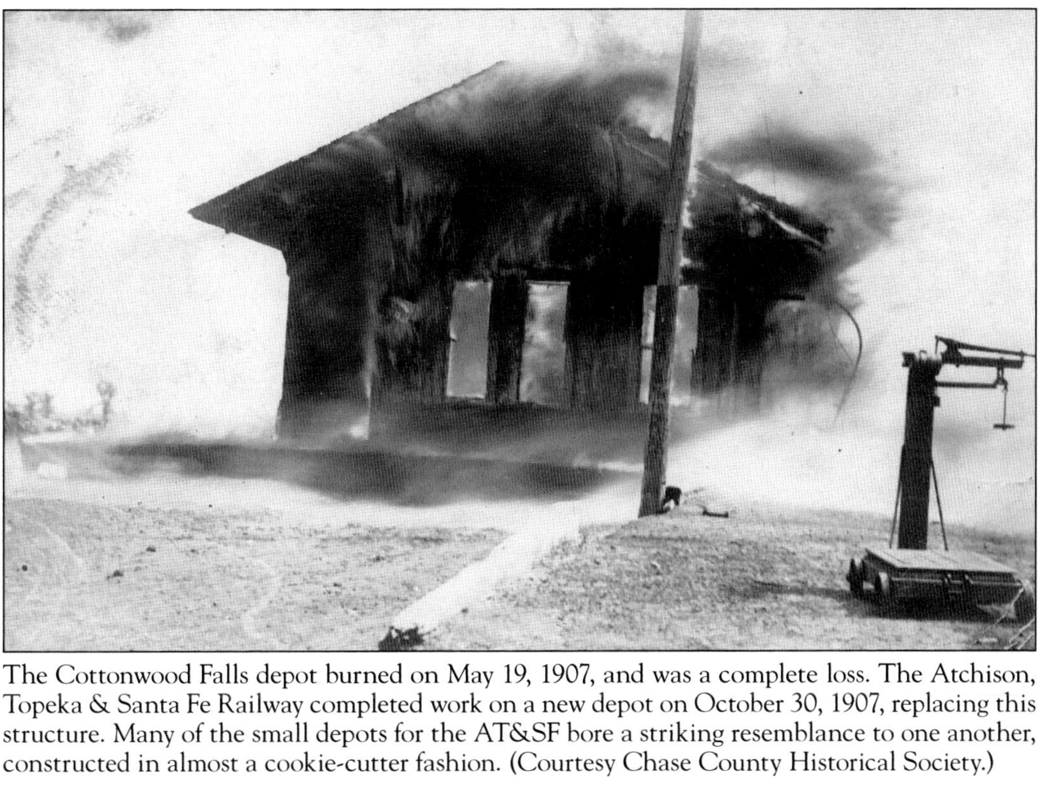

The Cottonwood Falls depot burned on May 19, 1907, and was a complete loss. The Atchison, Topeka & Santa Fe Railway completed work on a new depot on October 30, 1907, replacing this structure. Many of the small depots for the AT&SF bore a striking resemblance to one another, constructed in almost a cookie-cutter fashion. (Courtesy Chase County Historical Society.)

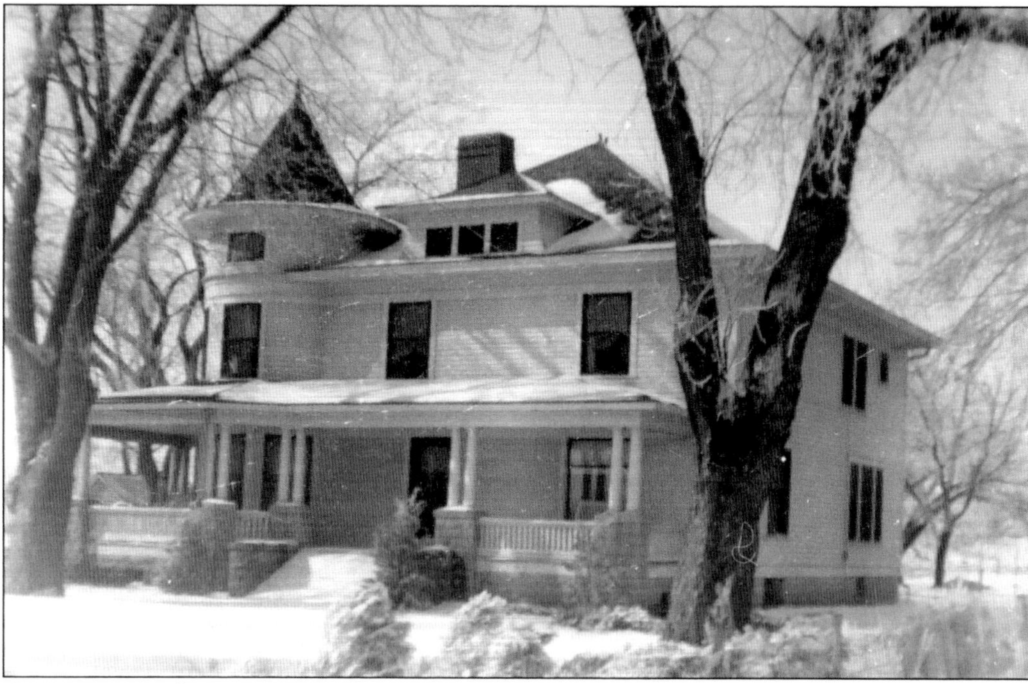

Erastus B. Crocker came to Chase County in 1866, homesteading north of Matfield Green. Crocker served two terms in the state legislature and engaged in cattle ranching. His sons, Ed and Arthur Crocker, were prominent cattlemen in Kansas in the early 1900s. Seen here in 1940, the Crocker Ranch, the home of Ed and Maud Brandley Crocker, was located 1.5 miles north of Matfield Green. (Courtesy Fred Howard II.)

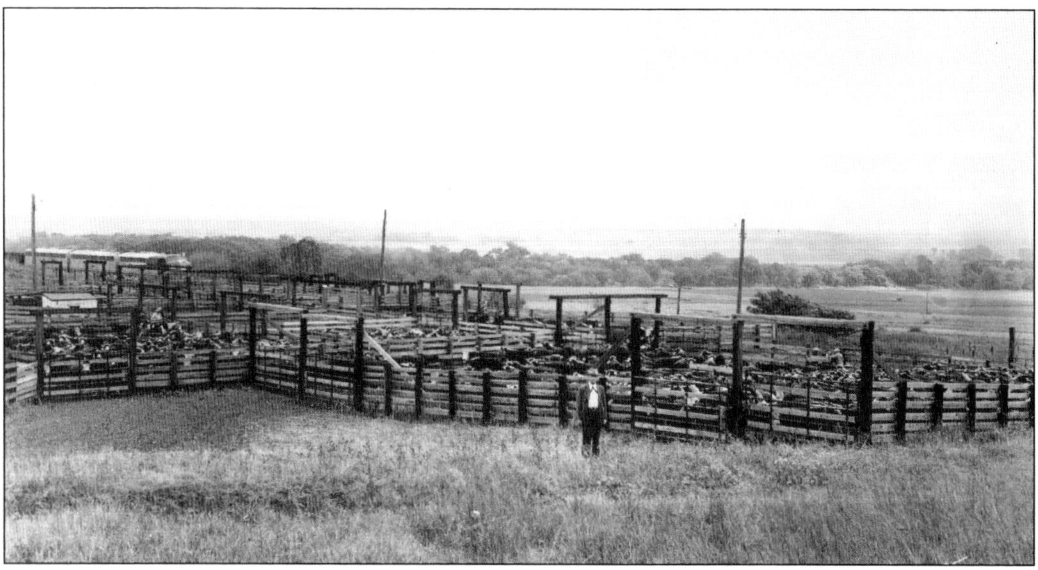

The cattle-loading pens at Matfield Green are seen here in a photograph from the fall of 1950 as a group of two-year-old steers from the Davis Ranch are waiting to be loaded into cattle cars. The Z Bar steers, fattened on Chase County grass, were sold to Vince Donahoe of Kansas City, Missouri, standing in the foreground, and were transported to feedlots in Iowa. (Courtesy Phyllis Scherich collection.)

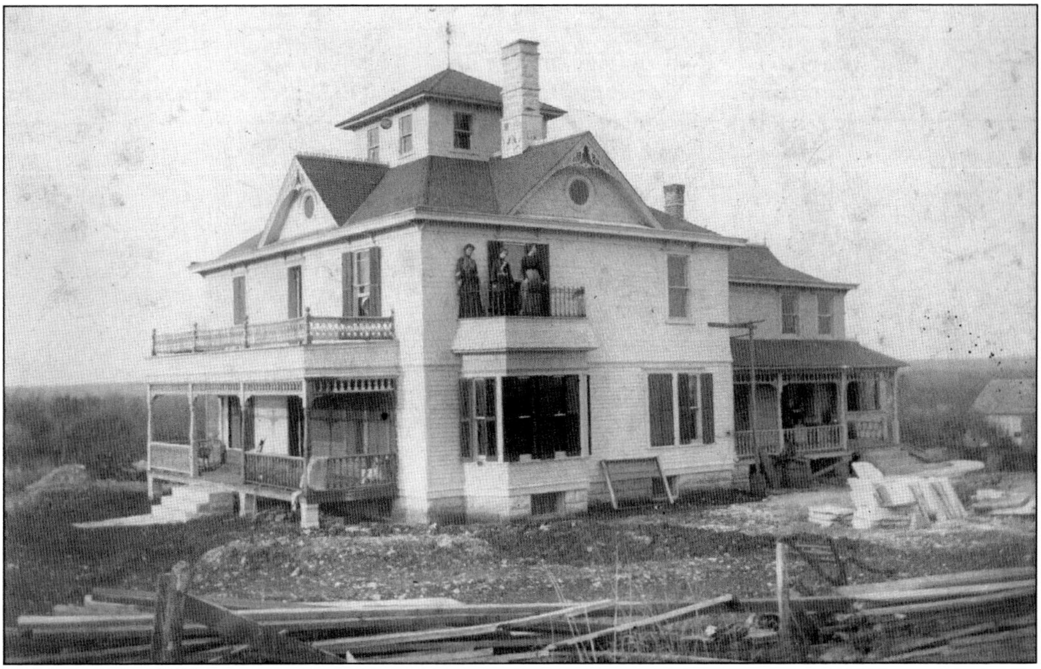

Henry Brandley came to America at age 12 from Switzerland with his family and met Charles W. Rogler, who had emigrated alone from Austria at age 17, when both young men were living in Iowa. The two boys walked from Iowa to Cottonwood Falls in 1859, both homesteading in Chase County. The Brandley home, seen here, burned on October 26, 1924. (Courtesy Chase County Historical Society.)

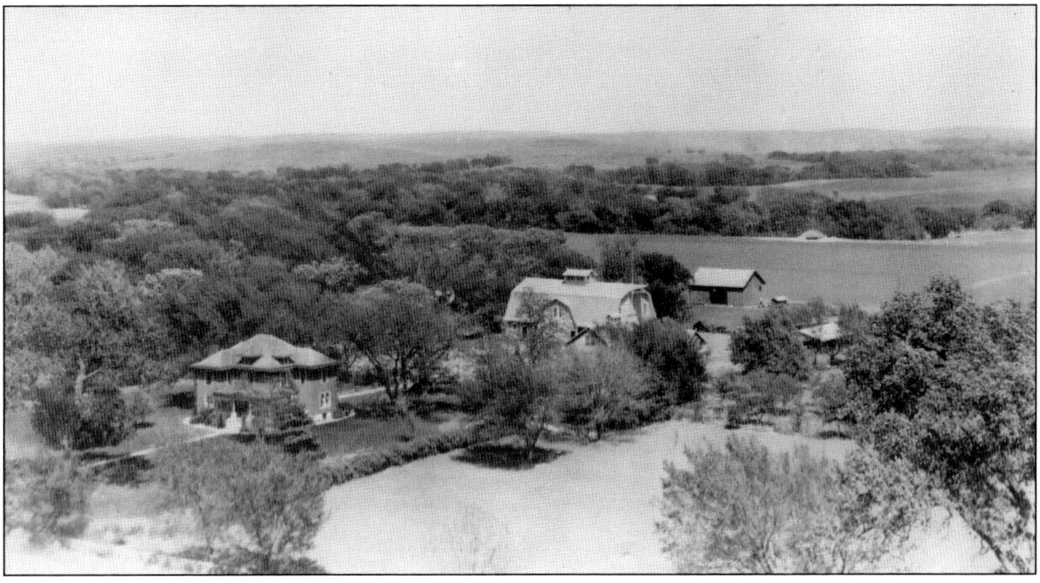

The Charles W. Rogler ranch, located on Highway 177 just south of the Crocker house seen on page 80, was homesteaded in 1859 and remained in the Rogler family until 2006 when it was sold at auction. The house, barn, and 12 acres sold to the Pioneer Bluffs Foundation, which operates a nonprofit foundation that celebrates the tallgrass prairie and ranching history while providing a resource for community involvement programs. (Courtesy Chase County Historical Society.)

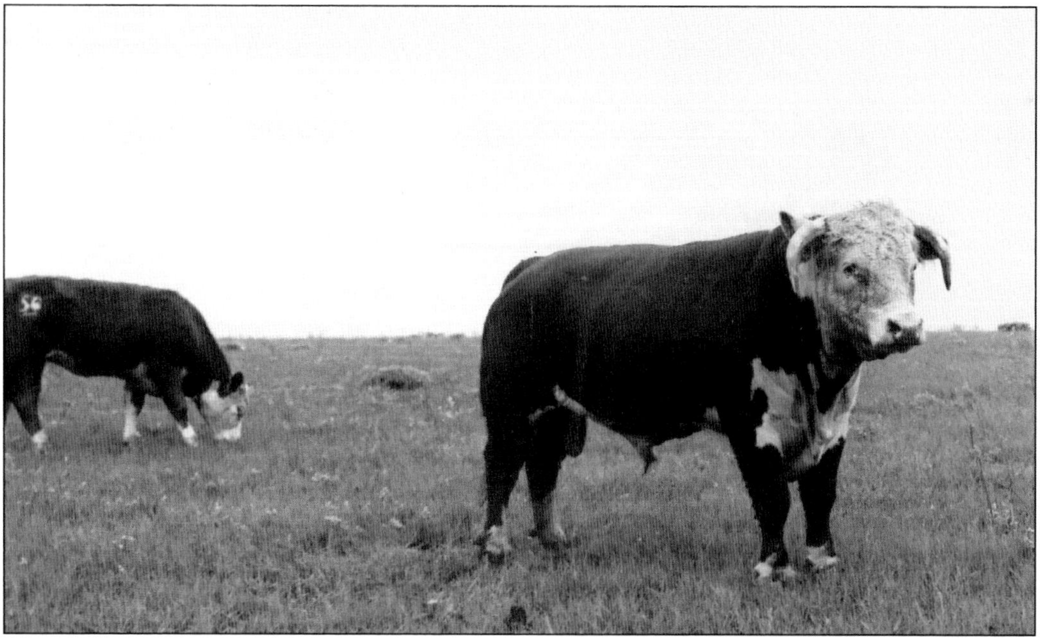

These two photographs were both taken by the United States Department of Agriculture (USDA) offices in May 1947 during a tour of Chase County ranches. Above, this Hereford bull is standing on the spring grass in A.J. McCabe's pasture. Below, steers are seen in a pasture at Henry Rogler's ranch, a half mile west of Matfield Green. Many changes occurred in ranching during the middle of the 20th century, including the marketing of year-old steers, finished at feedlots and processed regionally. However, the Flint Hills pastures have sustained the industry for 150 years. (Both, courtesy Chase County Historical Society.)

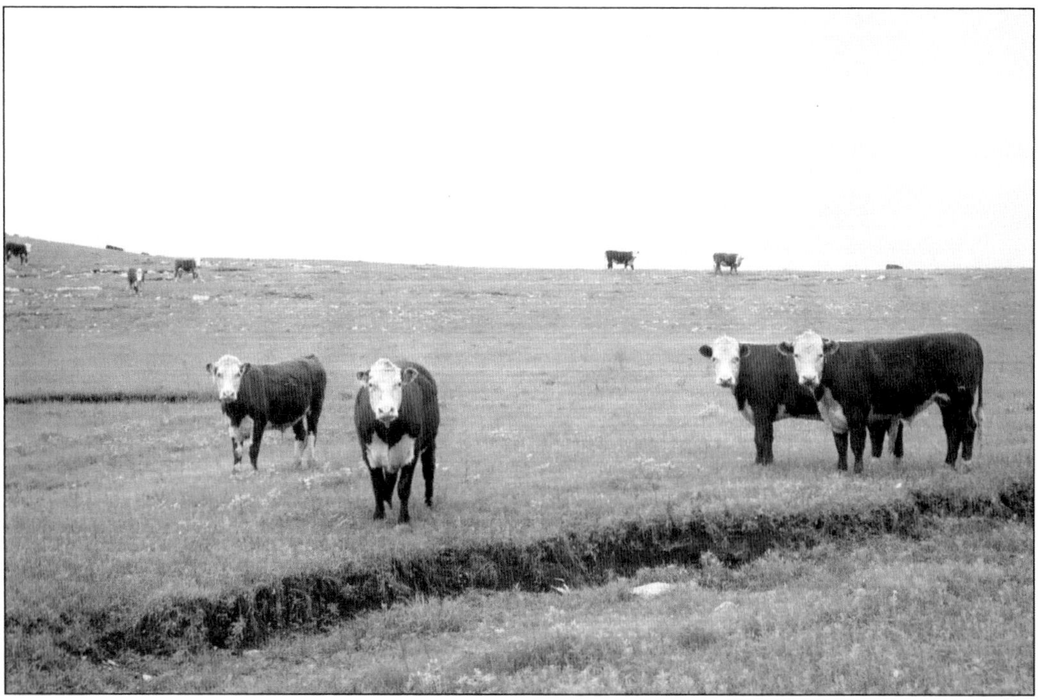

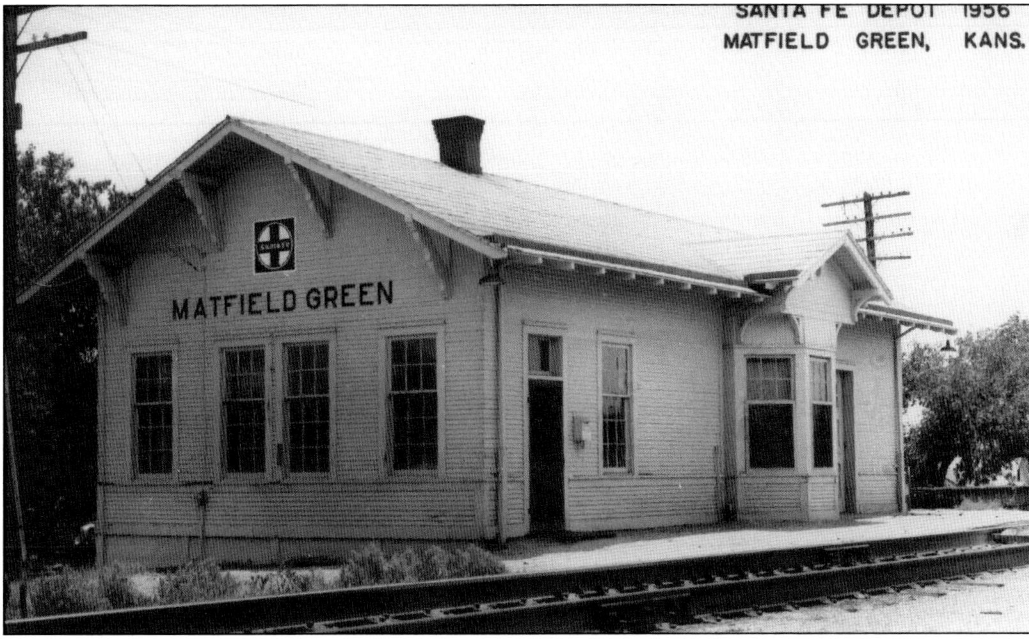

The Atchison, Topeka & Santa Fe depot at Matfield Green is seen in this real-photo postcard dated 1956. While the AT&SF had built tracks as far south as Bazaar in 1887, the railroad failed to provide service to Matfield Green. Finally, on July 31, 1923, a branch line arrived in Matfield Green, making the movement of cattle much more convenient. (Courtesy Greg Hoots.)

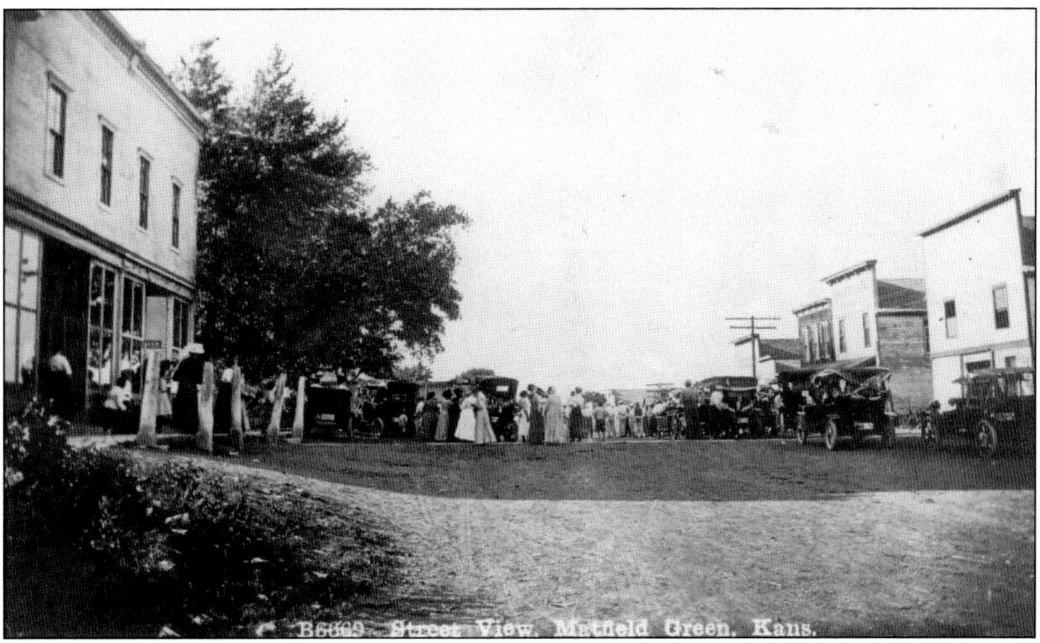

This real-photo postcard street scene from Matfield Green dates from the late 1910s. The first settler at Matfield Green was David W. Mercer, who arrived in 1858. In 1870, Mercer was named postmaster, and the first post office was established in his cabin. Ranching and farming are the primary industries in the area, as they have been for the last century and a half. (Courtesy Chase County Historical Society.)

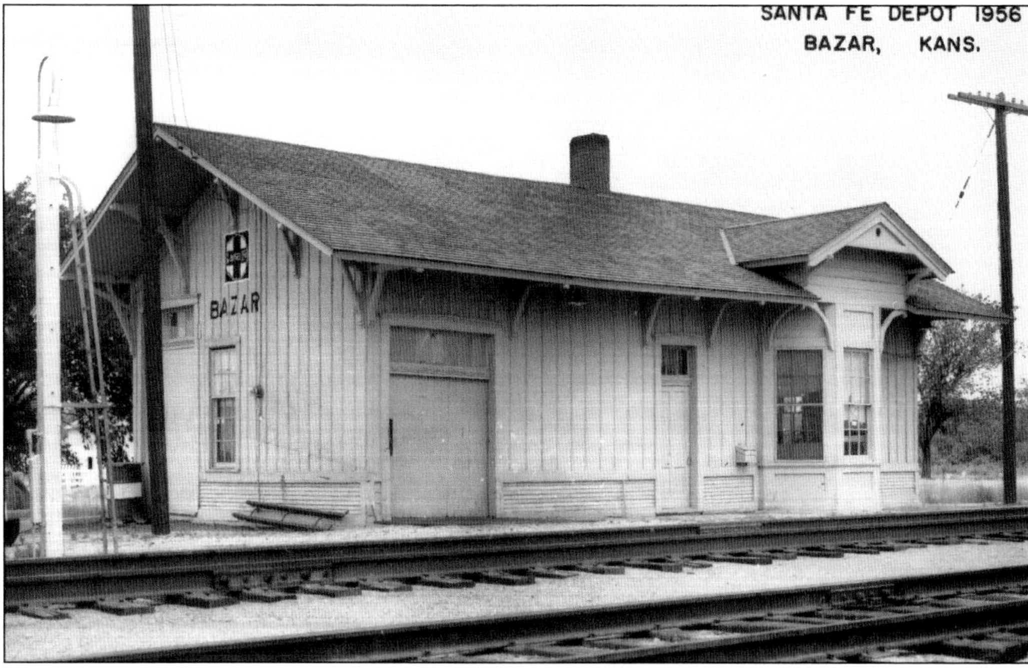

Settled in March 1856, the first post office opened in Bazaar in 1860. The Atchison, Topeka & Santa Fe Railway built the first depot in 1887, and almost immediately the railhead became one of the busiest in the nation for shipping cattle. In a bizarre twist, the AT&SF misspelled the name of the town painted on the depot seen in this real-photo postcard produced by the railroad in 1956. (Courtesy Greg Hoots.)

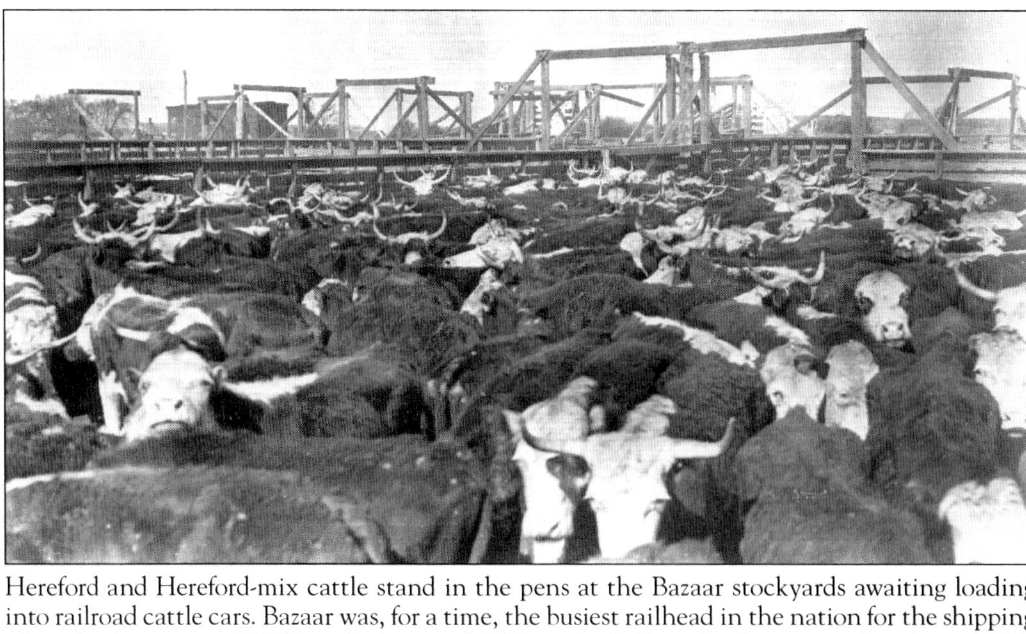

Hereford and Hereford-mix cattle stand in the pens at the Bazaar stockyards awaiting loading into railroad cattle cars. Bazaar was, for a time, the busiest railhead in the nation for the shipping of cattle. As many as 2,000 cattle cars would ship animals from the Bazaar stockyards each fall. (Courtesy Chase County Historical Society.)

Four

Davis Ranch

The story of the Davis Ranch begins with George H. Davis, born in 1876, the youngest of three children. His father, James Davis, worked for the railroad, and the family moved several times before coming to Kansas City, Kansas, when George was eight years old. Tragedy struck when James Davis lost his leg to amputation after a work accident, and his children, including George, were forced to begin working directly out of elementary school. George Davis's first job was as a messenger boy for a grain company in Kansas City's West Bottoms district. By age 20, Davis was promoted to manager of the company's New Orleans office. Within a year, the owner of the grain enterprise died, and Davis was called upon to return to Kansas City to conclude the company's business.

Davis had made valuable contacts in the grain industry, and at age 24, he obtained a seat on the Kansas City Board of Trade and partnered with A.L. Ernst, forming Ernst-Davis Grain Company. In 1912, Davis was elected president of the board of trade. Despite splitting with Ernst in 1914, Davis's grain business grew.

On March 16, 1923, Davis-Noland-Merrill Grain Company was formed, with Davis as president; Nicholas F. Noland, vice president; Harold A. Merrill, treasurer; and a longtime Davis employee, Minerva Gundelfinger, secretary. The three principals were members of the Kansas City Board of Trade. The firm assumed the leases of the Terminal Elevator and the Rock Island Elevator, with a total storage capacity of 2.6 million bushels. In 1924, the firm leased Santa Fe Elevator A, with a capacity of 10 million bushels, the nation's largest grain elevator.

The grain business thrived, despite the stock market collapse in 1929 and the economic upheaval in banking. By 1930, two significant changes were underway at Davis-Noland-Merrill. First, Nick Noland left the partnership, selling his interest back to the corporation. Harold Merrill became vice president, and Minerva Gundelfinger, now a stockholder, became secretary-treasurer. The second change was that George Davis began to think about investing in land. Thousands of acres could be had for less than $5 an acre. In 1931, Davis purchased the famed Dewey Ranch in Riley County, Kansas, buying 6,600 acres for $120,000. In 1932, Davis purchased six Johnson County farms for $160,000, and this was just the beginning.

Davis convinced Merrill and Gundelfinger to invest in land, and the Davis Ranch was born. In 1933, the firm purchased three adjoining ranches in Barber County, totaling 35,350 acres. Within a year, they acquired 17,000 acres in neighboring Comanche County, including the ranch headquarters of the former Comanche Cattle Pool at Evansville. Then the firm purchased a 12,500-acre ranch in Morris County and over 6,000 acres in Wabaunsee County. In 1935, they purchased 11,000 acres in Chase County, reuniting Barney Lantry's famed Deer Park Spring Hill Farm. Davis-Noland-Merrill also purchased 12 farms in Missouri, adding 11,200 acres to the 82,400 acres amassed in Kansas.

The second part of Davis's ranching strategy was to employ the best ranching talent that money could buy. He hired John Peavey "J.P." Lynn to be the ranch overseer and coordinate the efforts of the spreads. Because of the mild climate, the ranches in Barber and Comanche Counties were cow-calf operations where all of the calves were born. All of the steers were transported by rail to the ranches in Chase, Morris, and Wabaunsee Counties. Davis hired Fred Howard, former manager of the Crocker Brothers' ranch at Matfield Green, to manage the cattle operation in Chase and later in Wabaunsee County. Howard was considered by his peers to be the best in the business. Davis retained T.O. "Orville" Alley to manage the cow-calf operation on the vast Barber County property. Alley's brother Lester Alley was hired to manage the Comanche County ranch. At his spread in Riley County, Davis hired Orville Burtis Sr. to manage the ranch, and the two became partners in the cattle raised there. It became clear that Davis, never a rancher, sought out the services of the best cattlemen to guarantee his success.

In 1937 and 1938, Davis served as US Chamber of Commerce president. He and his wife, Elizabeth, moved to Washington, DC, where Davis represented business on Capitol Hill. During those years, Harold Merrill became more involved in the ranching business. In 1935, Merrill was elected president of the Kansas City Board of Trade, and he took an increasing role in the business when Davis was absent. By the early 1940s, there was increasing tension between Merrill and Davis. In 1944, Merrill resigned his position as vice president of Davis-Noland-Merrill and formed Harold A. Merrill Ranch and Grain Company. Due to legislation that prohibited corporations and grain companies from owning farms, all of the Davis-Noland-Merrill property had been deeded to Davis. In 1945, Merrill sued Davis, asking the court to place the property in the corporation's name. Davis won the suit; however, the ranch was split, with Merrill taking over 29,000 acres in Comanche and Morris Counties and a Buchannan County, Missouri, farm. In 1947, Davis-Noland-Merrill Grain Company ended its lease of Santa Fe Elevator A and ceased all grain trading.

Several other changes occurred in 1947. J.P. Lynn left the Davis Ranch and became Merrill's overseer of ranching, Lester Alley left the Comanche County ranch and went to work with his brother on the Barber County ranch, and Orville Burtis Jr. was named ranch overseer for the Davis Ranch holdings, replacing Lynn. There were no significant changes in the Chase County property, but Fred Howard also began managing the Wabaunsee County ranch.

In 1955, George H. Davis died from a heart ailment, and his personal ranches in Riley and Johnson Counties were soon sold. The remainder of the ranch continued unchanged, placed in a trust managed by the First National Bank, of which Davis was a director and longest-serving board member. Bank vice president Everett Ellis became president of the Davis Ranch. Orville Burtis Jr. assumed increasing responsibilities, as Ellis had no experience in ranching. When Ellis died in 1964, Orville Burtis Jr. became president of the corporation.

In the early 1970s, Burtis suggested to the board of directors that the name of the corporation be changed to the Z Bar Cattle Company. Burtis explained that the Z Bar brand was so recognizable and so respected in the industry that he believed the change would improve morale among the many employees. The board agreed, and the Z Bar Cattle Company was born.

The Z Bar continued to flourish until 1986, when the trust made a decision to cease cattle ranching. The reason given was that the corporation was paying corporate taxes, and then the stockholders were taxed on their profits, creating a situation paramount to double taxation. In 1986, that decision was implemented, and the Z Bar was offered for lease. Then, in 1994, the National Park Trust purchased 10,894 acres in Chase County from Boatman's Bank and Trust, which had acquired the First National Bank. In 1999, Ted Turner purchased the Barber County ranch for a reported $9 million. The remainder of the Davis Ranch property, including the Wabaunsee County and Missouri properties, remains in trust for heirs of George Davis.

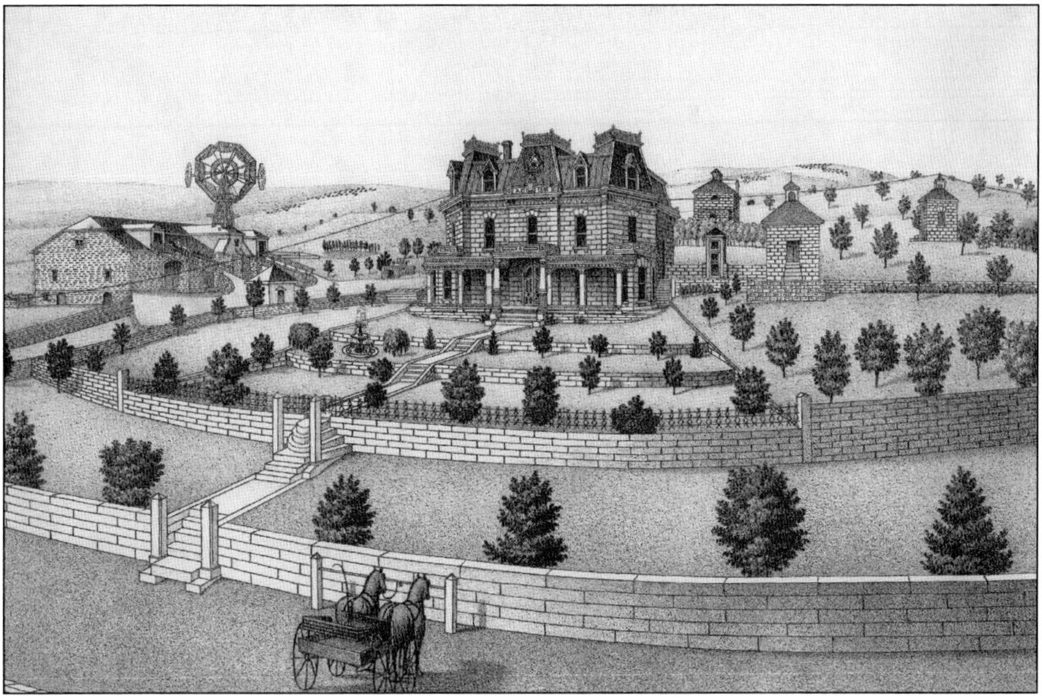

The Stephen F. Jones Spring Hill Farm and Stock Ranch was built on 160 acres that Jones purchased along Fox Creek for $2,000 in August 1878. In September, Jones contracted David Rettiger to construct the mansion, a three-story barn, and 30 miles of stone fence around the 7,000 acres that he soon added to the original quarter section. This etching is from the 1887 *Everts Atlas of Kansas*. (Courtesy Greg Hoots.)

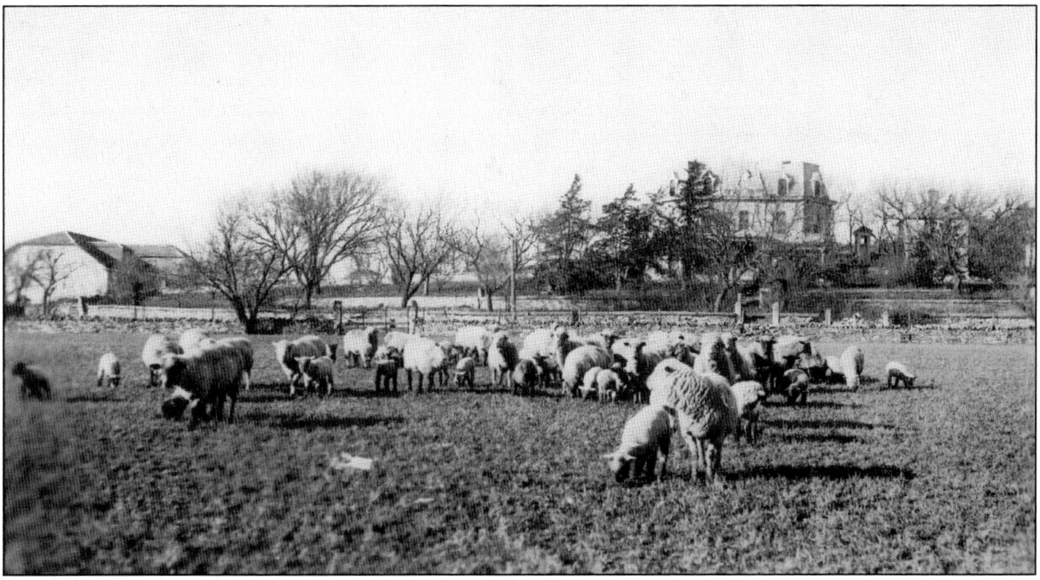

The Spring Hill mansion and barn can be seen in the background of this view of the property taken in the winter of 1930 while the ranch was owned by Flora Benninghoven. Benninghoven and her sons continued to ranch at Spring Hill after the death of her husband, Otto, in 1917. The Benninghovens raised sheep in the early 1930s. (Courtesy Phyllis Scherich collection.)

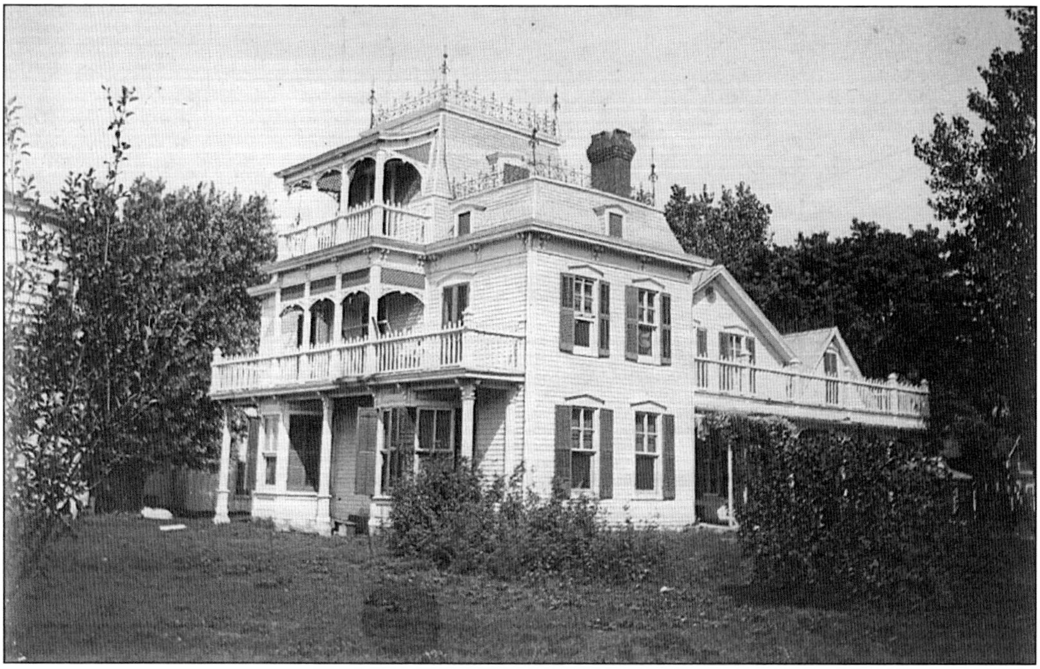

Above, Barney Lantry's mansion located at the north end of Strong City is seen in this c. 1900 photograph. Lantry raised his family in the rambling three-story house, though it also contained an area for offices for his many enterprises. When the house became the headquarters of the Davis Ranch, the Fred Howard family lived there. Quarters and office space were reserved in the back of the house for George Davis and the ranch headquarters. Below, Barney Lantry's Deer Park Farm is seen in the 1887 *Everts Atlas of Kansas*. It was said that Lantry named the ranch after the small herd of tame deer he kept on the property. (Above, courtesy National Park Service; below, courtesy Greg Hoots.)

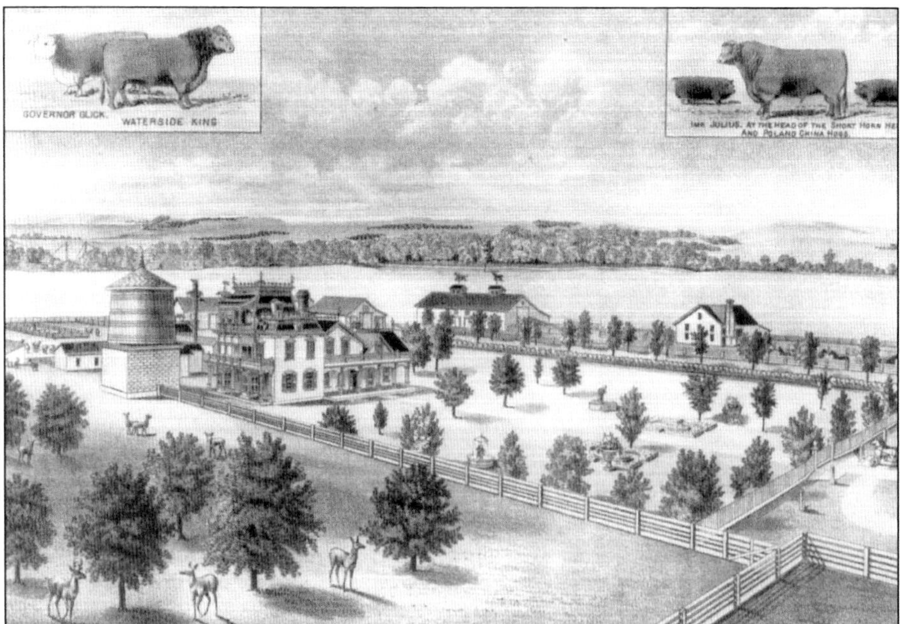

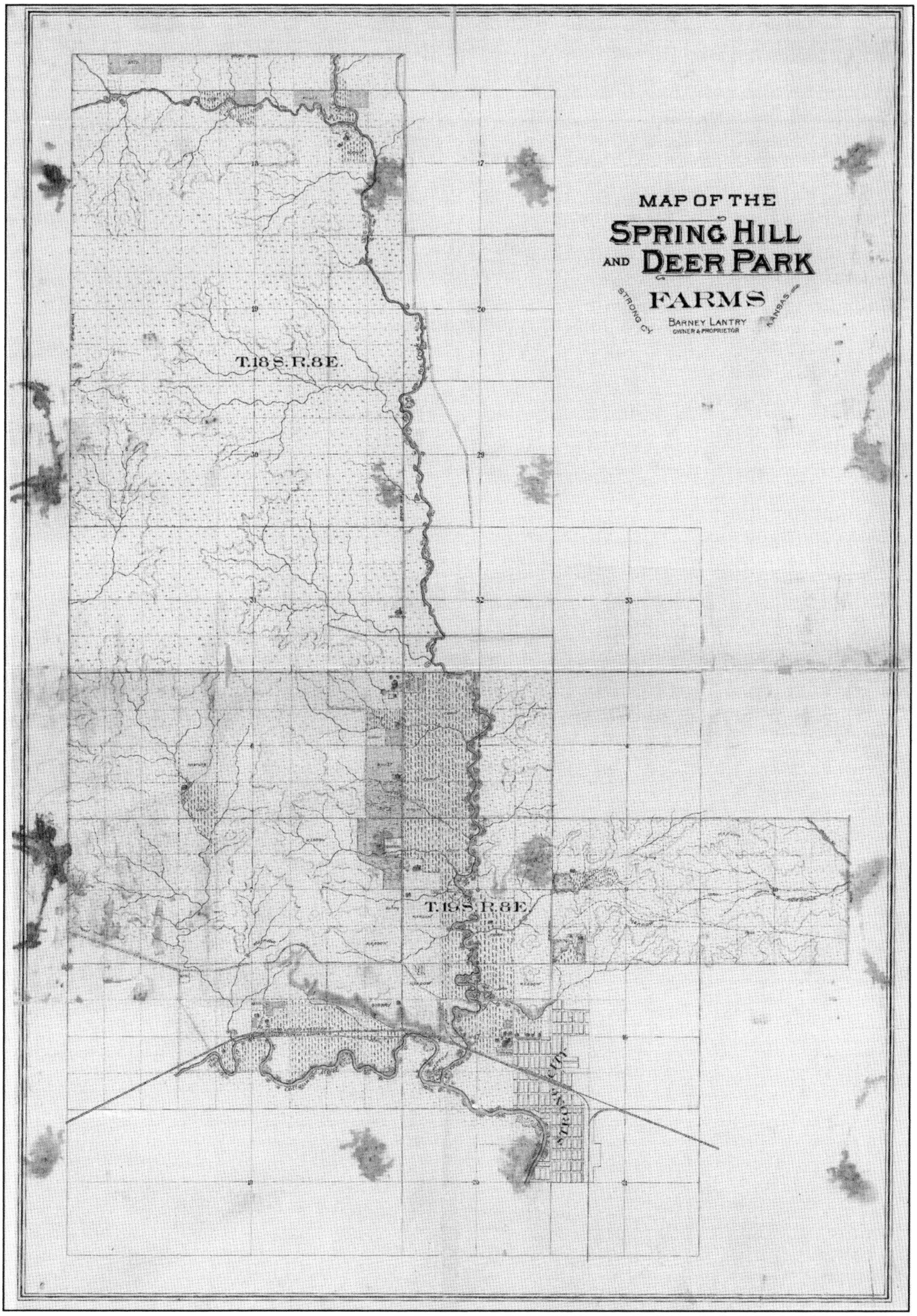

This map of the Spring Hill and Deer Park Farms was created for Barney Lantry after he purchased the Stephen F. Jones Spring Hill Ranch on February 13, 1888, and consolidated the two properties. Lantry's mansion can be seen on the map on the north edge of Strong City. At the time of Lantry's death in 1895, he was said to have been the wealthiest man in Kansas. His quarried stone had built railroad beds and depots across the western states. He was prominent in politics, having been the unsuccessful Democratic candidate for state treasurer in 1894 just months before his death. (Courtesy National Park Service.)

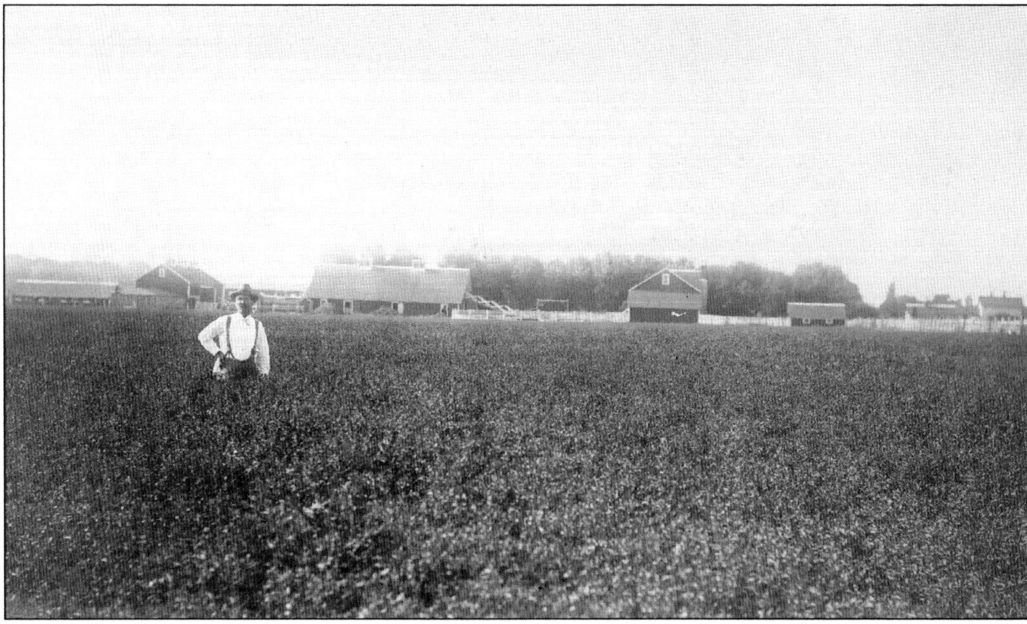

Barney Lantry is seen in his alfalfa field at his Strong City home, with the barns at the Lantry place in view. Lantry and his son Henry maintained a large ranching operation apart from their stone quarry business. After Henry's death in 1904, his brother Charles sold the family's holdings and moved to North Carolina to engage in railroad construction. (Courtesy Chase County Historical Society.)

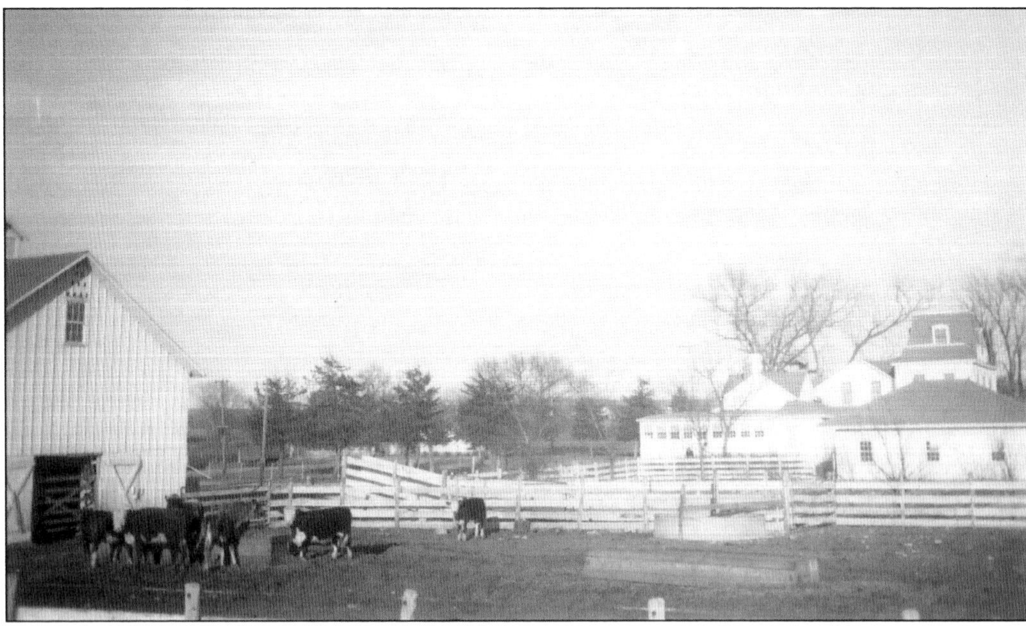

The Davis Ranch headquarters at Strong City is seen here in the early 1940s. The Lantry mansion became the home of Fred and Anna Marie Howard in 1935 when Howard accepted the position of ranch manager of the Davis Ranch property in Chase and Wabaunsee Counties. Howard had worked as ranch manager for his father-in-law, Ed Crocker, at Matfield Green, before the mighty Crocker Ranch was dissolved in the early 1930s. (Courtesy Fred Howard II.)

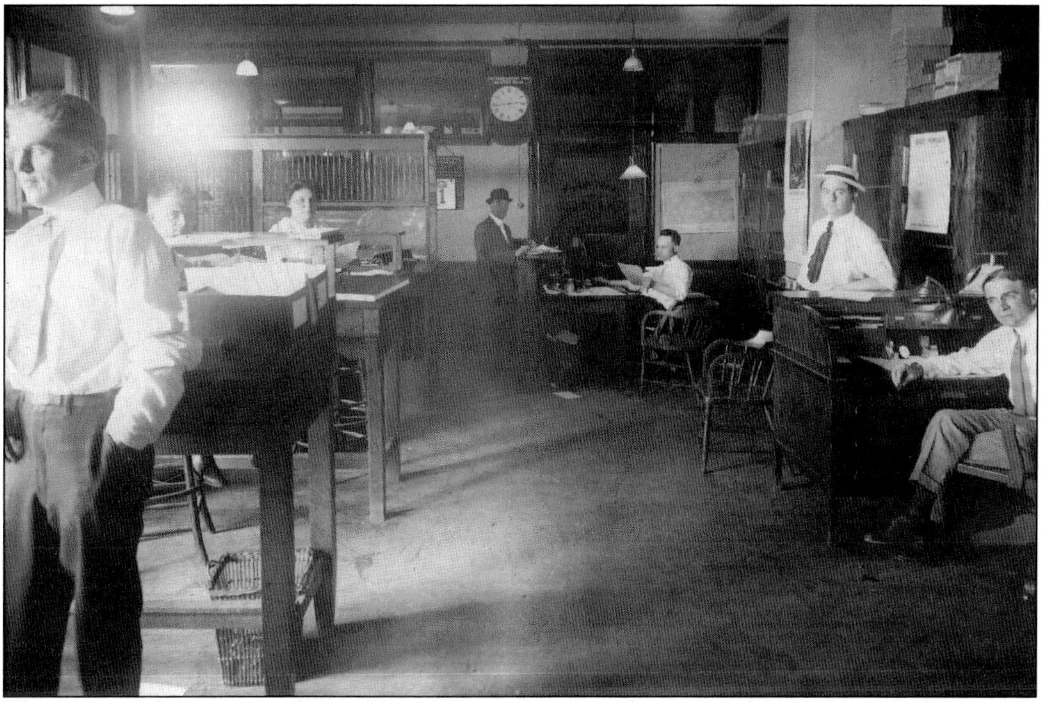

This view of the interior of Ernst-Davis Grain Co. was taken around 1905. Identified, from left to right, are Ed Parret, Charley Cheesman, Minerva Gundelfinger, J.F. Marion, Bill Simmons, and Paul Matthews. In 1914, Davis bought his partner's interest in the business, and in 1923 he formed Davis-Noland-Merrill Grain Company and commenced leasing Santa Fe Elevator A in Argentine, Kansas. (Courtesy National Park Service.)

This c. 1902 interior view of Ernst-Davis Grain Co. shows three unidentified staff members. Just out of elementary school when his father became disabled, Davis began his career in business as an office boy. In 1900, at age 24, he had become partners in Ernst-Davis, and he was elected president of the Kansas City Board of Trade in 1912. (Courtesy National Park Service.)

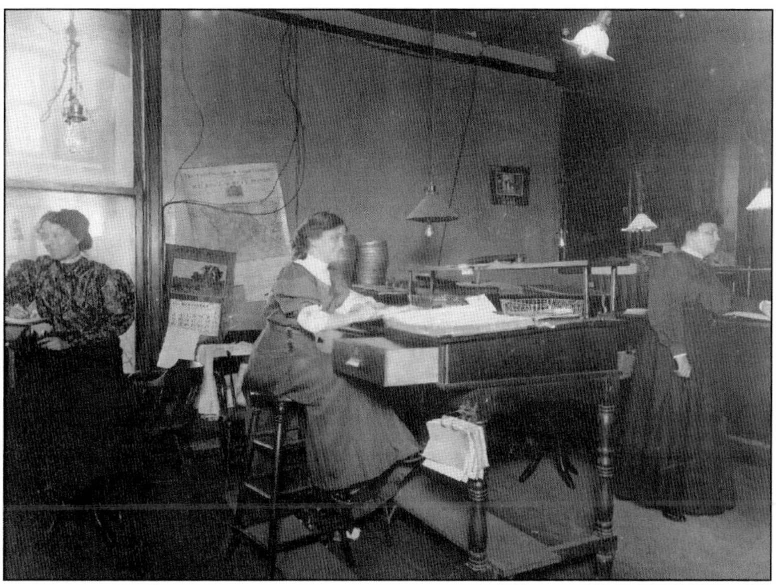

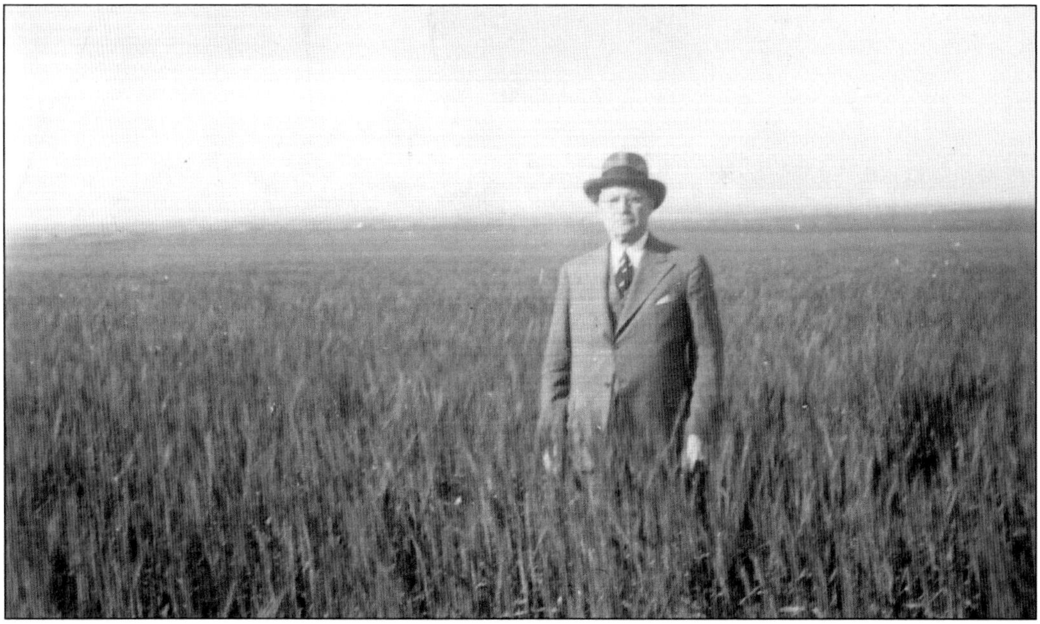

George Davis is seen in this vast pasture on the Temple Ranch, one of the three ranches he purchased in Barber County in 1933 on behalf of Davis-Noland-Merrill Grain Company. With the purchase of the Temple Ranch, Davis obtained the Z Bar brand, which was being used on cattle that came with the purchase. The Z Bar would become the most recognizable brand in the cattle industry. (Courtesy National Park Service.)

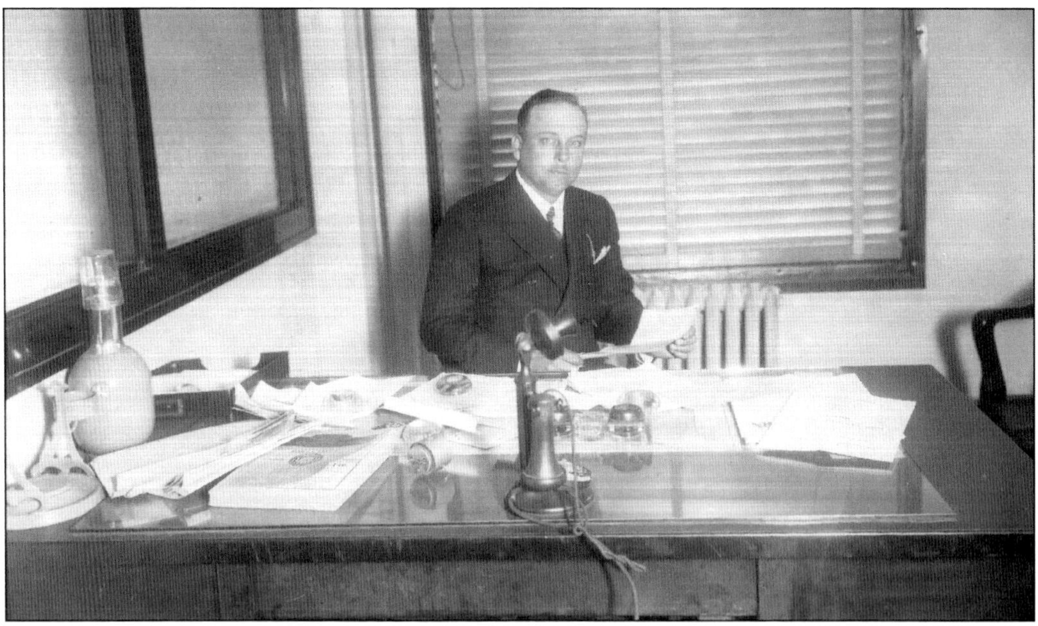

Nicholas F. Noland was the first vice president of Davis-Noland-Merrill Grain Company when it was formed in 1923. Little is known of Noland other than he was a member of the Kansas City Board of Trade. History records Noland as being one of the 22 members of the board of trade who built lodges on the newly constructed Lake of the Ozarks. By the early 1930s, Noland had left the partnership. (Courtesy National Park Service.)

Harold Merrill, left, is seen in 1962 with Mildred Scherich and her husband, Virgil, who was manager of the Merrill Ranch in Comanche County from 1944 to 1976. The Scherichs lived in the ranch headquarters house on the 17,000-acre spread at Wilmore that had once been part of the Davis Ranch. In 1976, Larry "Dee" Scherich became manager of the Merrill Ranch and remains so today. (Courtesy Phyllis Scherich collection.)

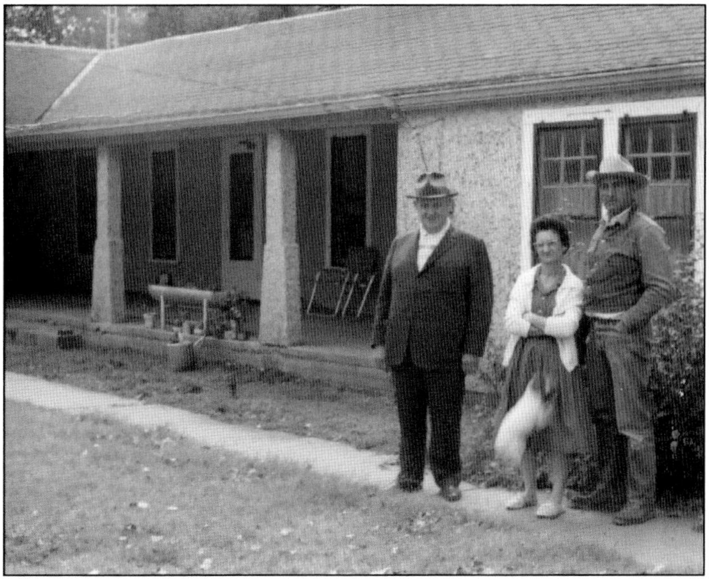

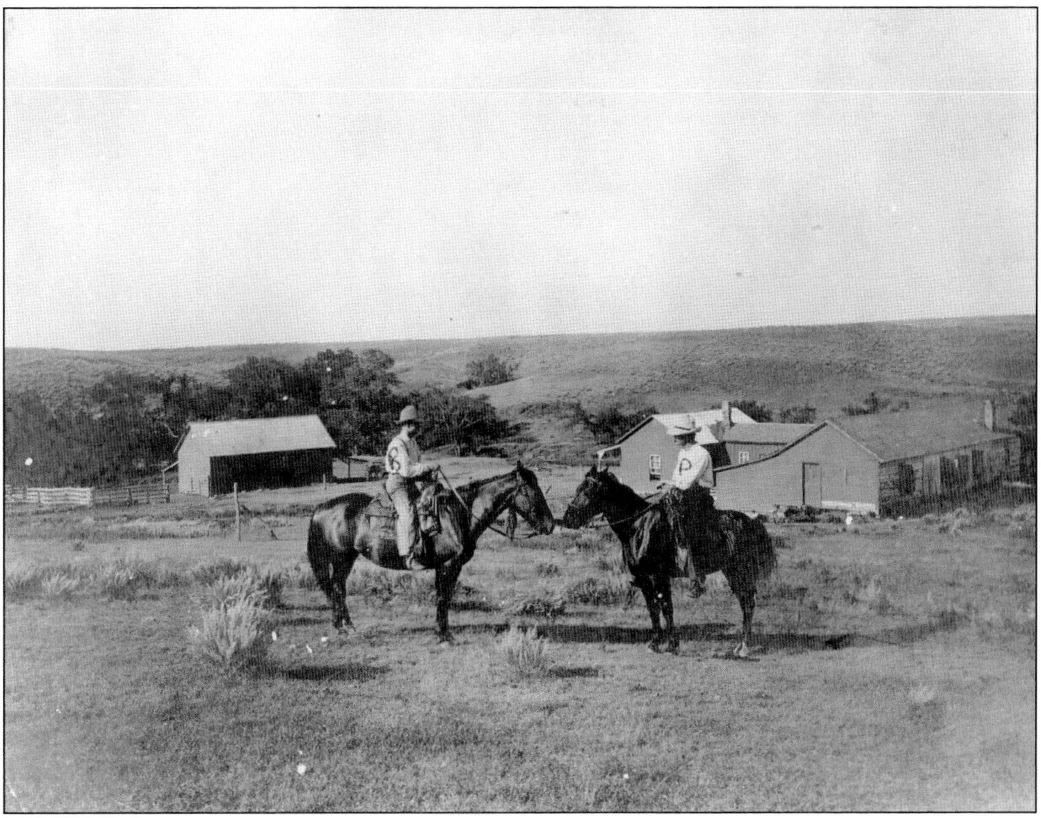

Billy Brown, left, and Ray Platt are seen in this 1910 photograph at Evansville, the former headquarters of the Comanche Cattle Pool from 1878 to 1886. The cattle pool was a 1.5-million-acre, open-range cattle cooperative headquartered at a site named after its founder, Jessie Evans. The Davis Ranch headquarters in Comanche County was located here, and the original house was expanded several times. (Courtesy Phyllis Scherich collection.)

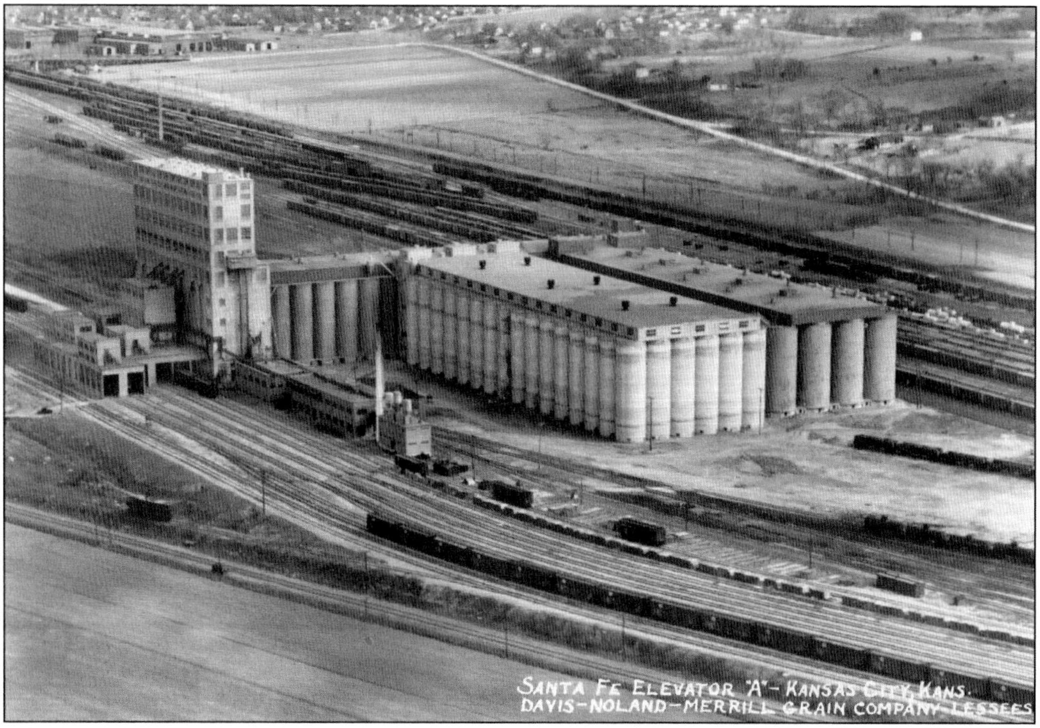

The Santa Fe Elevator A, located in the Argentine rail yards of Kansas City, Kansas, was leased by Davis-Noland-Merrill Grain Company in March 1923. The company laid claim to the largest grain storage facility in the world. This elevator was demolished in 1996, and railroad tracks were laid where the elevator had stood. (Courtesy Phyllis Scherich collection.)

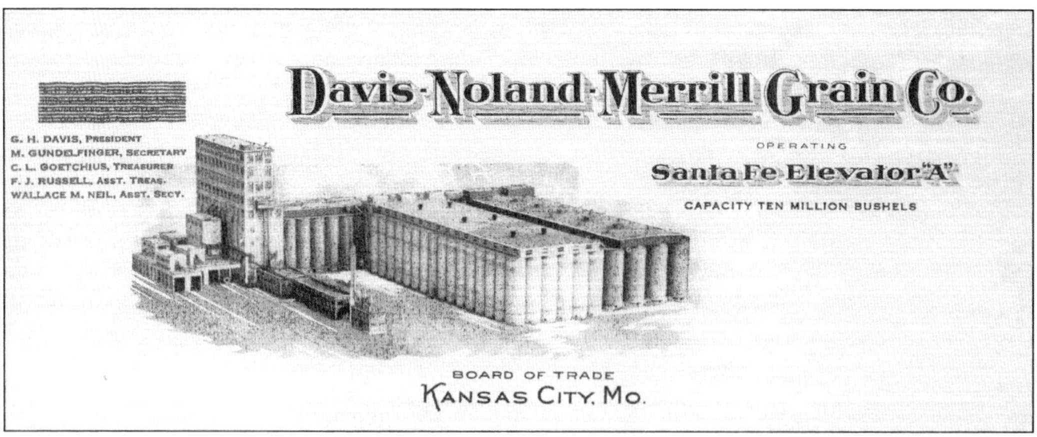
Davis-Noland-Merrill Grain Co.

G. H. DAVIS, PRESIDENT
M. GUNDELFINGER, SECRETARY
C. L. GOETCHIUS, TREASURER
F. J. RUSSELL, ASST. TREAS.
WALLACE M. NEIL, ASST. SECY.

OPERATING
Santa Fe Elevator "A"
CAPACITY TEN MILLION BUSHELS

BOARD OF TRADE
KANSAS CITY, MO.

This piece of letterhead for Davis-Noland-Merrill Grain Co. dates from the mid-1940s. When Nicholas Noland, vice president of the company, left the partnership by the mid-1930s, the company had begun pursuing ranching interests, and Harold Merrill became vice president. When disputes between Merrill and Davis led to Merrill's departure in 1944, rather than print new letterhead, the company overprinted the earlier letterhead, deleting Merrill's name. (Courtesy Phyllis Scherich collection.)

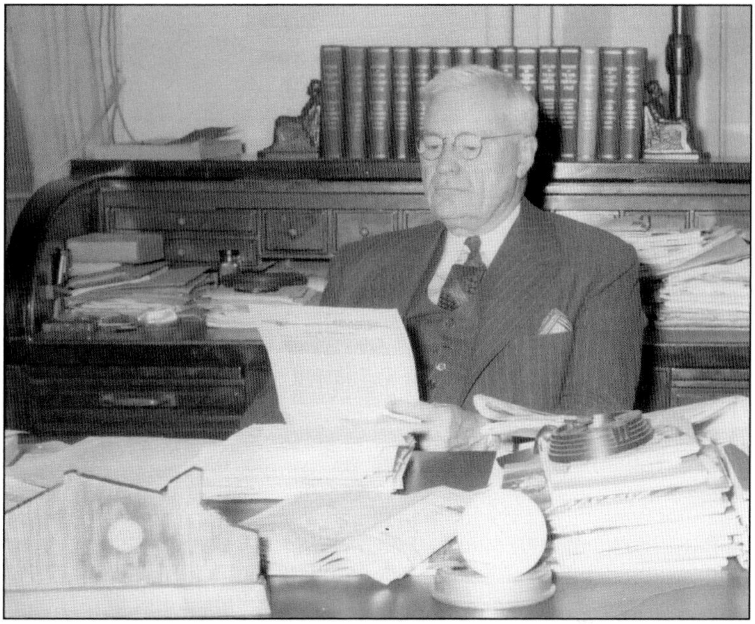

George Davis is seen at his desk in the Kansas City Board of Trade building in this 1951 photograph. That year, Davis was named one of the leaders of Kansas City by the *Kansas City Star*, and his accomplishments were lauded in an extensive article in the paper in which this image appeared. Davis's work area looks to be located between two rather busy and large desks. (Courtesy National Park Service.)

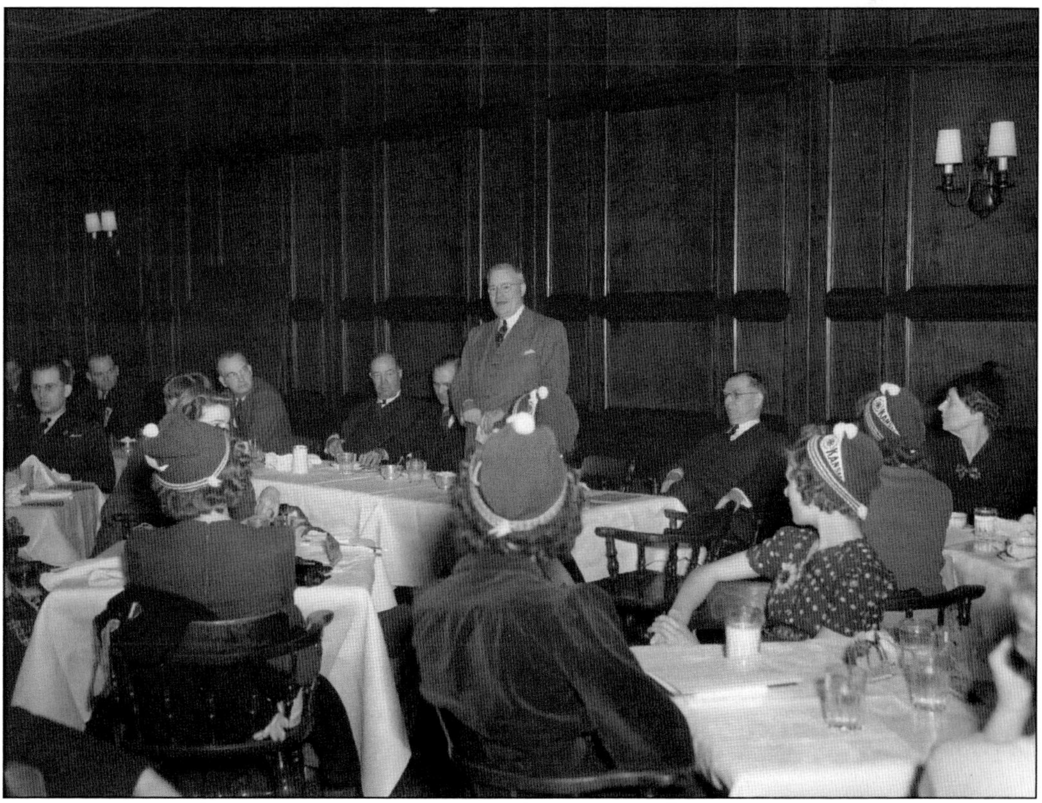

George Davis addresses a group at the national convention of the 4-H Club in Chicago at a breakfast meeting in the fall of 1940. Davis, at that time, was president of the American Royal Livestock Show, in addition to his role as the owner of the largest ranch in Kansas. One of Davis's many interests was promoting the involvement of youth in agriculture. (Courtesy National Park Service.)

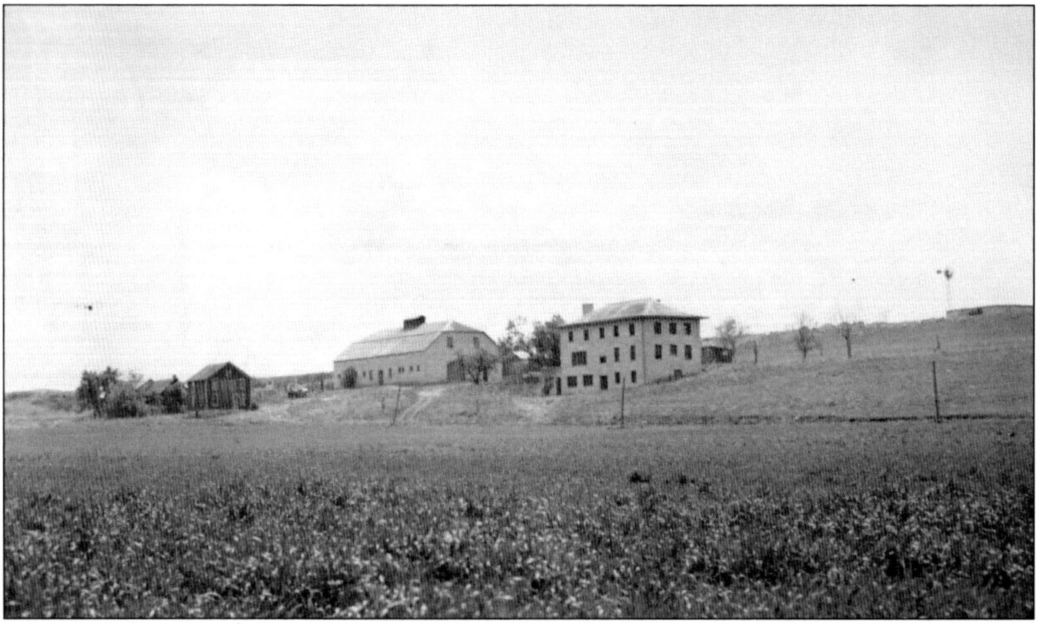

In 1931, George Davis purchased the 6,600-acre Dewey Ranch (seen here) in Riley County, his first ranch property. This ranch and the six Johnson County farms he bought in 1932 were owned by Davis individually, before Davis-Noland-Merrill Grain Company began buying ranches. The stone house, home to ranch hands, and the barn seen here in this 1938 photograph were constructed in 1914 by stonemason Walter Burr. (Courtesy National Park Service.)

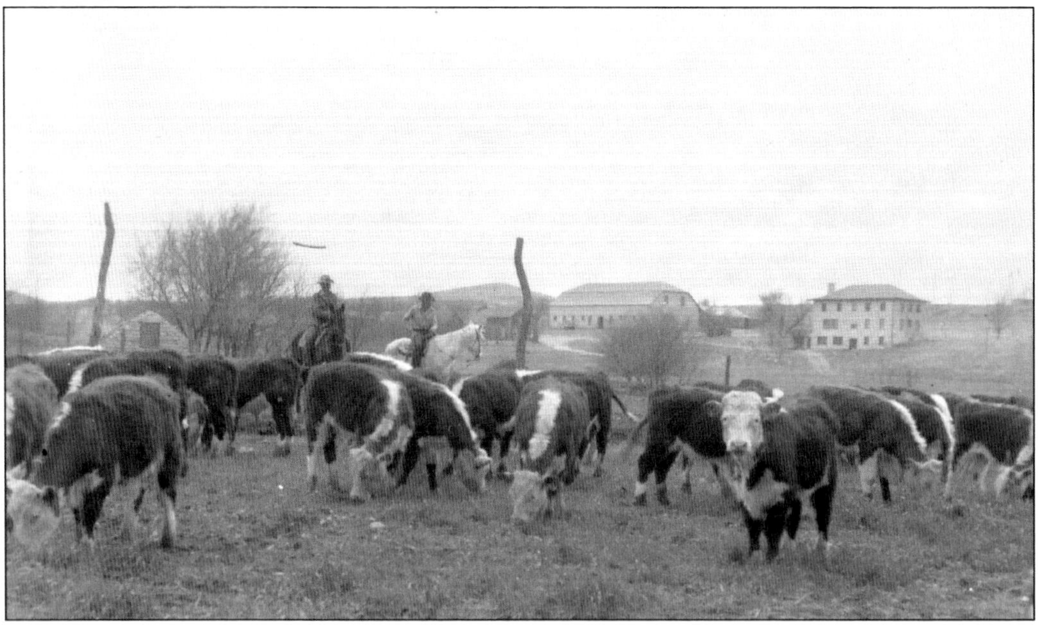

George Davis hired Orville Burtis Sr. to manage his Riley County ranch shortly after purchasing the property. Burtis lived in the stone ranch house, and he and Davis were partners in the cattle that they raised on the ranch. Burtis's son Orville Burtis Jr. began working for Davis in the ranch offices in Kansas City in 1947. This photograph was taken in 1948. (Courtesy National Park Service.)

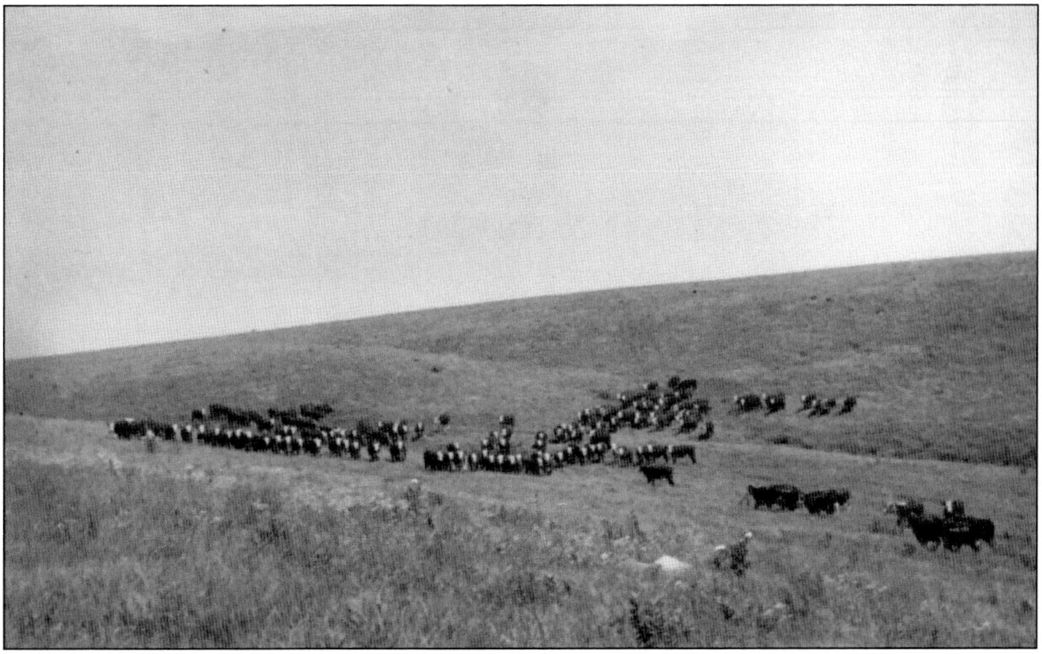

In spring 1938, the Davis Ranch purchased 3,800 year-old steers located in El Paso, Texas, from the Palomas Cattle Company. The cattle were rounded up, placed in cattle cars, and transported to the Flint Hills. Davis dispersed the steers throughout his Flint Hills ranches. In this view, several hundred are seen on the Dewey Ranch in Riley County. (Courtesy National Park Service.)

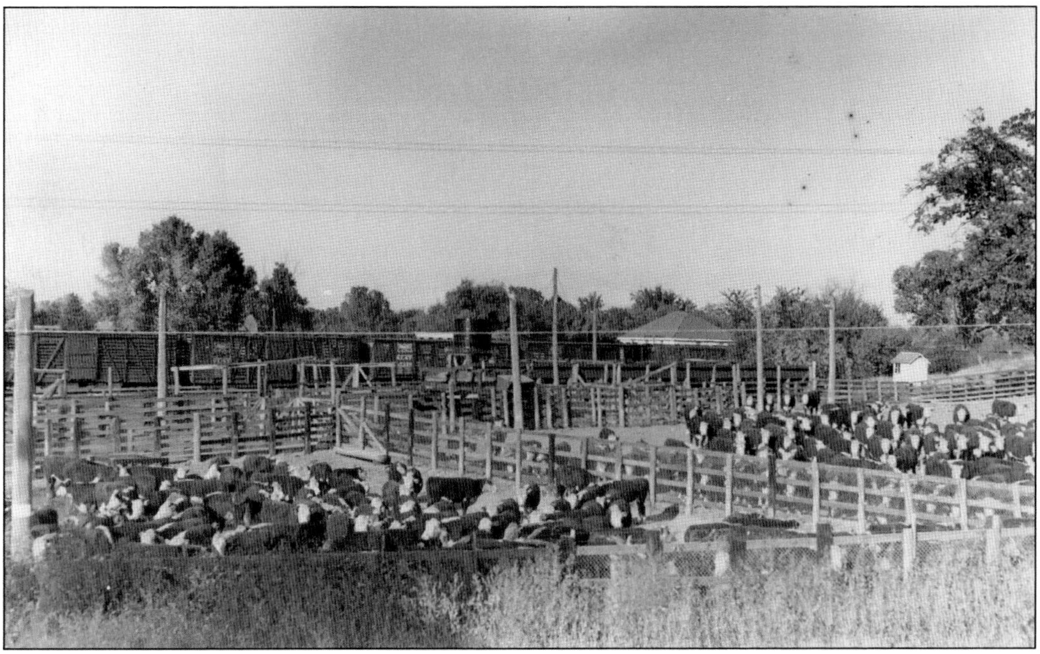

Cattle buyer Vincent Donahoe, a frequent customer of Davis Cattle Company and later the Z Bar Cattle Company, purchased these 302 steers from the Riley County ranch for shipment to feedlots in Iowa. The cattle are seen here in the stockyards in Manhattan, awaiting loading into cattle cars. A photograph of Donahoe can be found on page 100. (Courtesy National Park Service.)

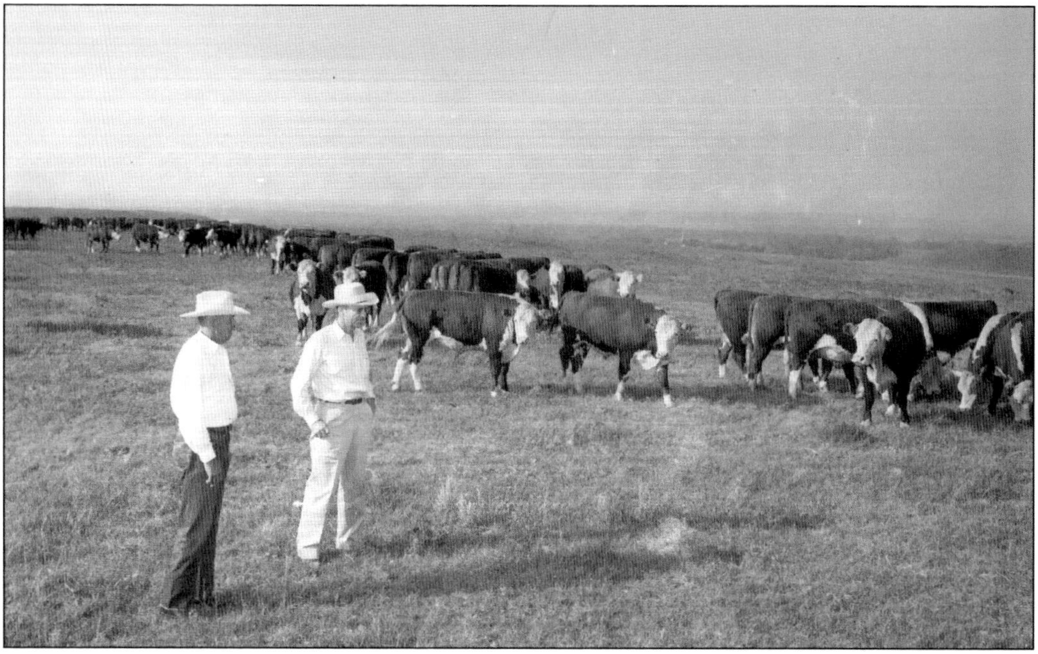

In this 1955 photograph, Fred Howard Sr. (left), considered to be one of the most accomplished cattlemen in the Midwest, is seen here with E.C. Crofoot of the Crofoot Feed Lot, Strong City, inspecting steers sold and bound for an Iowa feedlot. Howard spent more than 35 years managing the Chase County Davis Ranch, later known as the Z Bar Cattle Company, before his death in 1970. (Courtesy Fred Howard II.)

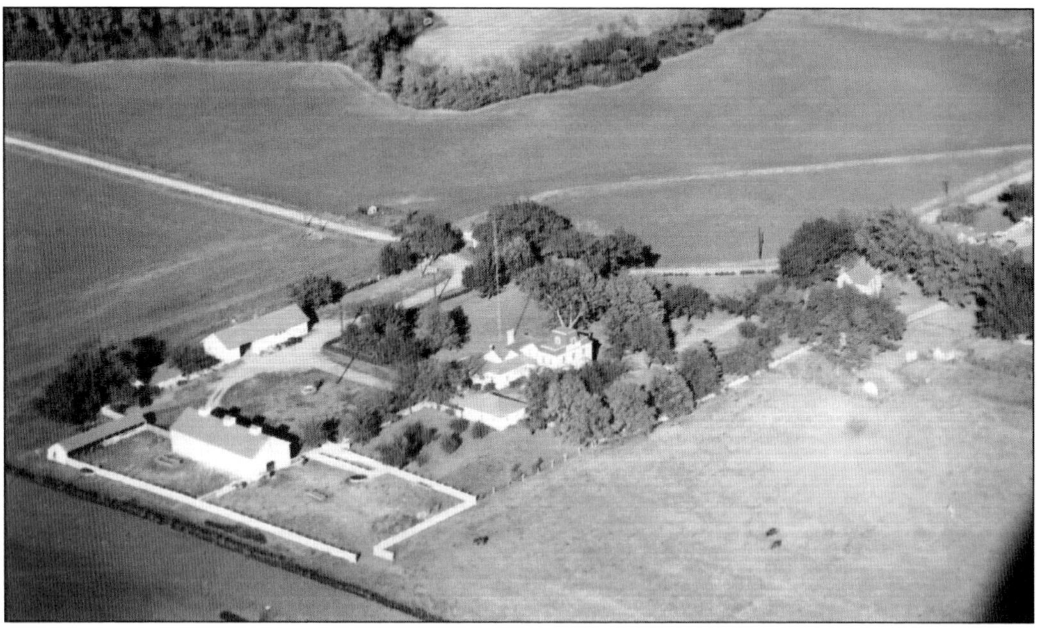

The Davis Ranch headquarters in the Flint Hills is seen in this c. 1950 aerial view. Formerly Barney Lantry's Deer Park Farm, in 1935 this house became known by all in Chase County as the Howard family's home. Fred and Anna Marie Howard raised five children—Robert, Pat, Bus (Donald), Sonny (Fred II), and Nancy—in the sprawling ranch house. (Courtesy Fred Howard II.)

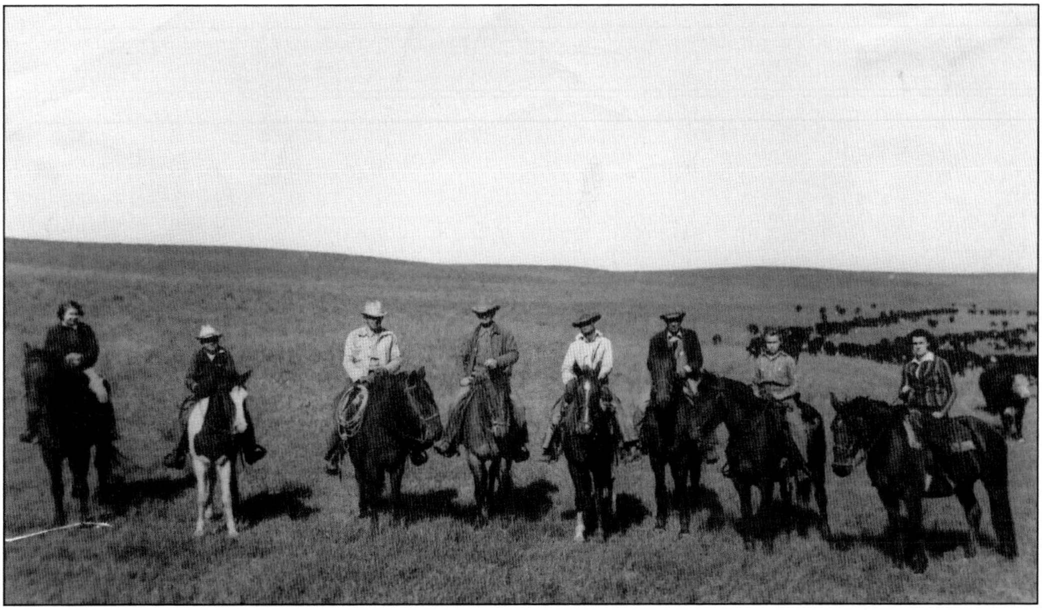

Fall roundup time on the Z Bar in Chase County was a time of excitement and anticipation for everyone. Seen in the photograph above are, from left to right, Catherin Vogrin, Donald "Bus" Howard, Fred Howard, Hazel Slabaugh, Delmar Hyman, Blackie Bullock, Mary Sharon Burnett, and Pat Howard. Going to work in the office, Vogrin joined Davis-Noland-Merrill Grain Company in 1926 at age 15. In 1947, Vogrin married Harold Merrill, vice president of Davis-Noland-Merrill, a widower. After Harold Merrill's death, Catherin Merrill maintained offices in Kansas City until the late 1980s, from where she would oversee the workings of "her ranch" in Comanche County. Below, the same riders are moving away from the camera. (Both, courtesy Fred Howard II.)

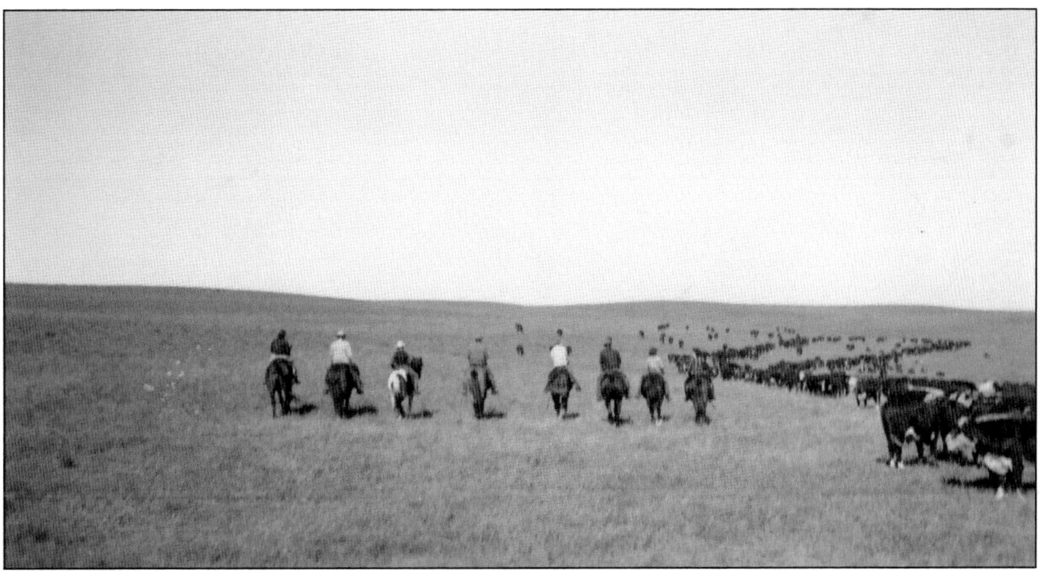

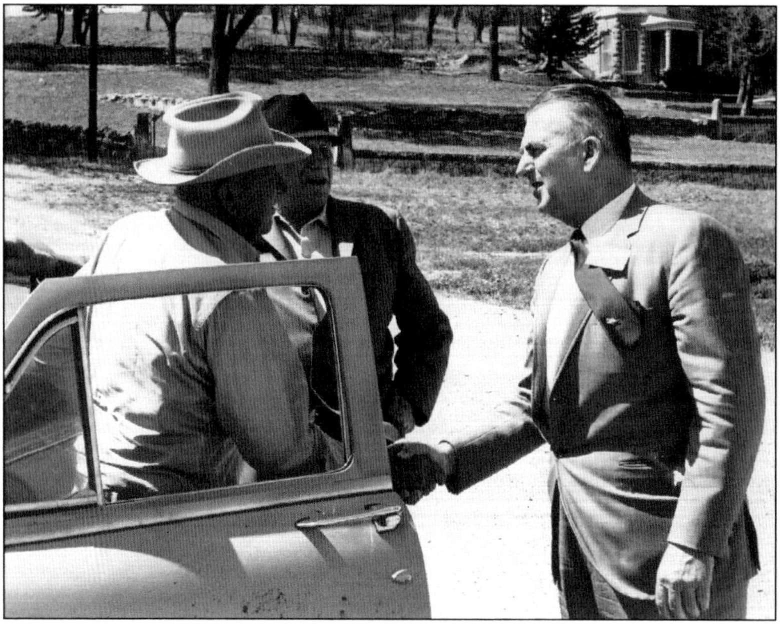

Fred Howard, left, greets Vincent Donahoe, a Kansas City cattle buyer, with a handshake in the driveway of the Jones house at Strong City in this photograph from fall 1951. In the autumn, cattle buyers like Donahoe would purchase the fattened steers from the Davis Ranch and send them to feedlots for "finishing." (Courtesy Phyllis Scherich collection.)

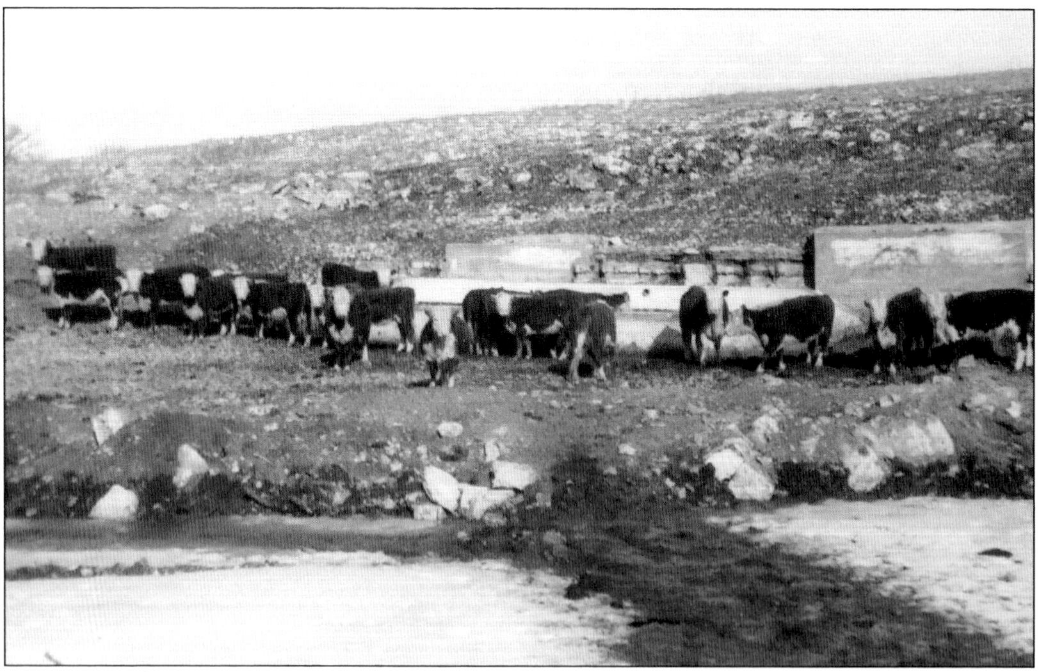

Water was a huge concern for ranchers during the 1930s when the Davis Ranch was born. In Chase County, Fred Howard and his men built many concrete water troughs where springs were located on hillsides, the tanks collecting the steady flow of springwater. This view is from the Spring Hill ranch during the 1930s. Fourteen lakes were also constructed on the Chase County ranches between 1935 and 1955. (Courtesy Fred Howard II.)

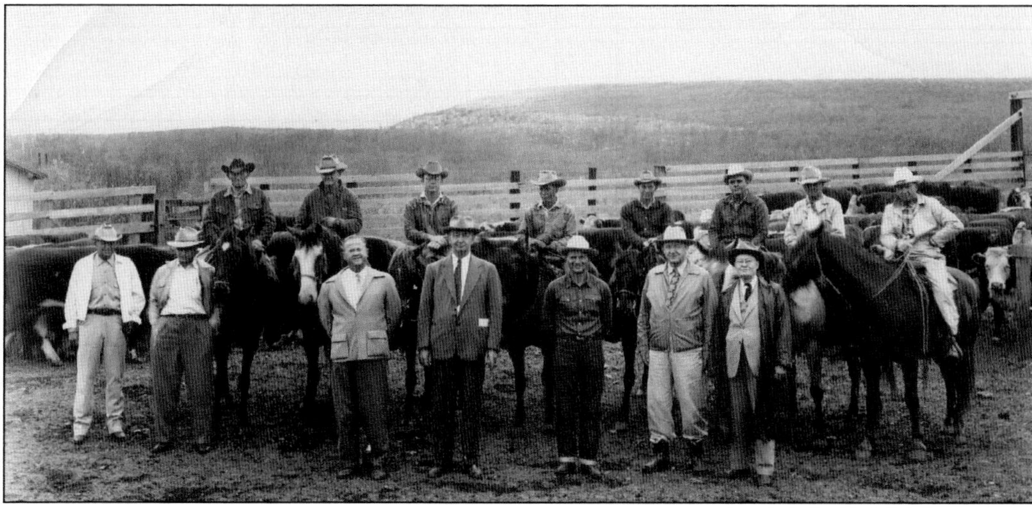

Above, cattle buyers, sellers, and cowboys pose for this photograph at Strong City in fall 1951. George Davis brought a professional photographer along for the trip. Standing in the first row are, from left to right, Fred Howard, Orville Burtis Jr., Davis's pilot, Vincent Donahoe, Bridwell's foreman, Joe Bridwell, and George H. Davis. Cowboys in the second row include, from left to right, two unidentified, Eugene Talkington, June Talkington, Wilber Talkington, Max Shaw, Jesse Bailey, and Wayne Rogler. Below, the cattlemen and cowboys seen above are photographed here at the Strong City stockyards standing at the pens where cattle will be loaded on railcars for shipping. There are long lines of cattle cars parked along the horizon. (Both, courtesy Phyllis Scherich collection.)

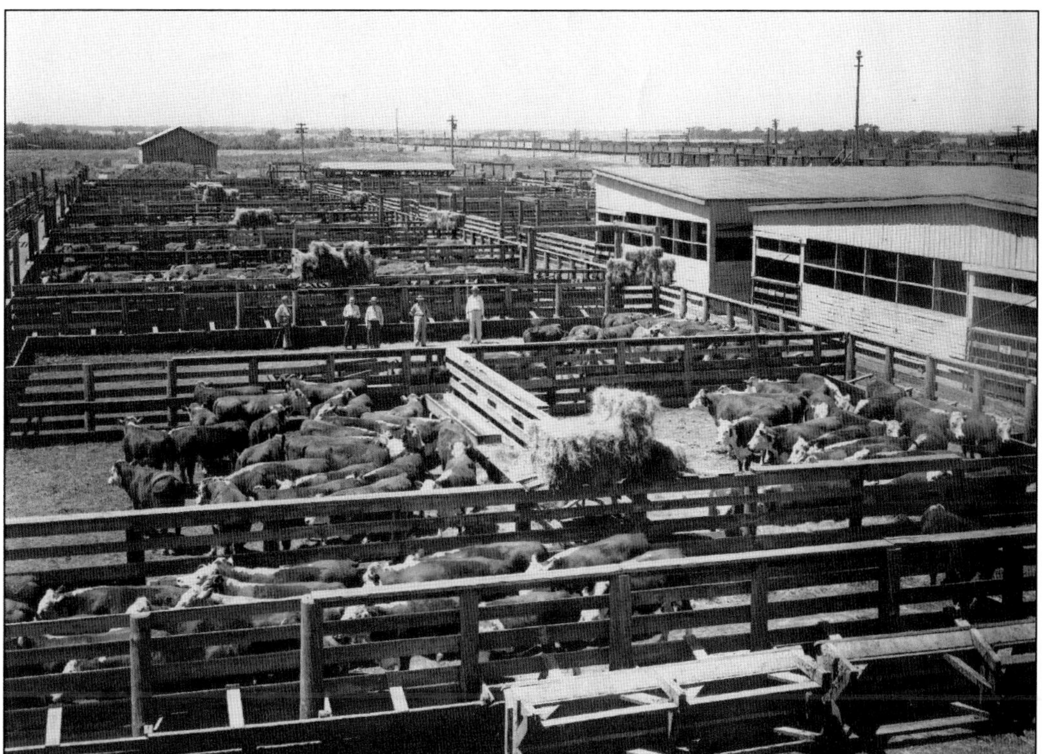

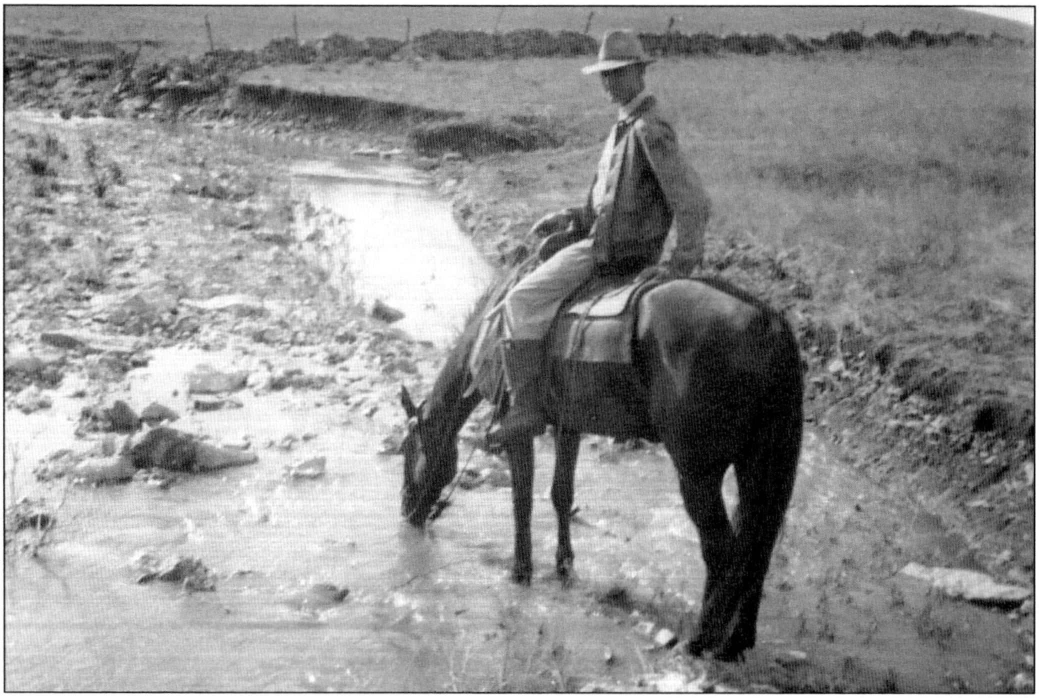

Curt Benninghoven is seen on the Chase County Davis Ranch. On the back of this photograph is written, "5/21/38 Benninghoven giving his horse a drink after turning Palomas steers loose in a 4000 acre pasture, Chase County Kansas." Davis had purchased 3,800 Texas steers in early May, and they arrived in Strong City on May 21. (Courtesy Phyllis Scherich collection.)

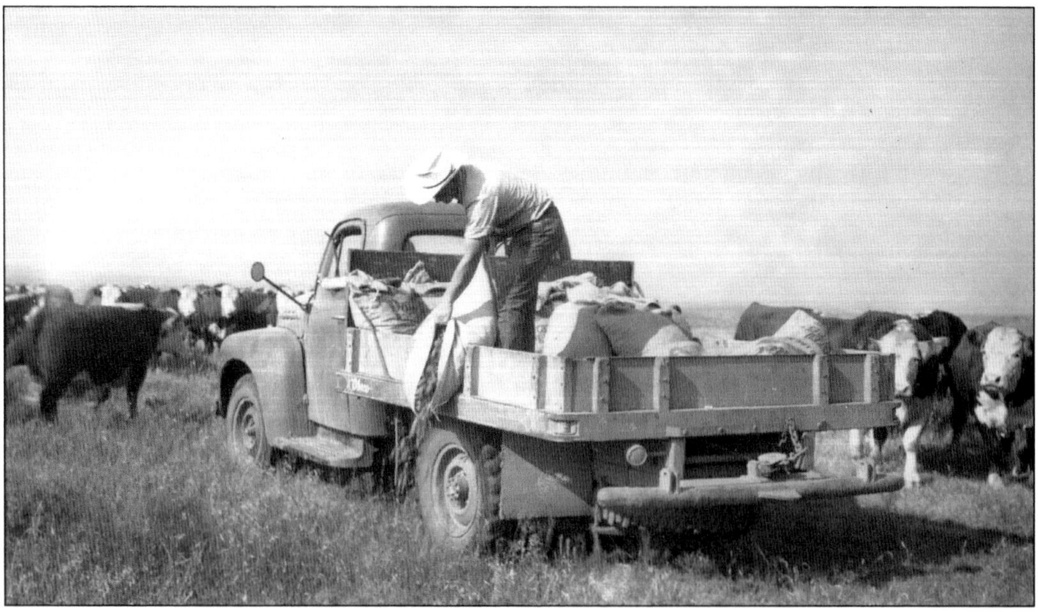

An unidentified Davis Ranch cowboy is seen feeding cattle on the Chase County ranch. The ranch would sell steers every fall, but cattle would also be fed during the winter on the Chase County property. In 1954, the Chase County ranch fed 1,500 steers during the winter months. (Courtesy Phyllis Scherich collection.)

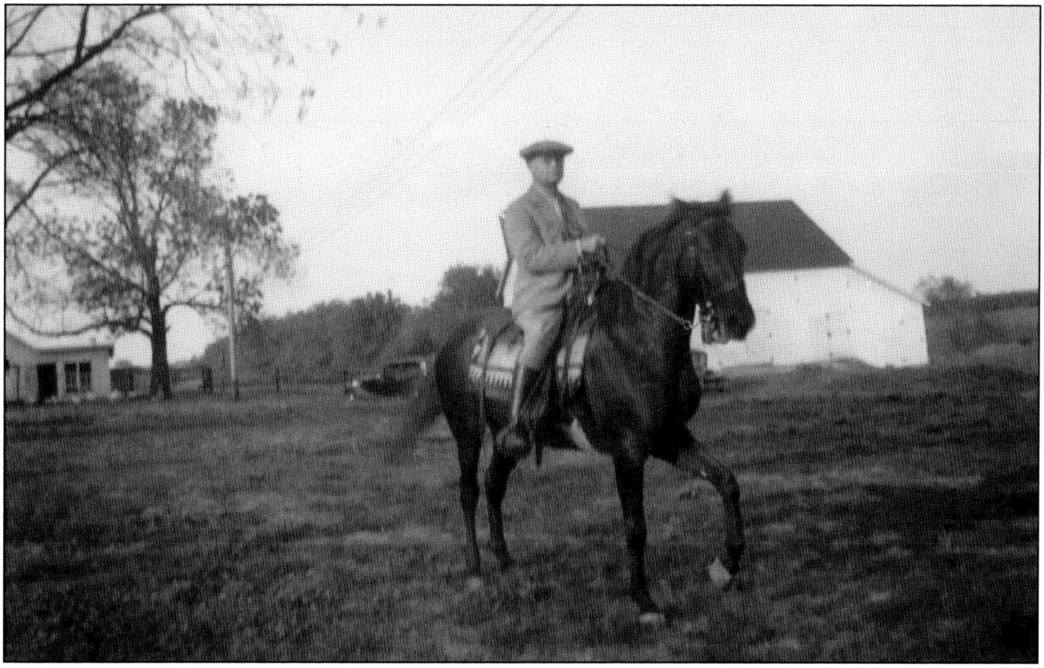

After purchasing the Dewey ranch in 1931, Davis purchased six Johnson County, Kansas, farms in 1932. Above, Davis is seen on horseback at his Johnson County ranch in October 1934. Below, Percy Schrader (left) and George Davis are seen at Davis's Johnson County property. Ninety-two-year-old Orville Burtis Jr., the last president of the Z Bar Cattle Company, looked at this photograph, chuckled, and remarked about his old friend Davis, "A guy who isn't a real cowboy shouldn't dress up like one." Davis probably agreed, for this is the only known photograph of the mighty rancher dressed in Western attire. (Both, courtesy National Park Service.)

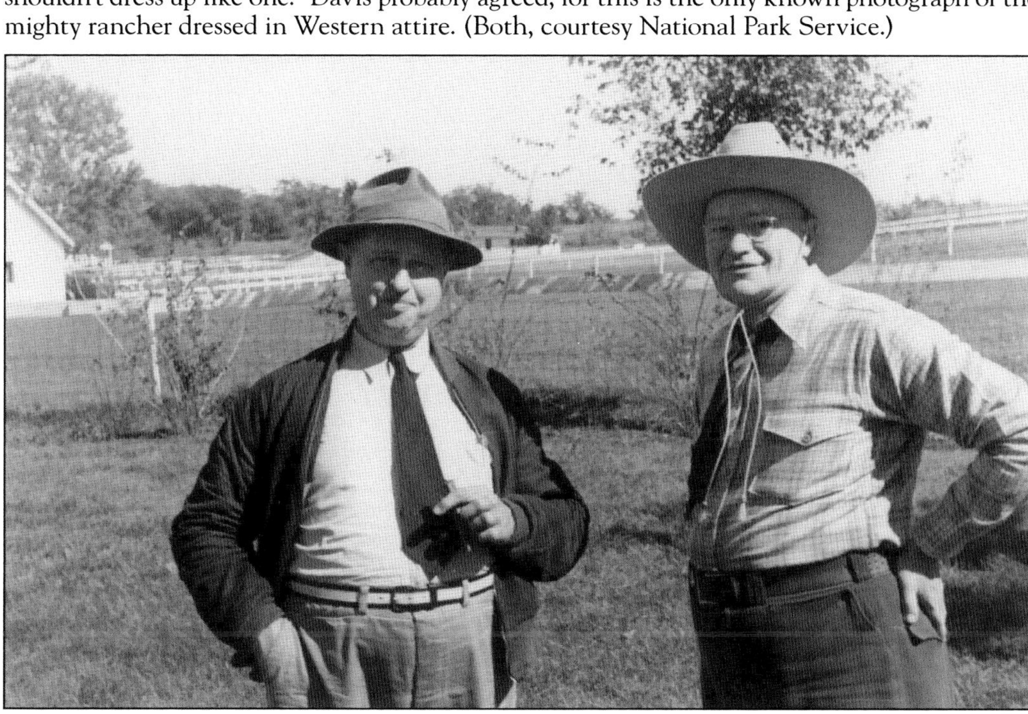

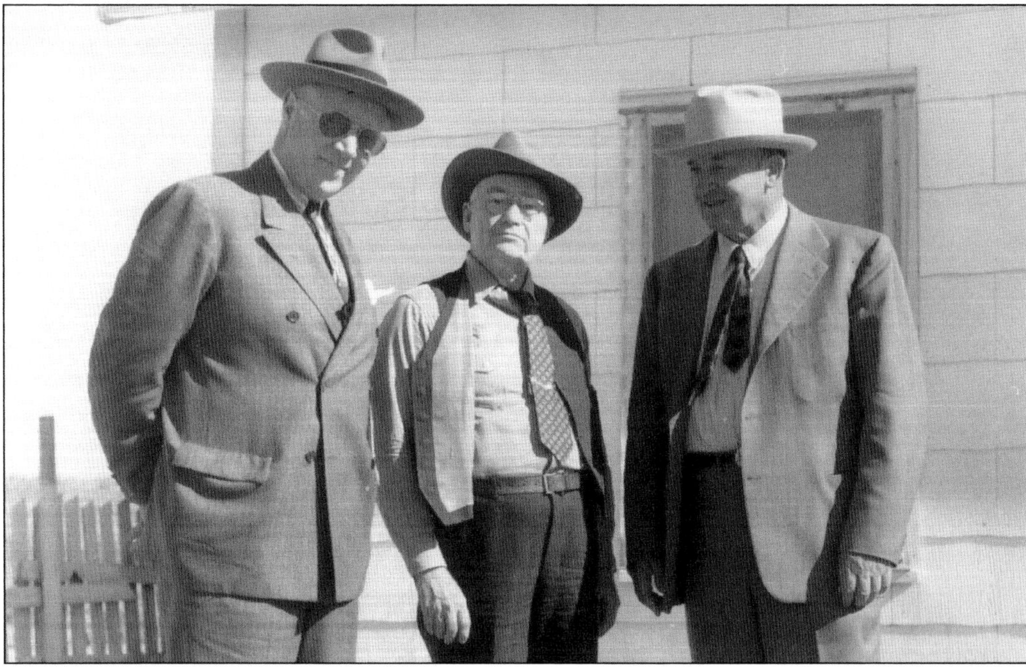

This photograph dated May 13, 1948, was taken on the Davis Ranch in Barber County, Kansas. Seen are, from the left to right, Gates Williams, of St. Louis, Missouri; George Davis; and Joe Bridwell, of Wichita Falls, Texas. Involved in both the purchasing and sale of cattle, Davis enjoyed taking a very active role in the ranching endeavor. The Barber County ranch was the first ranch acquired by Davis-Noland-Merrill Grain in 1933. (Courtesy National Park Service.)

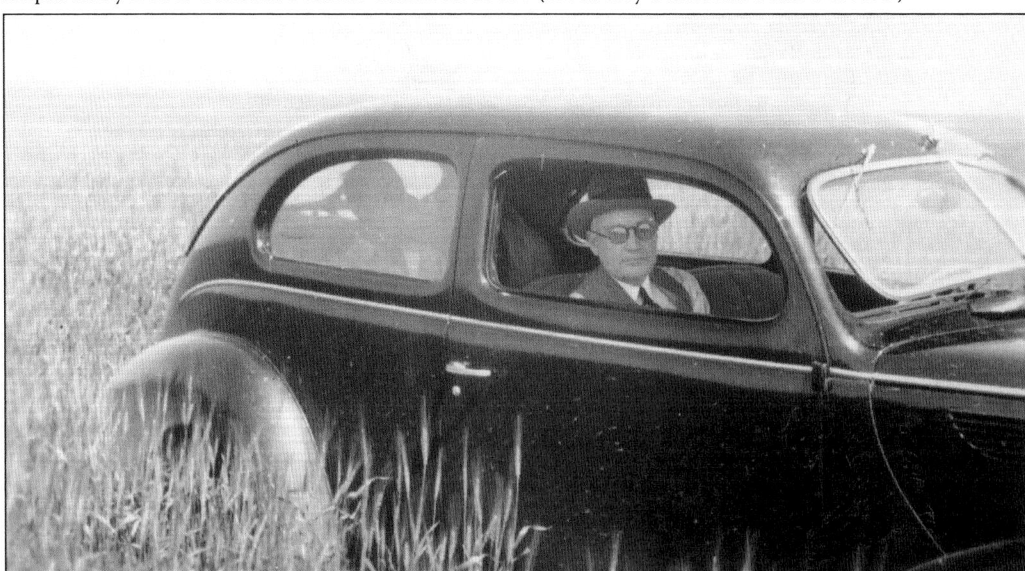

George Davis, seated in the front passenger seat, is seen in a pasture on his Barber County ranch in this 1936 photograph. The southern ranches in Barber County and Comanche County were selected for their geographic location in Kansas, which has a mild climate in the winter. Davis believed that the temperate winter enjoyed on these southern Kansas ranches was ideal for the birthing of calves. (Courtesy National Park Service.)

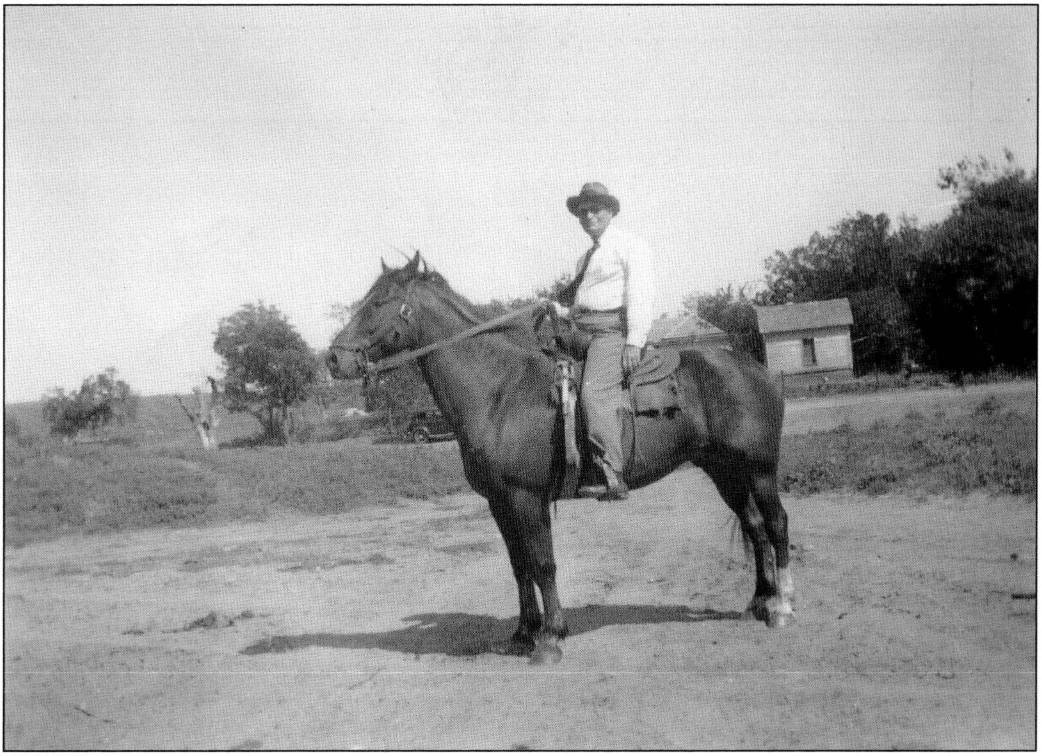

Above, George Davis sits astride a horse on the former Temple Ranch, a part of his Davis Ranch in Barber County, Kansas. This photograph, dated September 19, 1934, was taken just months after Davis had acquired the property for Davis-Noland-Merrill Grain Company. The Temple Ranch had the distinction of having cows and calves that came with the ranch, all bearing the Z Bar brand. Davis acquired the brand with the purchase of the property. Below, cattle are seen in the main pens at the ranch headquarters in Barber County in this 1930s photograph. (Both, courtesy National Park Service.)

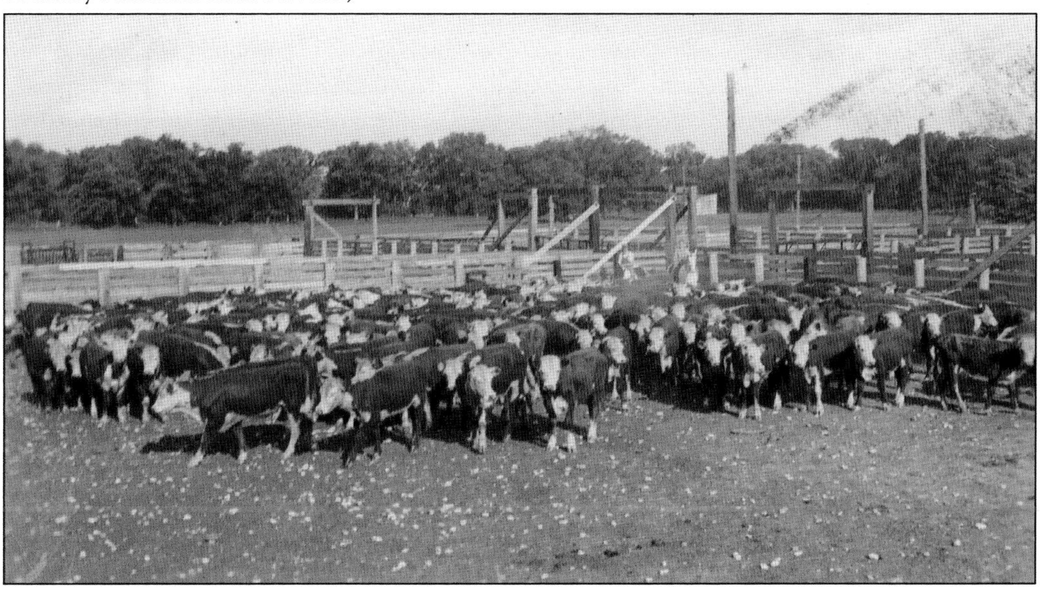

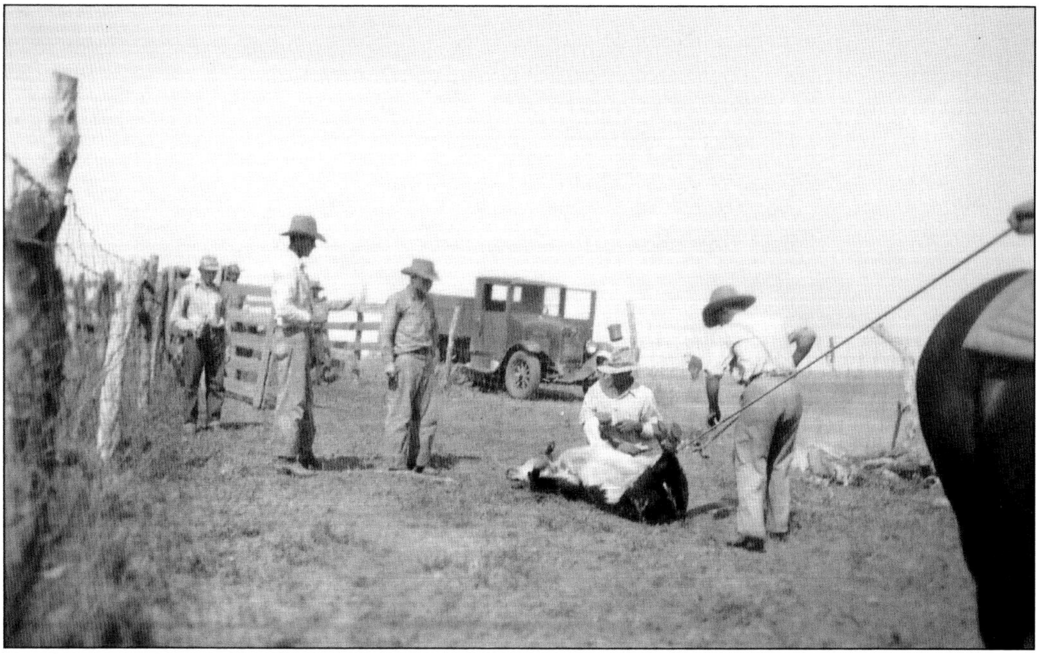

Cowboys on the Davis Ranch in Barber County, Kansas, are seen branding steers in this mid-1930s photograph. The process remained unchanged for decades—one man on a horse with a lariat, one to wrestle the steer, and one with the red-hot iron. In this view, the brand is the Z Bar. (Courtesy National Park Service.)

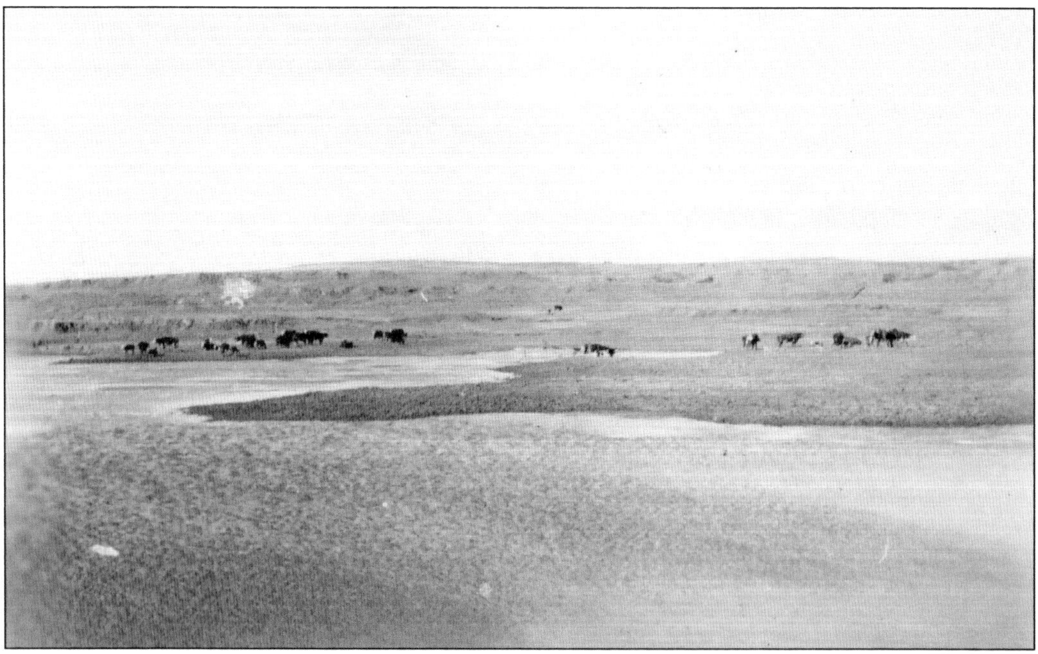

Cattle graze in a big pasture on the Z Bar Ranch in Barber County. Because of water shortages experienced during the 1930s, George Davis constructed over 25 lakes on the Barber County ranch, guaranteeing a year-round supply of water for livestock. This is one of the lakes on the Barber County Z Bar. (Courtesy National Park Service.)

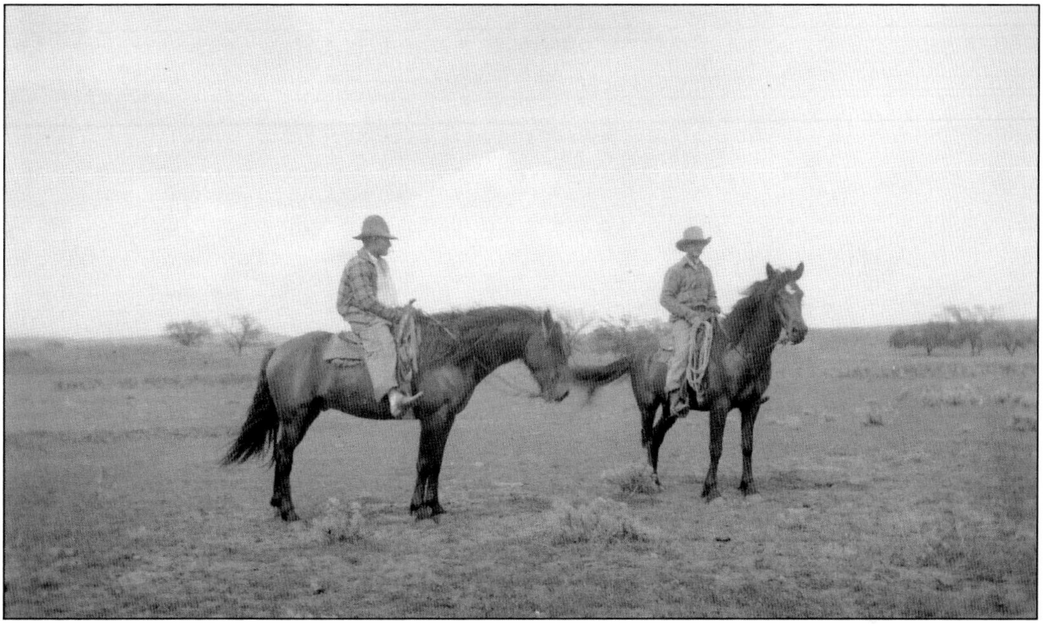

Cole Goff, left, and Orville Alley are seen on horseback on the Davis Ranch in Barber County in this early 1930s photograph. Alley was the longtime ranch manager for the Davis Ranch in Barber County from 1933 to 1951. Alley's brother Lester Alley managed the Davis Ranch in Comanche County from 1934 to 1947, when Harold Merrill took ownership of that ranch. (Courtesy National Park Service.)

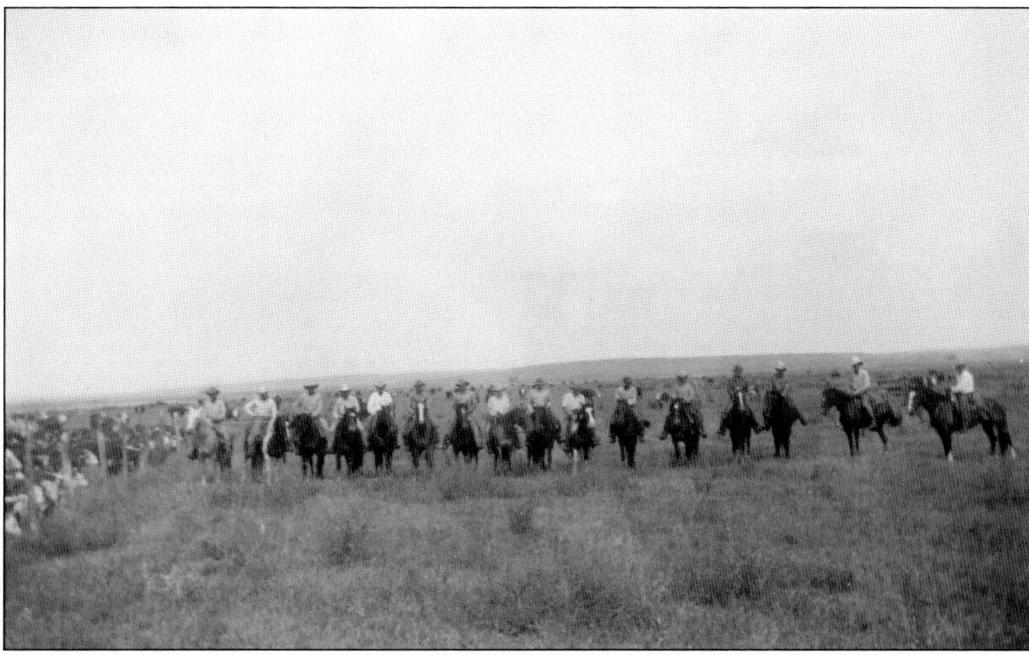

This photograph from the Barber County Z Bar Ranch and dated May 26, 1936, shows 16 cowboys lined up ready to work cattle. In the spring, the steers were branded and driven to the stockyards to be loaded on cattle cars headed to the lush pastures of the Flint Hills. (Courtesy National Park Service.)

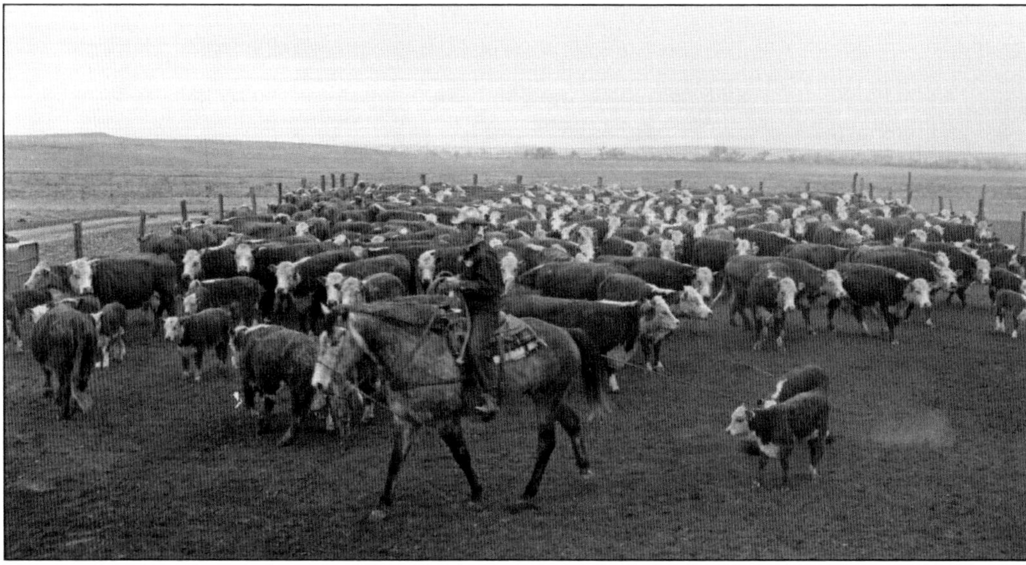

The weather was cool in May 1972 when these photographs were taken of the steer roundup and branding on the Z Bar Ranch in Barber County. Above, the steers are moved into pens where cowboys on horseback lasso a steer, a second cowboy brings it to the ground, and the third man wields the branding iron. In the photograph below, one modern convenience the ranch employed by 1972 was a propane gas–fired burner to heat the branding irons. At the far left in the lower photograph is Lloyd "Bud" Liggenstoffer, ranch manager in Barber County from 1951 to 1983. (Both, courtesy National Park Service.)

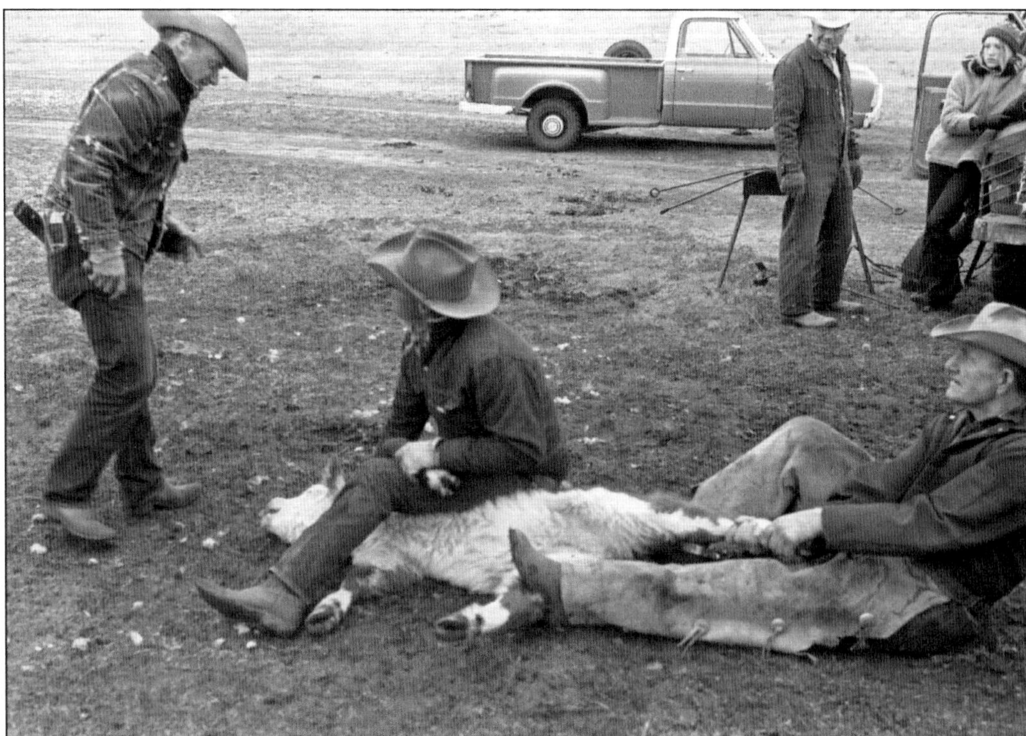

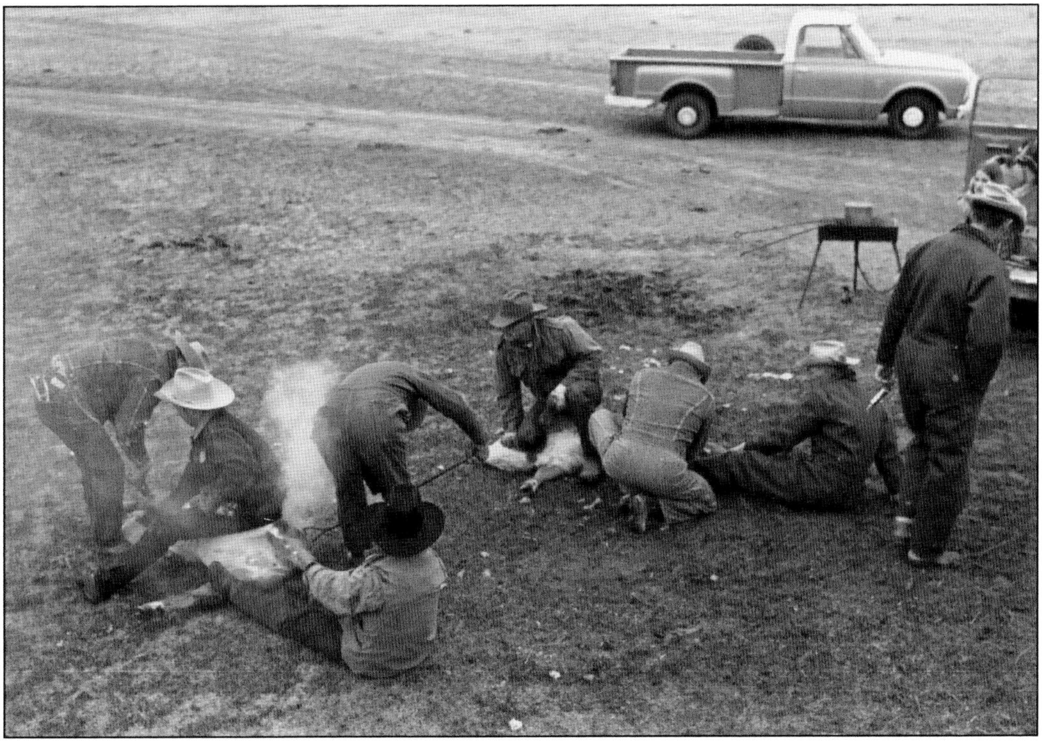

In the Barber County photograph above, taken in May 1972, cowboys are seen working in two teams branding calves. Two more branding irons are seen heating in the burner at the right side of the photograph. Below, one cowboy sits on a steer while a second applies the Z Bar brand. The brand originated for the Davis Ranch on this very Barber County property. When Davis purchased the Temple Ranch, cattle included in the purchase bore the Z Bar brand, which he kept. (Both, courtesy National Park Service.)

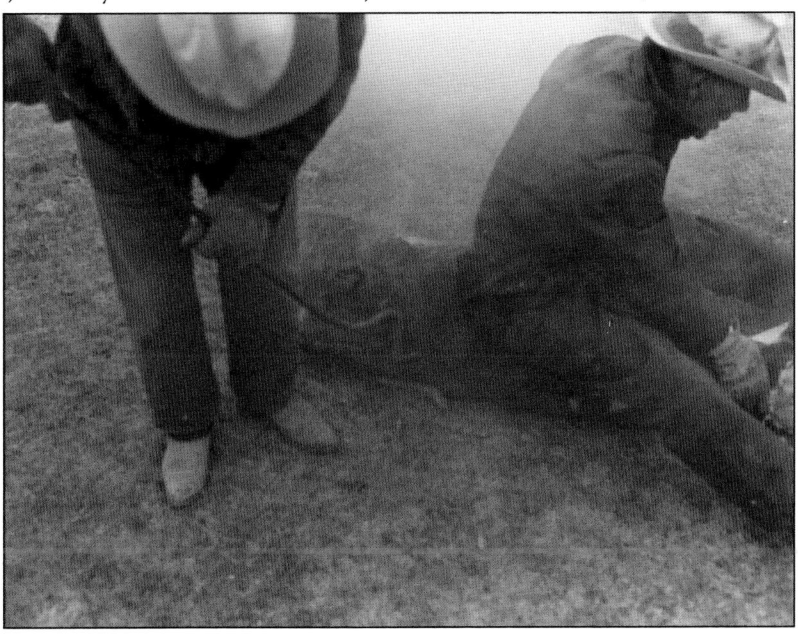

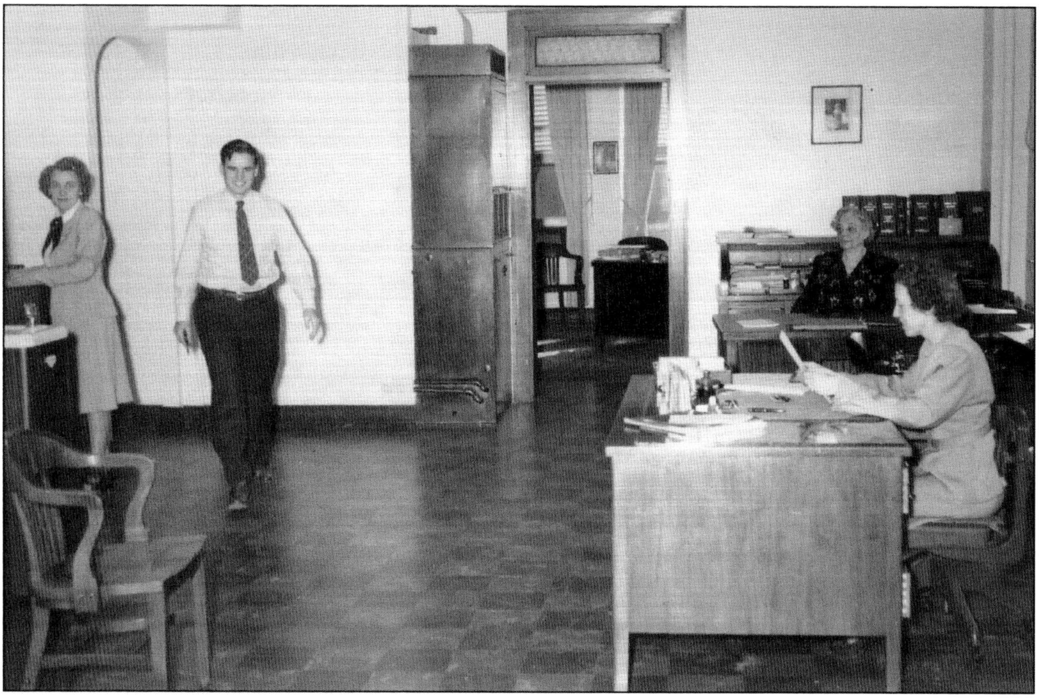

After the reorganization of the Davis Ranch in 1947 with the closing of Davis-Noland-Merrill Grain Company, some new faces arrived in the Kansas City office and some familiar ones remained. Above are, from left to right, Winnie Westman Brown, Orville Burtis Jr., Minerva Gundelfinger, and Hilda Burke. Below, Gundelfinger is seated while Burke, Burtis, and Brown are seen behind her; both of these photographs are from 1948. Gundelfinger was not only the ranking staff member, having begun working for Davis in 1902, but she was also a stockholder in the corporation. Burtis began working for Davis in 1947, replacing J.P. Lynn as overseer of the ranches. Lynn left the Davis operation that year to become overseer of Harold Merrill's ranches, a position he held until 1960. (Both, courtesy National Park Service.)

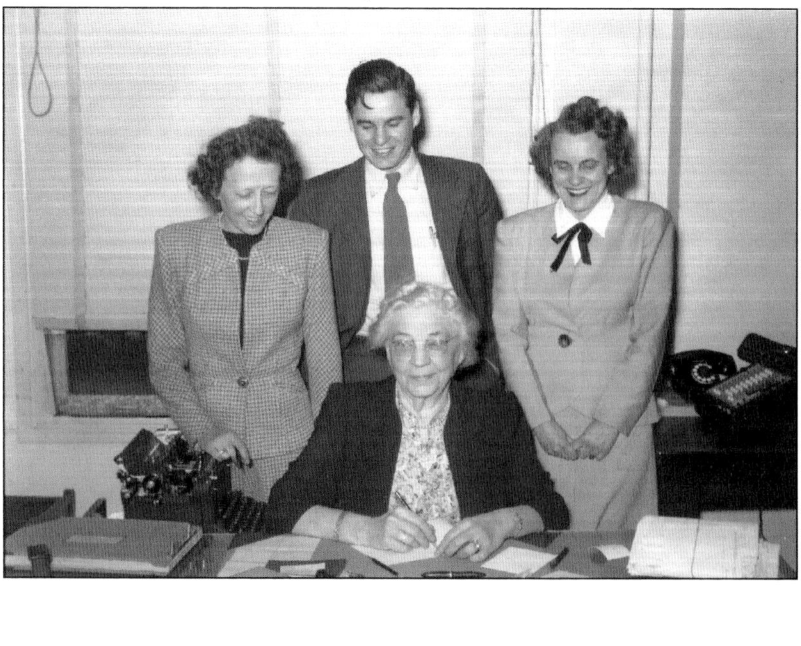

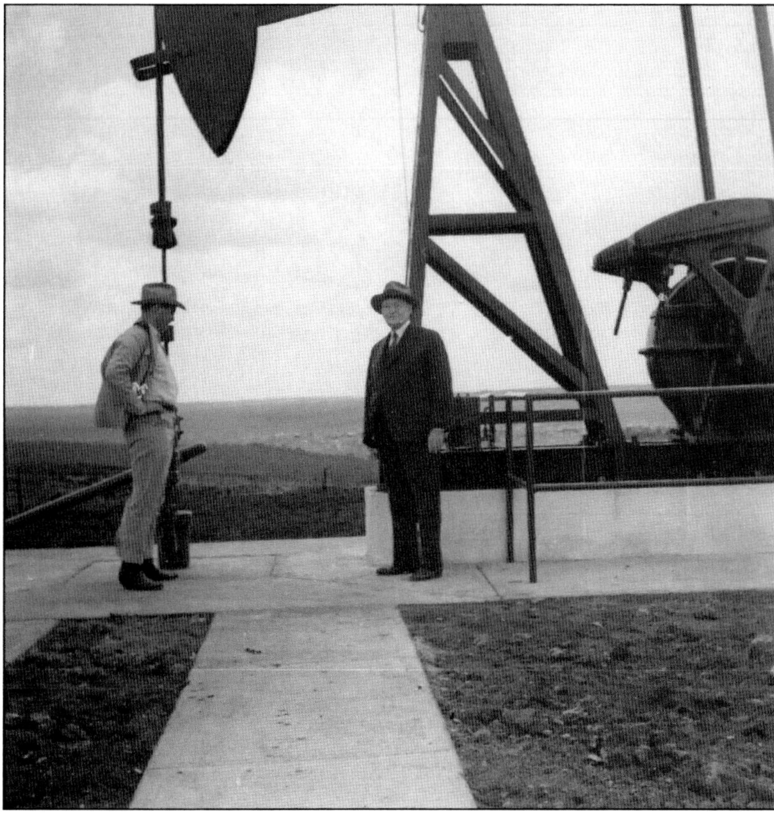

Orville Burtis Jr., left, and George H. Davis stand on the well platform at the Davis Ranch in Wabaunsee County in May 1949. Only a month earlier, Carter Oil Company had struck oil while wildcatting on the Davis Ranch, 10 miles south of Alma, Kansas. In May, Davis and Burtis toured the first well. By February 1, 1951, the Davis Pool had 18 producing oil wells. (Courtesy Phyllis Scherich collection.)

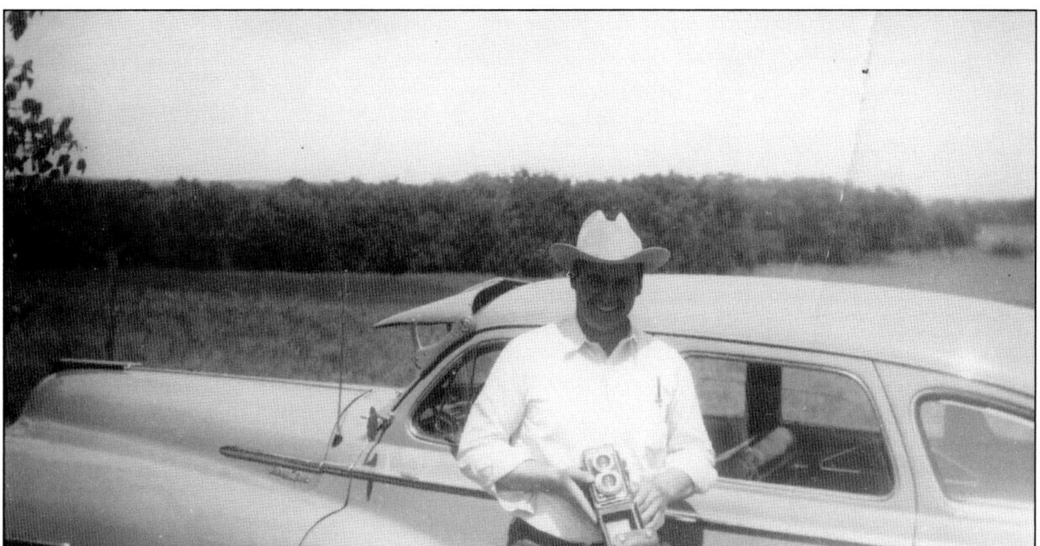

Orville Burtis Jr. is seen on the Davis Ranch in Wabaunsee County, camera in hand. Burtis had become acquainted with Davis when Burtis's father, Orville Burtis Sr., managed George Davis's Dewey Ranch in Riley County. Davis hired Burtis Jr. when J.P. Lynn left to work for Harold Merrill. In 1964, Orville Burtis Jr. became president of Davis Cattle Company upon the death of Everett Ellis, who had succeeded Davis as president. (Courtesy National Park Service.)

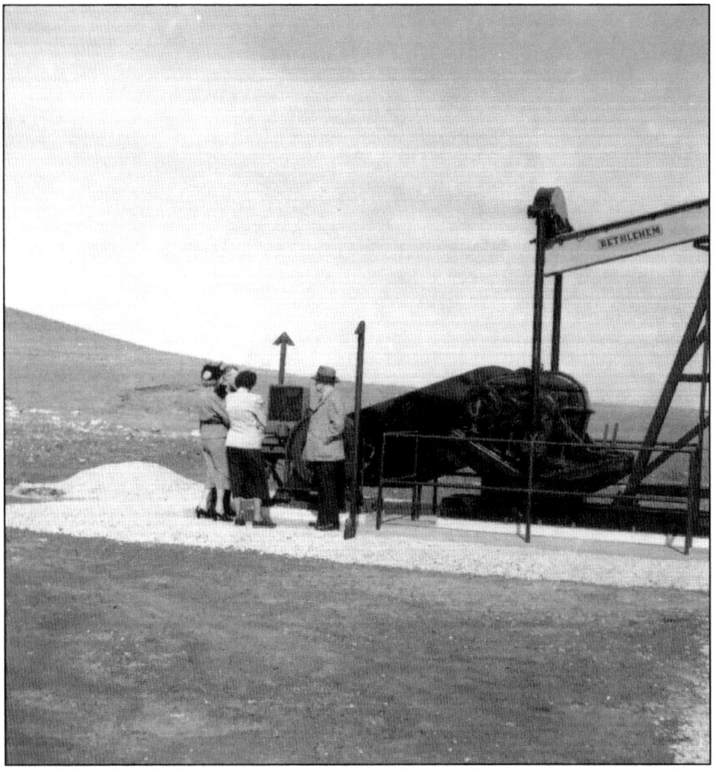

Elizabeth and George Davis, right, and James D. and Dorothy Tinklepaugh visit the Davis Ranch in Wabaunsee County on November 11, 1949, inspecting yet another new oil well in the Davis pool. Dorothy Tinklepaugh was George Davis's niece, and her husband, J.D., had gone to work for Ernst-Davis Grain Company as an office boy in 1914, remaining with Davis his entire career and becoming a director and treasurer of the corporation. Below, cattle from the Davis Ranch bearing the Z Bar brand are grazed among the two dozen oil wells drilled on the property. (Both, courtesy Phyllis Scherich collection.)

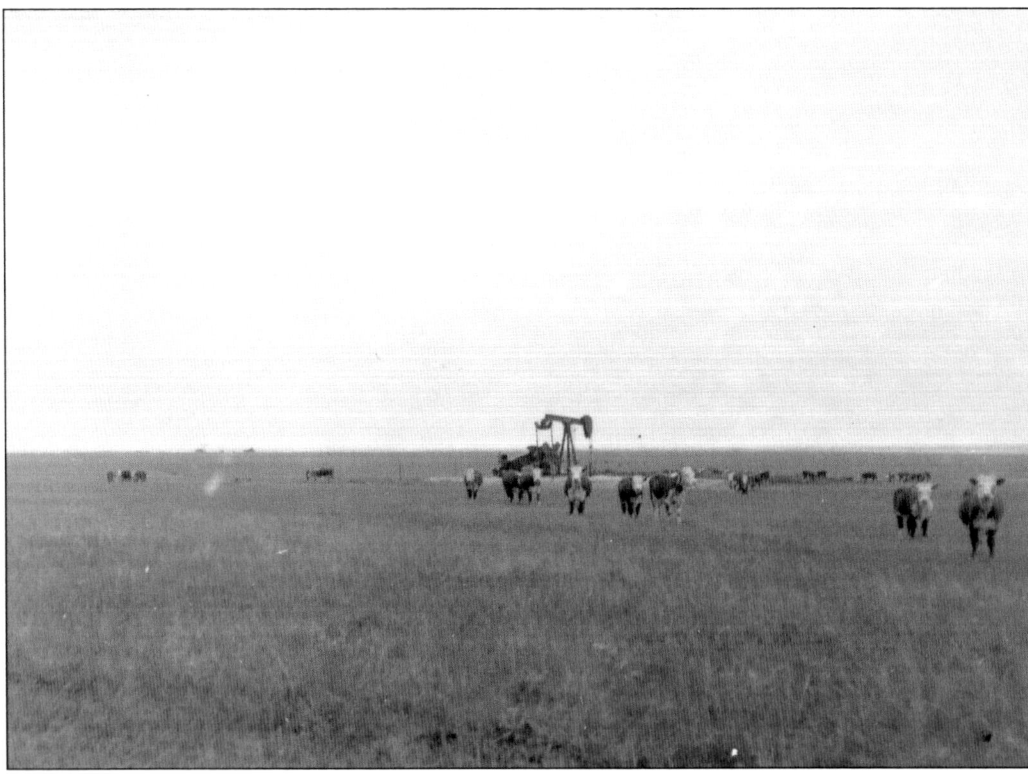

Five

Real Cowboys of the Flint Hills

Their life has been romanticized in movies, books, and song. The American cowboy has long been regarded a maverick, a free spirit, and hard as nails, yet always ready for fun. It is easy to see why this portrayal has been so prevalent. The job is a tough one—handling livestock and dealing with uncontrollable adversities ranging from severe weather to illness affecting herds. Often the movie script overlooks the endless hours and no available days off experienced by many real cowboys trying to make a living raising cattle.

However, there are times when the stereotype seems to fit. It is not uncommon to find young cowboys in cheerful competition with their peers, riding, roping, and manhandling cattle—the same activities that they perform while working. For a century, rodeos have been the sport and entertainment for cowboys and those who enjoy watching cowboys. They began, often enough, as a group meeting in a pasture, a circle of parked cars and trucks serving as the arena fence. Young men jump on the backs of untamed horses and bulls and the crowd anxiously watches the outcome. It is a tough sport when hanging onto a wild animal for only eight seconds is a victory. But the cowboys who participate in such activities love it. They often endure injuries far more severe from competing in rodeo than those suffered by football players or professional boxers.

It is hard sometimes to decide which is more difficult, the rodeo sport or being a real cowboy and raising cattle. Both require endurance, stubbornness, and quickness. Both require a passion for the business and compassion for animals, horses, and cattle. This chapter contains views of real Flint Hills cowboys pursuing their livelihood: raising cattle. Also included are views of real Flint Hills cowboys competing in rodeo events.

Pictured in this chapter are views of a number of Flint Hills rodeo venues. Virtually every county in the Flint Hills hosted a rodeo after World War II, when the sport became increasingly popular. Every rodeo arena has 1,000 stories to tell of famous cowboys who rode famous bulls and broncs within the arena walls. Likewise, every arena has a story of its origin, and those, too, are as noteworthy as the tales of great rodeo stars. Here are two accounts of rodeo arenas: one venue has grown to be the site of the most prestigious rodeo in the Midwest, and the second faded into obscurity, with little left except old photographs and memories.

The Flint Hills Rodeo in Strong City is the record of the Emmett C. Roberts family, for the story of the family and the rodeo are inexorably tied. E.C. Roberts and his wife, Clara, moved to Strong City around 1920, where Roberts engaged in ranching. The couple raised six children on their Flint Hills ranch, and insofar as horses were E.C. Roberts's passion, there were always horses around to break to ride. The three older children— Marge, Ken, and Gerald—were all interested in riding, and their father let them break young horses. All three excelled at the enterprise. In 1929, at age 13, Marge joined Clyde Miller's Wild West Show and became a renowned trick rider. Each summer, she worked for the show until graduating from high school, and then she joined the production full-time. Her brothers, Ken and Gerald, worked in the show as well. In 1940, Marge won the world championship in women's bronc riding. Her brother Ken was the World Champion Bull Rider in 1943, 1944, and 1945. Gerald Roberts was the All-Around Champion cowboy of the world in 1942 and 1948. The Roberts family was a dynasty in the sport.

In 1937, Emmett Roberts held his first rodeo in a pasture on his ranch. In 1938, Roberts and son Ken and Marge's husband, Eddie Boysen, held what they called the First Annual Chase County Rodeo. The next year, it was renamed the Flint Hills Rodeo. The event has been held every year since. In 1948, it moved into a new arena facility, and its popularity increased annually. Rodeo cowboys from all over the country travel to Strong City every June to compete in this storied event. Today, the Flint Hills Rodeo at Strong City is considered one of the most prestigious rodeo events in the Midwest.

In Alma, Kansas, in the years following World War II, members of the local 4-H Clubs looked for a location to hold a rodeo event for their members. For a few years, the football field at Alma High School was used as an arena. However, in 1951, spring rains saturated the ground and threatened to cancel the 4-H rodeo, as bringing livestock onto the wet field would destroy the grass. Alma rancher Lester Marten, whose son Gerald "Cheese" Marten was a hopeful participant in the event, offered his pasture two miles south of Alma for the rodeo. The Lester Marten Rodeo Arena was born. Spring and fall, 4-H rodeos were held at the arena. Marten made improvements in the pens and constructed a judges' and announcer's tower. He installed lights so the rodeos could go into the night. Marten began holding weekly jackpot roping events on Saturday nights. They opened a little concession stand, and there was always a crowd. And it was always exciting. For a quarter of a century, Marten's arena was a regular spot for Flint Hills cowboys and spectators. Cheese Marten compiled a list of cowboys who had competed at his father's arena. It was a roll of every active rodeo cowboy in the Flint Hills in the 1960s. Marten's Rodeo Arena came to an end in 1976. It was a big event, on the Fourth of July in the bicentennial year. The pasture was filled with vehicles. DeLong Livestock Company from Scranton, Kansas, provided the rodeo stock. And they brought a buffalo along for an entertaining show at intermission and the possibility that some young cowboy might want to ride it. Some young fellow did, indeed. However, in the course of the presentation, a horse was gored badly by the buffalo that really "wasn't broke to ride," and the horse had to be shot. After the event, Marten's wife, Yvonne, gave her Lester a clear choice: it was her or the rodeo. There was never another event held at Marten's Rodeo Arena.

Cecil "Whitey" Butts, longtime rodeo cowboy from Alma, Kansas, is seen here competing in the bull riding competition at an unidentified 1959 rodeo. Whitey Butts traveled the rodeo circuit during the late 1950s and 1960s competing in bull riding, bareback bronc riding, and saddle bronc riding as well as other rodeo events. (Courtesy Whitey Butts.)

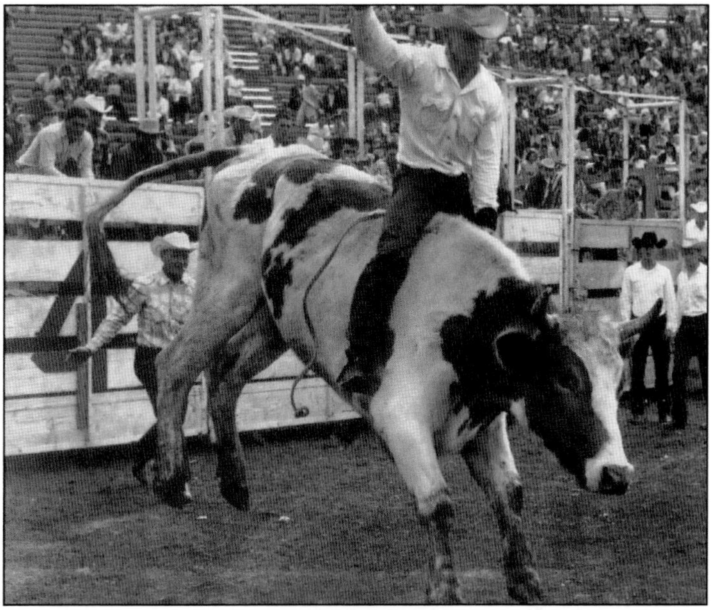

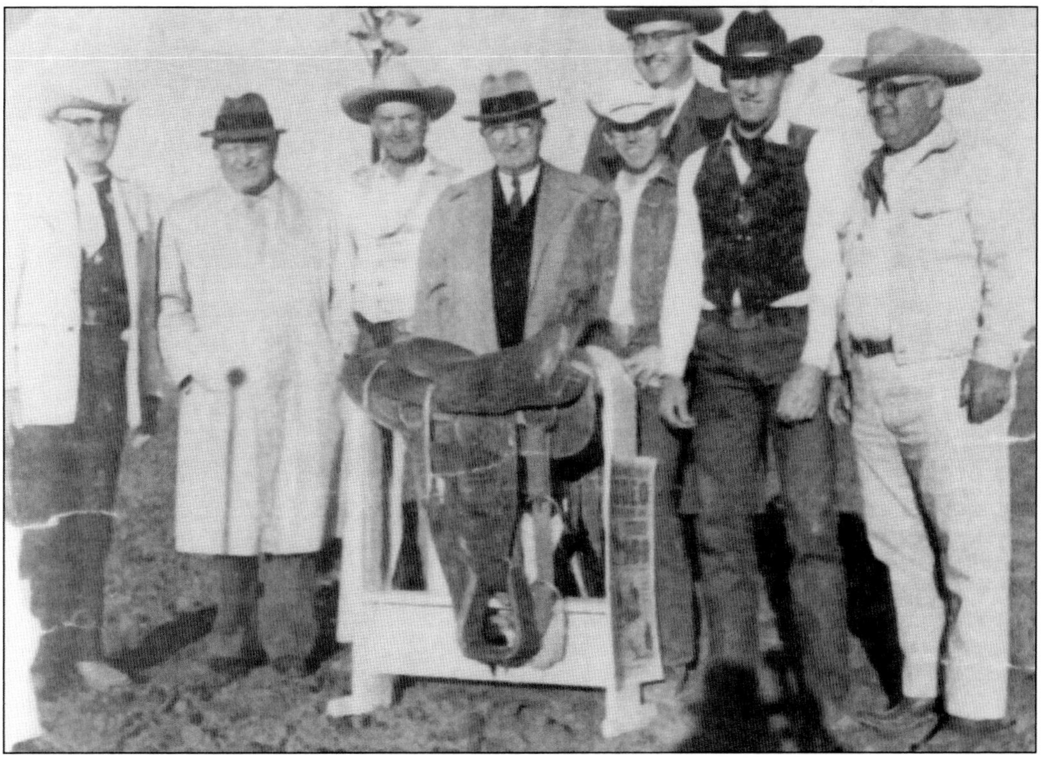

Whitey Butts won the all-around cowboy Trophy Saddle at the 1959 Independence Missouri Police Rodeo. Butts had this unidentified newspaper picture in his rodeo photograph collection. Identified, from left to right, are Louis Howell, Bill Serman, E.C. Roberts, Pres. Harry Truman, Whitey Butts, Ken Roberts, Mike Westwood; in the background is Les Milgrim. When asked what happened to the saddle, Butts replied, grinning, "I sold it for a hundred silver dollars." (Courtesy Whitey Butts.)

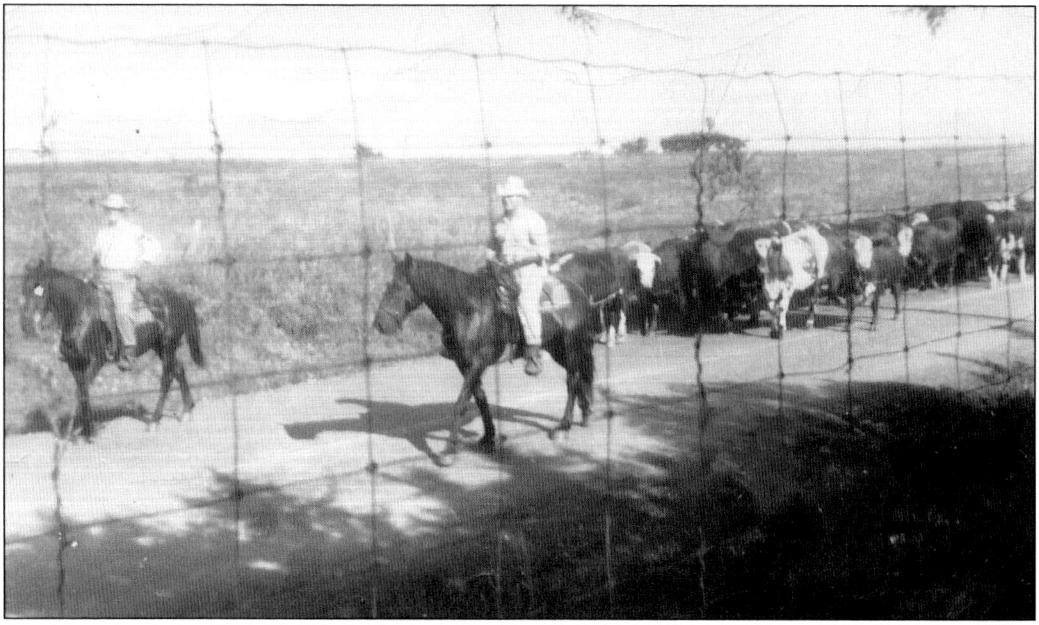

Cowboys drive cattle down K-99 Highway at the intersection of McFarland Road in this 1940s photograph. Moving cattle from horseback was a standard for over a century in the Flint Hills. Often, the highways and roads made perfect "cattle lanes," as they were usually fenced on both sides. Cowboys still move cattle on horseback today; however, at many ranches all-terrain vehicles have replaced horses for this task. (Courtesy Rob Meseke.)

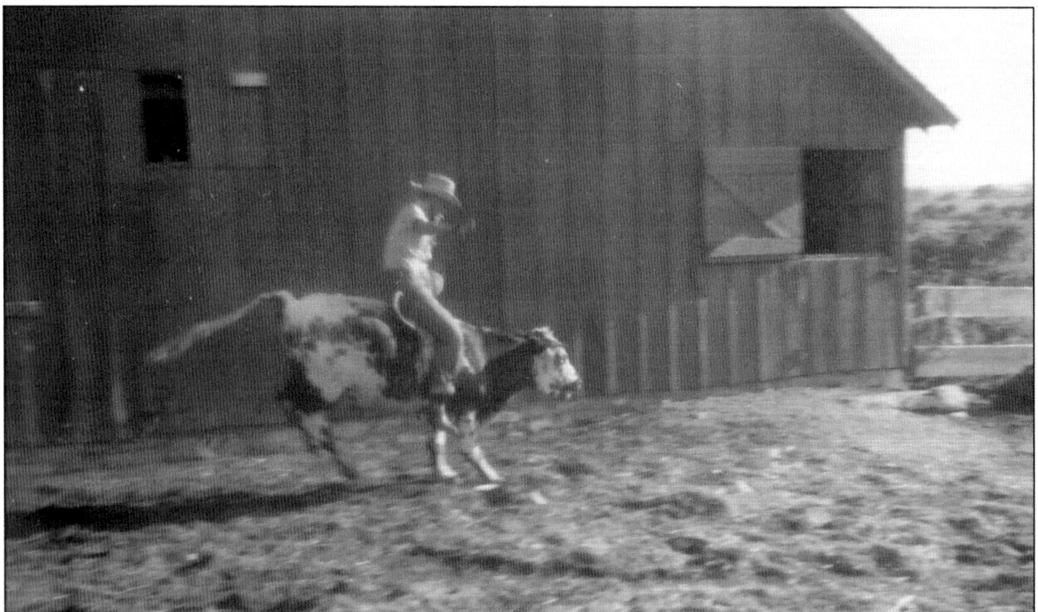

A 16-year-old Ron Pletcher is seen in the corral by the barn at his parents' home place on Missile Base Road, Eskridge, practicing bull riding for the first time. The practice paid off; Pletcher became an accomplished bull rider and rodeo competitor in the late 1950s and 1960s. A photograph of Ron competing in bull riding is found on page 127. (Courtesy Shirley Pletcher.)

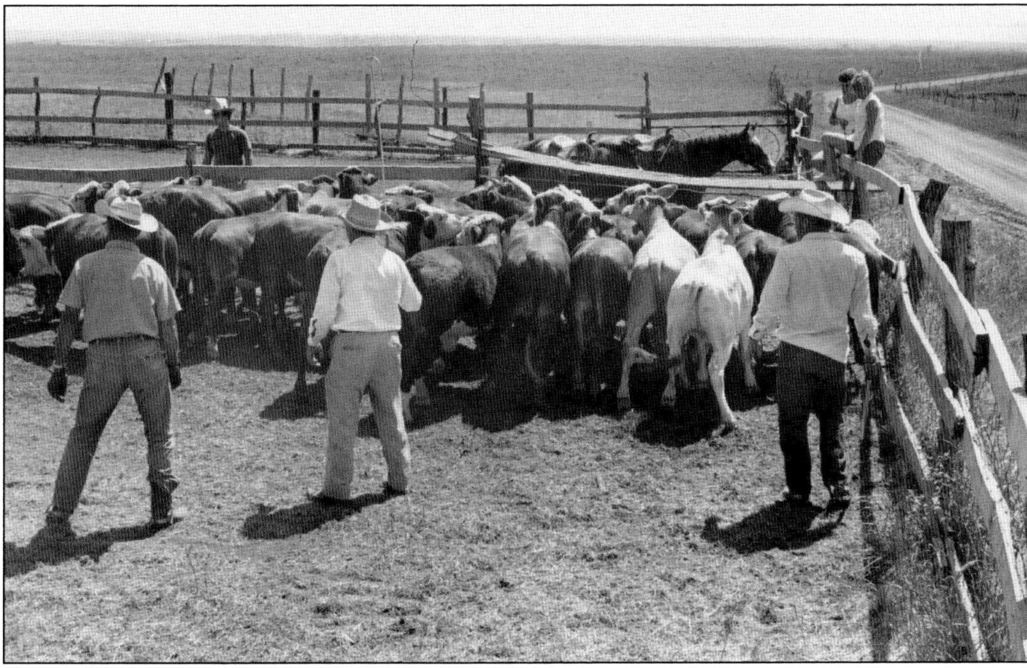

This August 1970 photograph by Jerry Engler was taken at the Munzer pasture pens, located south of Volland, Kansas. In the foreground, with their backs to the camera, are, from left to right, Bill Schultz, Art Schultz, and Keith Schultz. Facing the camera are, from left to right, Jim Hollenbeck, Julie Schultz, and Carol Schultz. (Courtesy Cleo and Julie Schultz.)

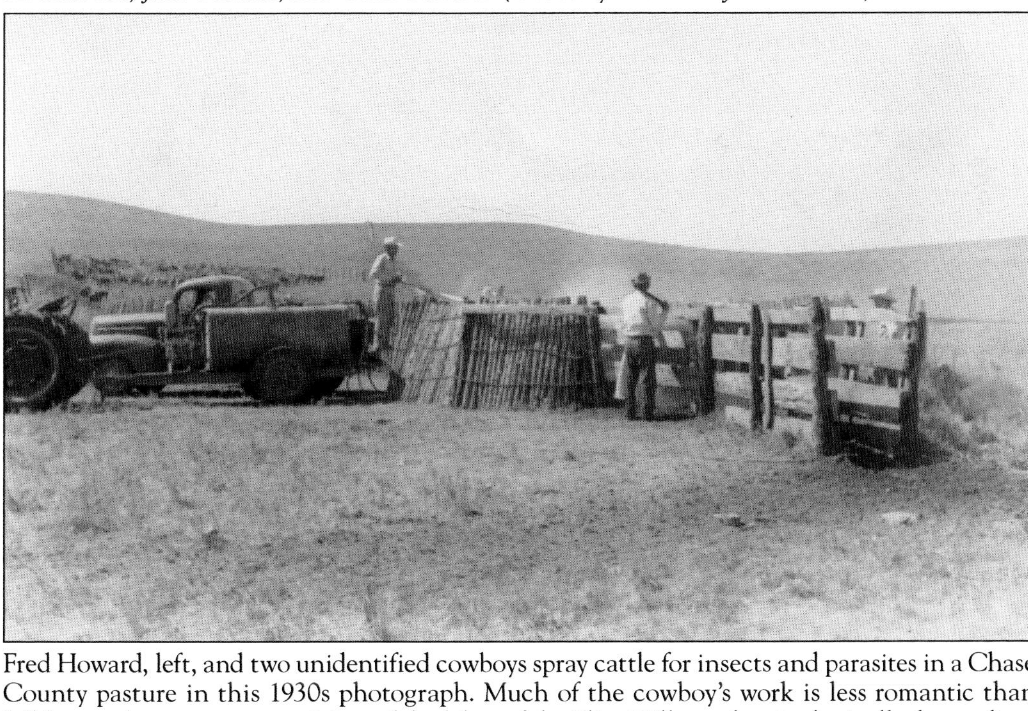

Fred Howard, left, and two unidentified cowboys spray cattle for insects and parasites in a Chase County pasture in this 1930s photograph. Much of the cowboy's work is less romantic than folklore and songs represent. Most of the labor of the Flint Hills cowboy is physically demanding, uncomfortably hot or cold, and oftentimes dangerous. (Courtesy Fred Howard II.)

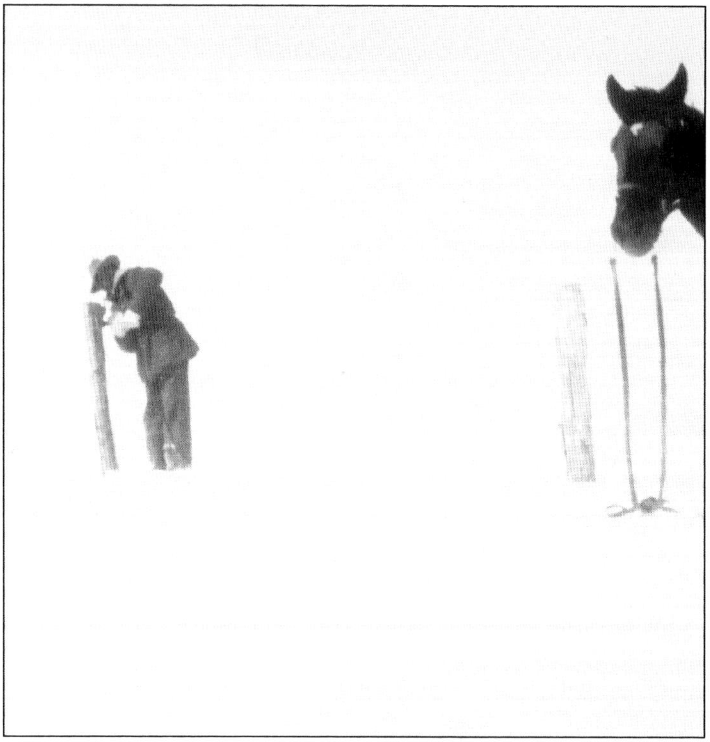

Art Schultz, a lifelong resident of the Volland community, is seen here fixing a fence in a blinding snowstorm. In fact, Schultz suffered severe snow blindness from excessive exposure to bright sunlight coupled with a heavy snow cover. Broken fences and loose or sick cattle have respect for neither the weather nor the day of the week. Ranching is an around-the-clock job. (Courtesy Keith Schultz.)

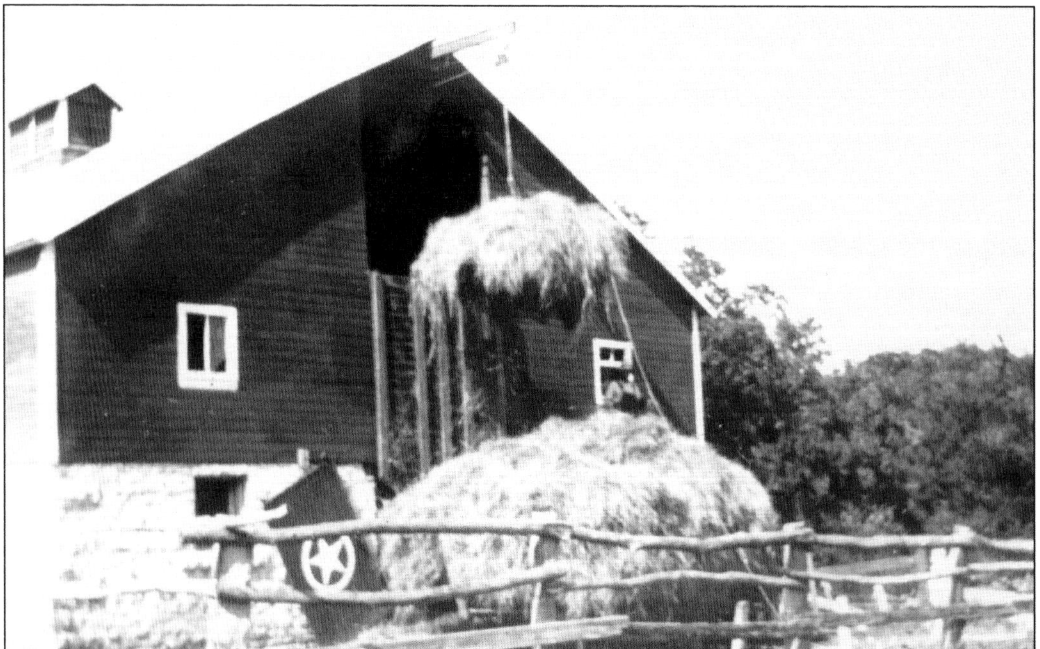

Growing, harvesting, and storing hay has always been the job of every rancher in the Flint Hills. Winters are tough in the area, and times are tougher without adequate hay supplies stockpiled for cold weather. Here, workers use a hay carrier to load hay into a barn loft at the Fred Steinmeyer farm and ranch, located five miles south of Alma on K-99 Highway. (Courtesy Keith Schultz.)

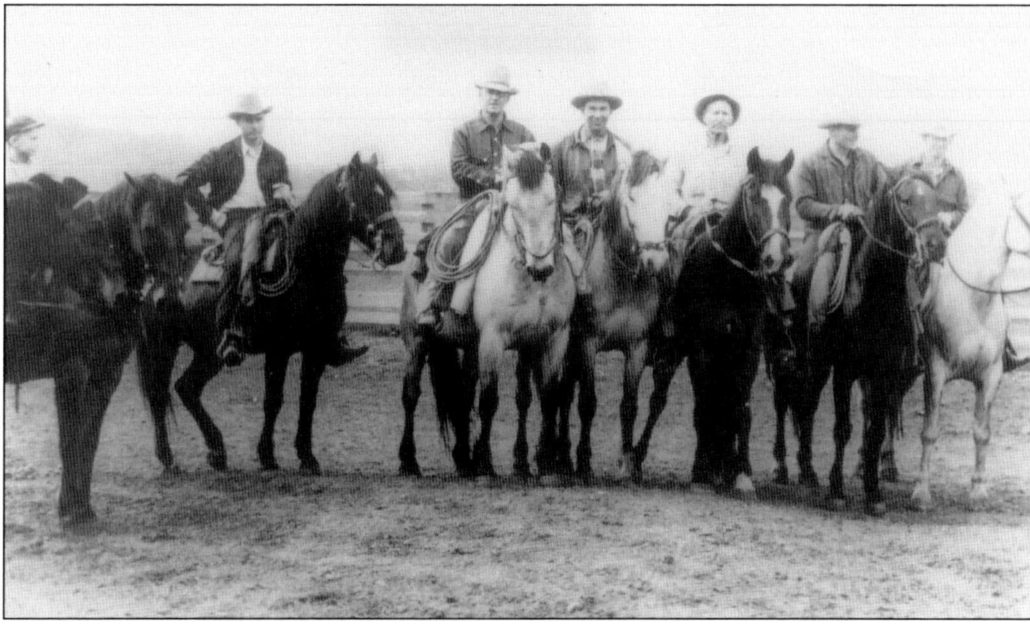

Above, cowboys prepare for the cattle roundup in Hessdale, Kansas, in this 1940s photograph. Seen from left to right are J.R. Maike, Oliver J. Hess, Earl Rock, Adolph Maike, Herman Sommer, Lyle Heder, and Clarence Meyer. Hessdale was one of the busiest railheads for the shipment of cattle in the nation in the first half of the 20th century. Below, cattle in the pens at the Hessdale stockyards and depot are prepared for loading into an AT&SF cattle train. By 1960, the AT&SF had discontinued the use of cattle trains in the Flint Hills. (Both, courtesy Wabaunsee County Historical Society.)

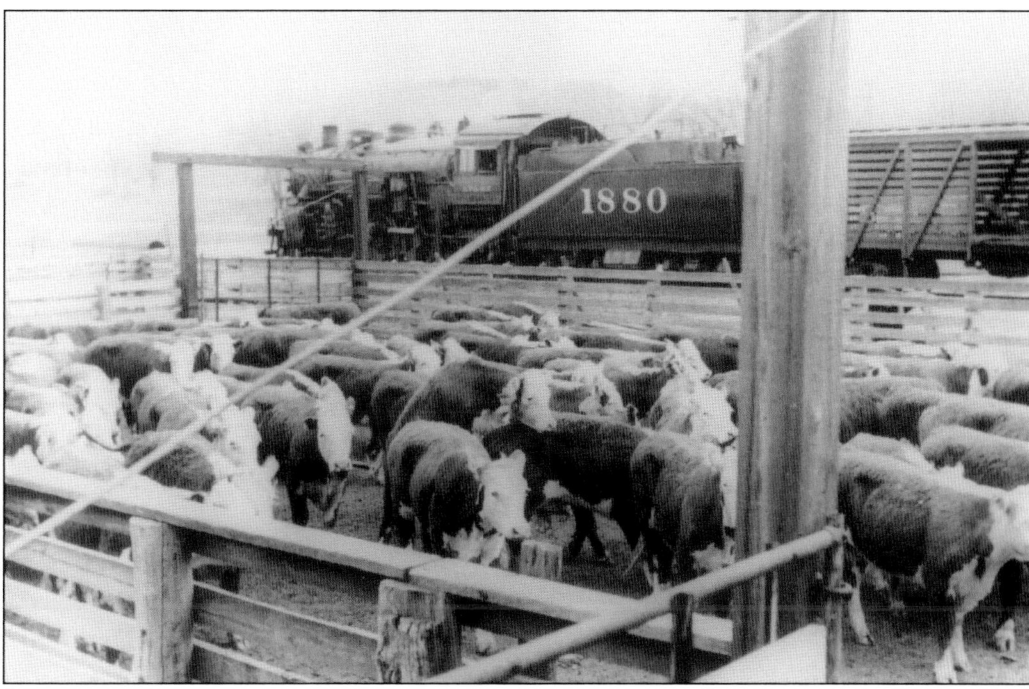

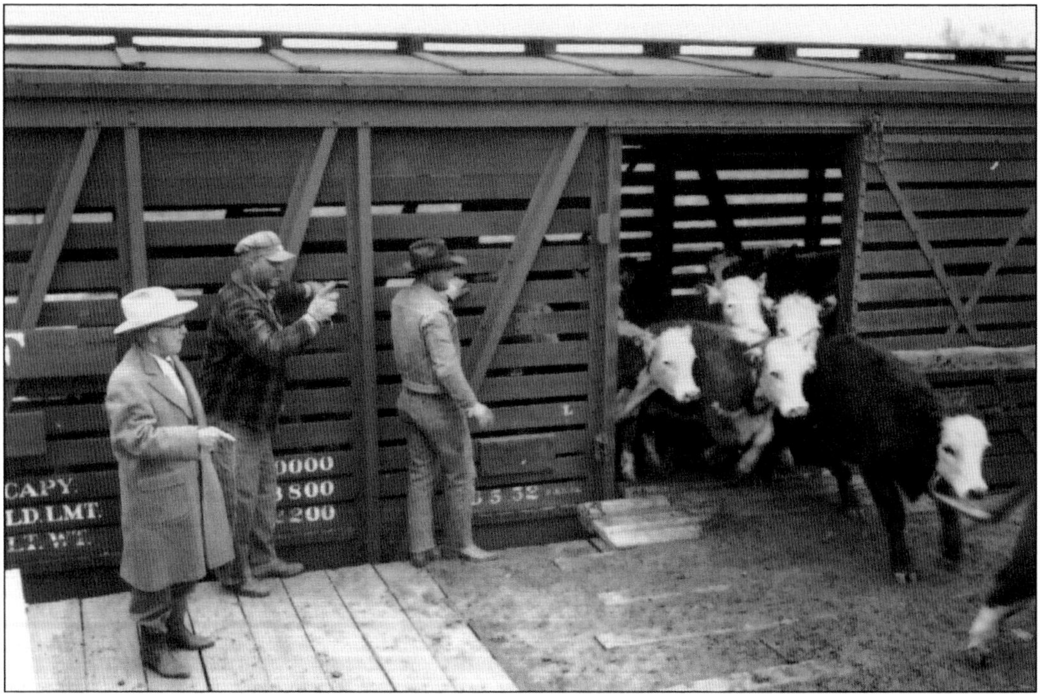

Above, cattle purchased by William K. Waugh, left, are being unloaded at the Eskridge stockyards and depot. Bud Kraus, center, and Wendell Tranter help move the cattle into the pens. Below, one can see the cattle moving into the stockyard pens from the Atchison, Topeka and Santa Fe cattle cars. The stockyards in Eskridge were located on North Cedar Street where the senior citizen apartments are today. Fenced cattle lanes led from the stockyards to the huge pastures that lay to the north and west of town. (Both, courtesy Bruce Waugh.)

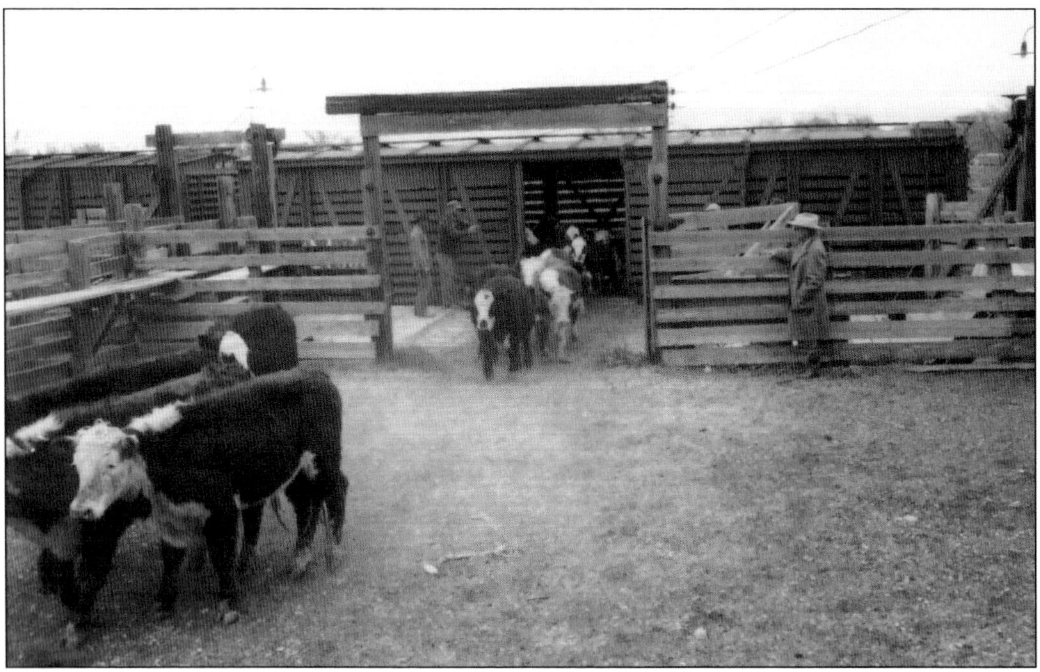

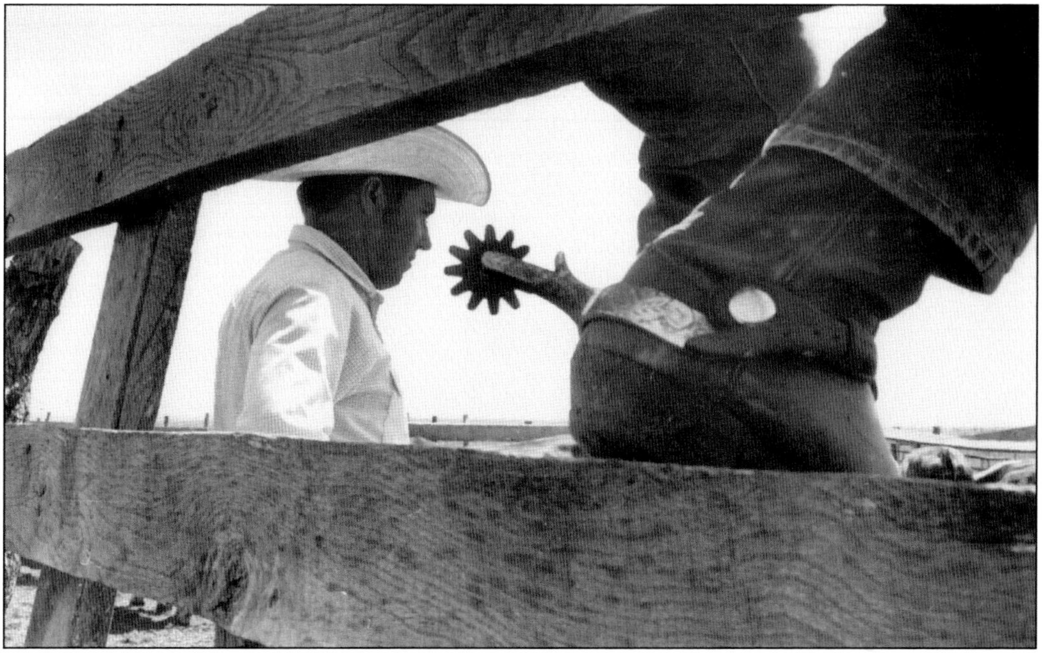

Keith Schultz is seen in the cattle pens at the Munzer Pasture in this photograph taken by Jerry Engler on August 6, 1970, south of Volland, Kansas. The cowboy sitting on the fence with the spur on his boot is Keith's uncle Bill Schultz. Both of the Schultzes are lifelong residents and ranchers of the Volland community. (Courtesy Carol Schultz.)

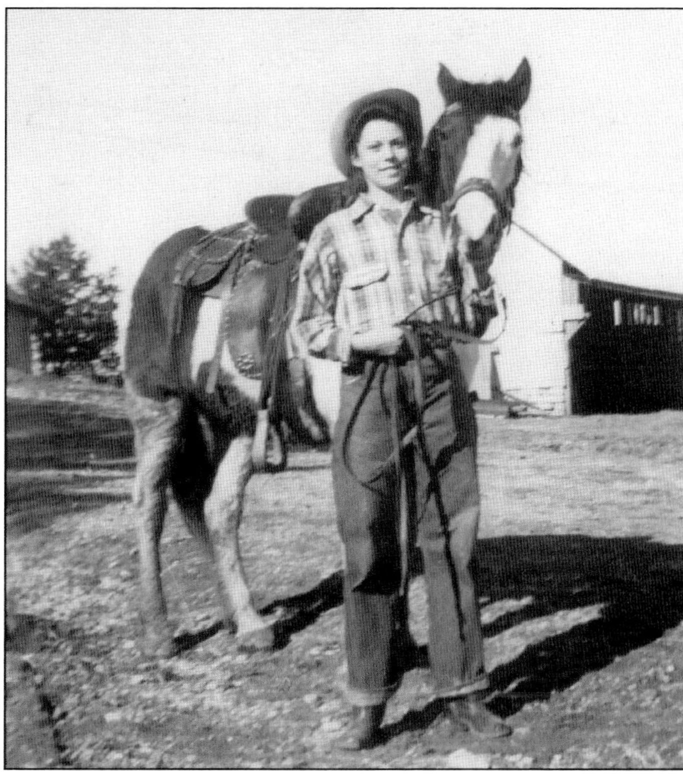

Sometimes, the real cowboys are not boys at all. This view of Laura Gnadt (Barthuly) dates from the 1940s. Laura's brother Martin Gnadt donated this photograph, saying, "She was really good on a horse, she could ride as good as all of the guys. And, she was good handling cattle, too." Indeed, she was. She married Winston Barthuly, and the couple operated a dairy farm at Paxico, Kansas, for decades. (Courtesy Martin Gnadt.)

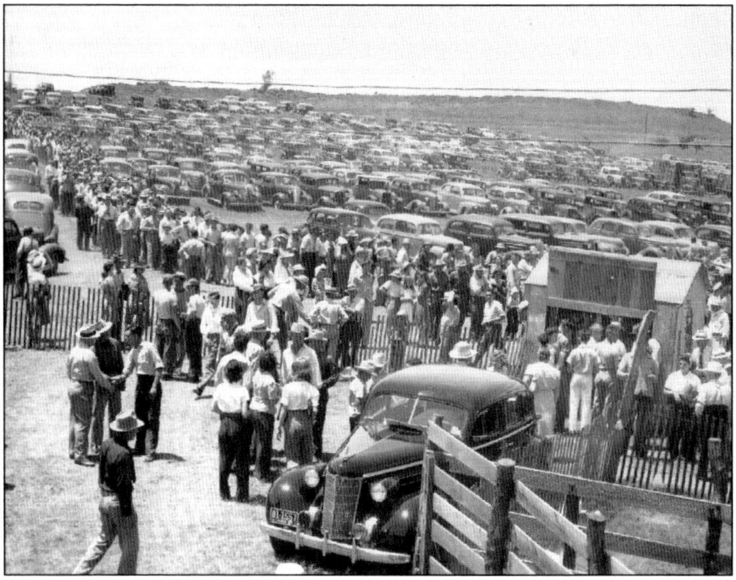

The parking lot was full, and spectators wait to enter the rodeo grounds at Strong City in this early 1940s view. The old rodeo grounds were located a half mile west of Strong City, and the Flint Hills Rodeo was held there from 1940 through 1947. The annual rodeo had its birth at Emmett Roberts's ranch at Strong City in 1937. In 1939, it was renamed the Flint Hills Rodeo. (Courtesy Chase County Historical Society.)

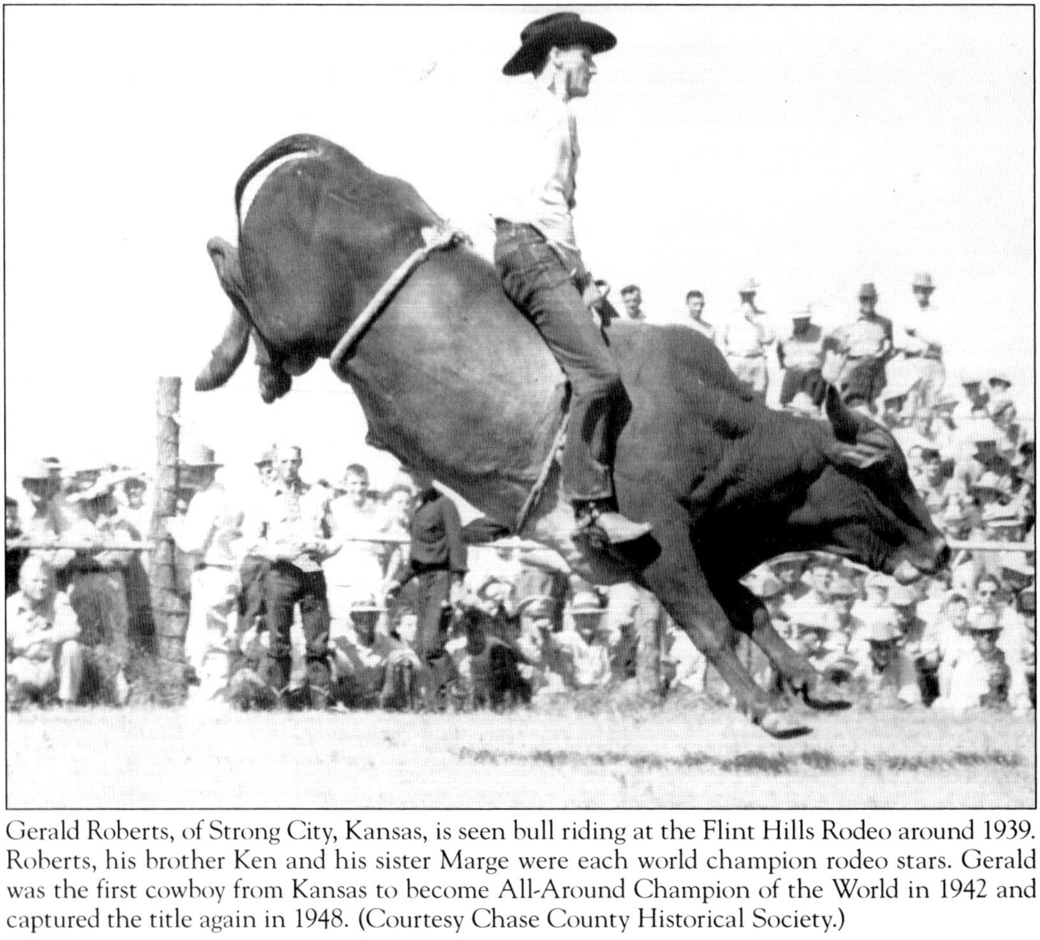

Gerald Roberts, of Strong City, Kansas, is seen bull riding at the Flint Hills Rodeo around 1939. Roberts, his brother Ken and his sister Marge were each world champion rodeo stars. Gerald was the first cowboy from Kansas to become All-Around Champion of the World in 1942 and captured the title again in 1948. (Courtesy Chase County Historical Society.)

Marge Roberts performs her trademark stunt, "the dive," at the May 24, 1940, Flint Hills Rodeo. The eldest of Emmett Roberts's children, Marge started spending summers traveling with the Clyde Miller Wild West Show when she was 13 years old and soon became the best female trick rider in the nation. In 1940, when women were still competing in rodeo events, Marge won the World Champion Women's Bronc Rider championship. (Courtesy Chase County Historical Society.)

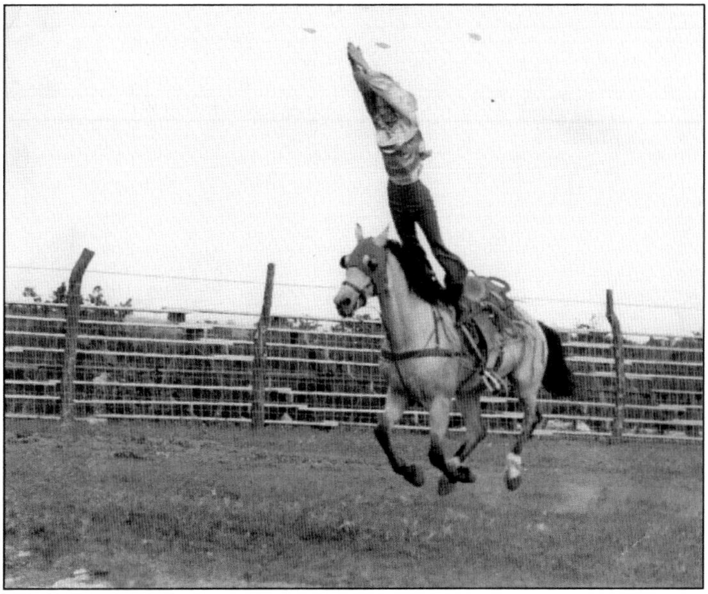

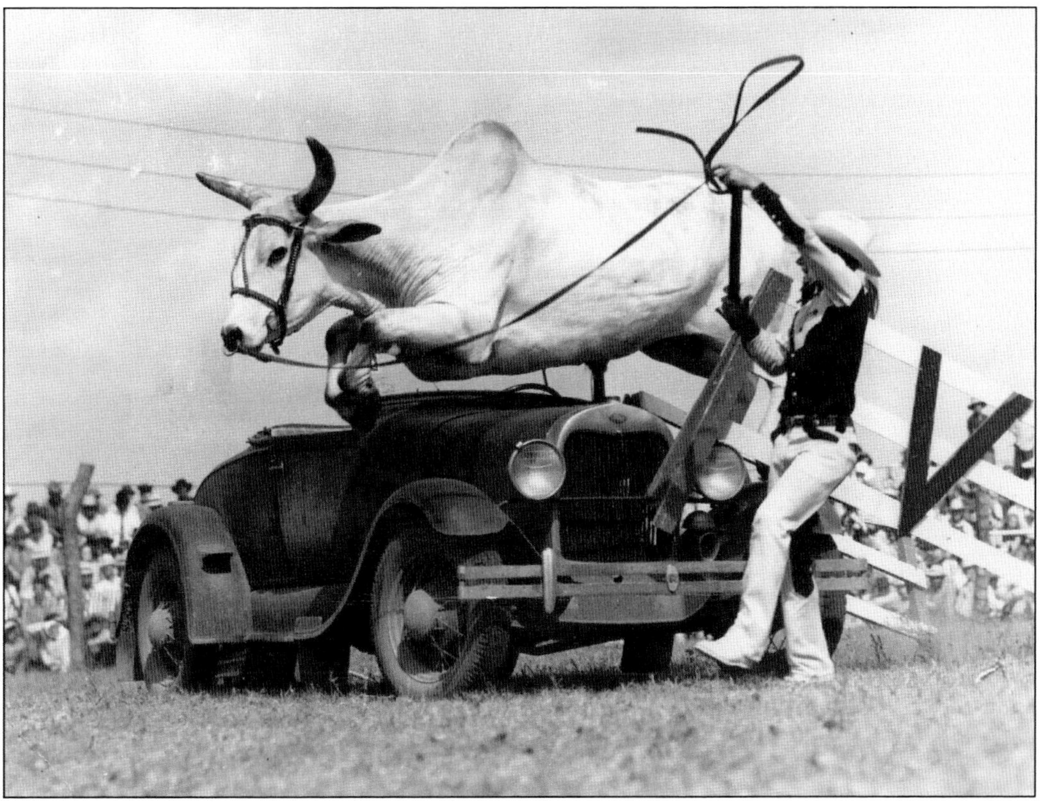

George "Kid" Roberts was a rodeo cowboy and trick performer in the late 1930s and 1940s. In 1941, Marge Roberts and her husband, Eddie Boyson, had divorced, and Marge married George "Kid" Roberts. In the 1940s, the couple performed at rodeos and wintered in Tucson, Arizona, working at dude ranches. Here, Kid Roberts is seen performing his act where he has a bull jump over a car. (Courtesy Chase County Historical Society.)

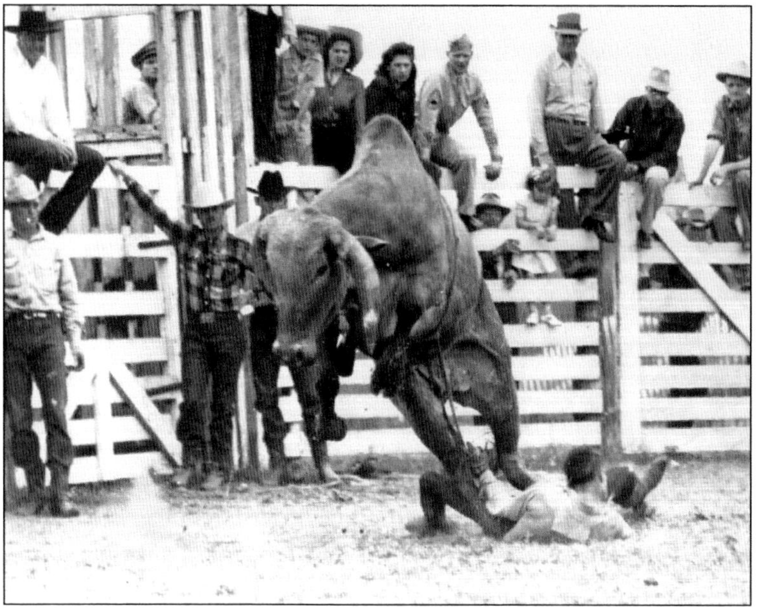

An unidentified bull riding cowboy is thrown from his ride at the Flint Hills Rodeo in Strong City in this photograph from the 1940s. Howard "Jiggs" Roberts, E.C. and Clara Roberts's fourth child, is seen wearing the black hat and sitting on the fence at the top left of this view. The Roberts family was a dynasty in the history of the rodeo sport in Kansas. (Courtesy Chase County Historical Society.)

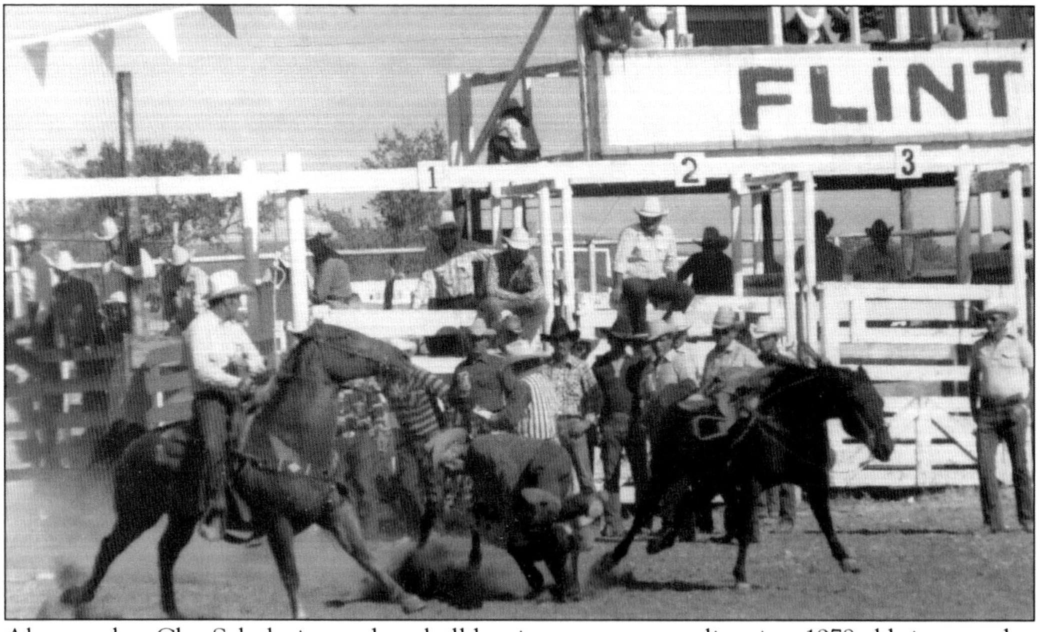

Alma cowboy Cleo Schultz is seen here bulldogging, or steer wrestling, in a 1978 old-timers rodeo event at the Flint Hills Rodeo in Strong City. To qualify for the event, participants must be at least 40 years old. Bulldogging entails leaping off one's horse onto the horns of a racing steer and then wrestling it to the ground. It seems like tough work for the over-40 crowd. (Courtesy Cleo and Julie Schultz.)

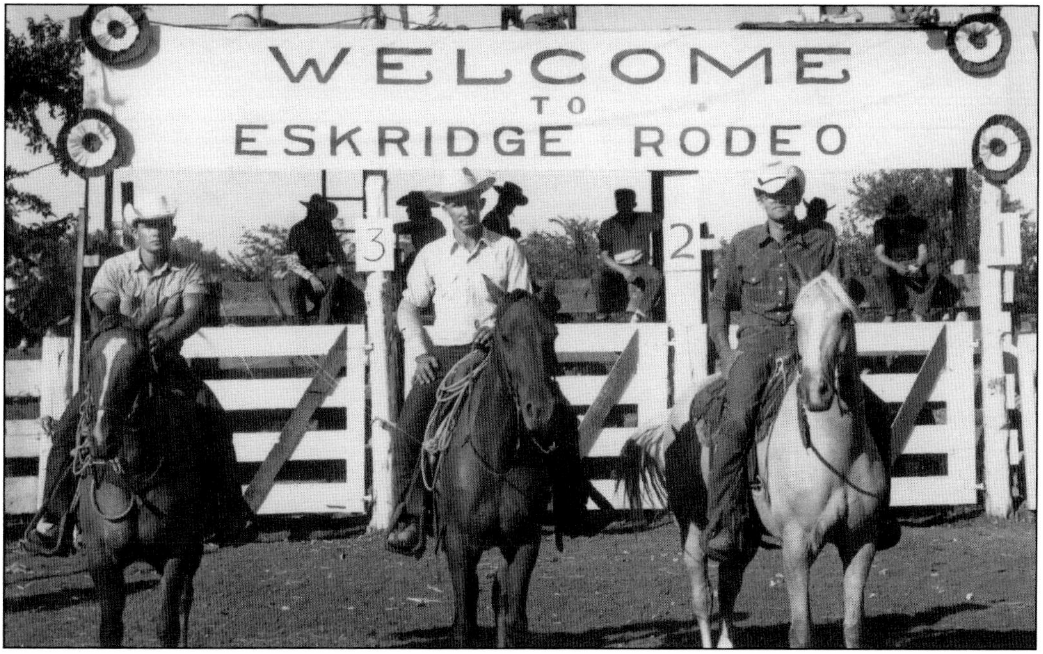

The founders of the Eskridge Labor Day Rodeo are seen here at the rodeo grounds in this 1953 photograph of the first Labor Day rodeo. From left to right are Wendell Tranter, Bob Widau, and Ed Van Petten. In 2010, Eskridge celebrated its 58th annual Labor Day rodeo with record attendance. (Courtesy Bob Widau.)

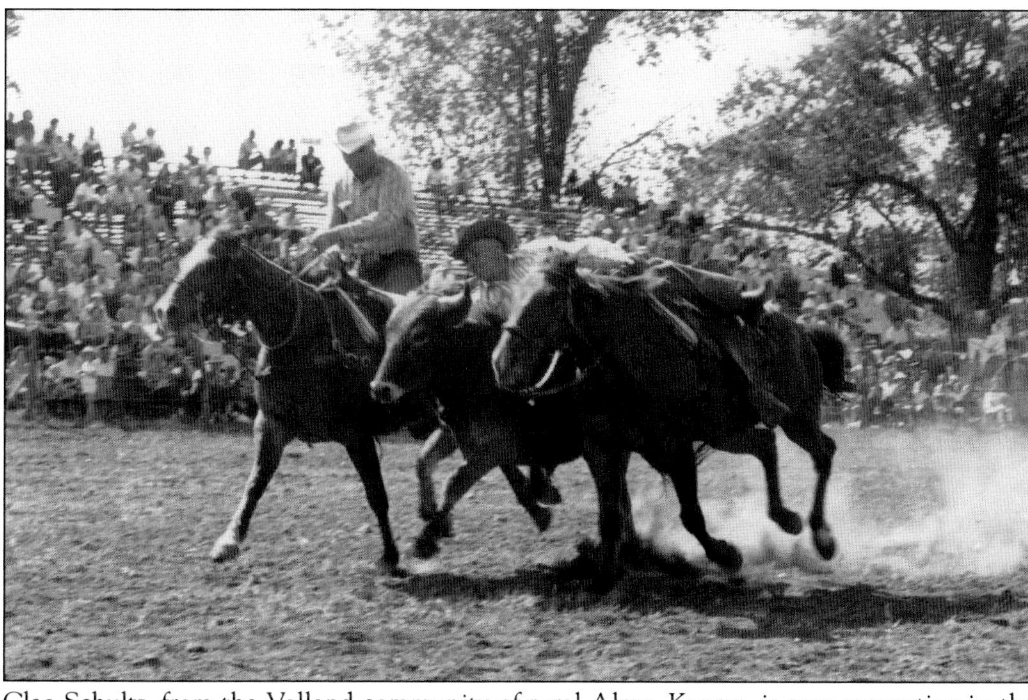

Cleo Schultz, from the Volland community of rural Alma, Kansas, is seen competing in the bulldogging event in this 1960s view from the rodeo grounds at Mayetta. Schultz was born at Volland and spent his life as a Flint Hills rancher and cowboy. (Courtesy Cleo and Julie Schultz.)

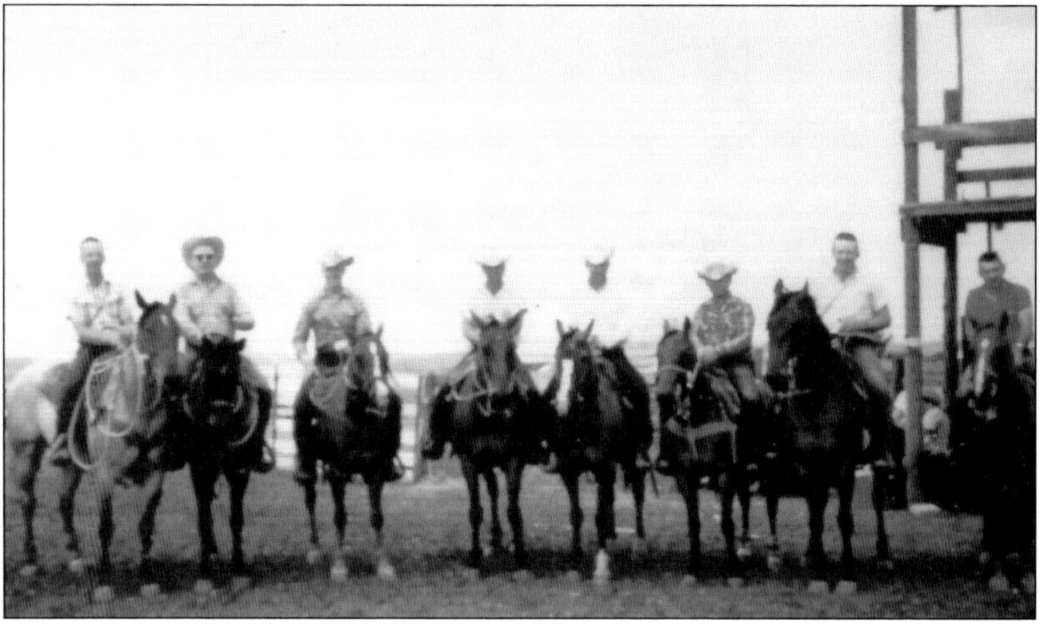

A group of Flint Hills cowboys competing in jackpot roping poses for a photograph at Lester Marten's Rodeo Arena, located two miles south of Alma, Kansas. Marten built the arena to host area 4-H rodeos, but soon it was used for weekly jackpot roping and rodeos. Seen are, from left to right, John Webb, Curley McCary, Bobby Lee, Reece Jackman, Clark Jackman, R.W. Alexander, Gerald "Cheese" Marten, and Jon McCormick. (Courtesy Cheese Marten.)

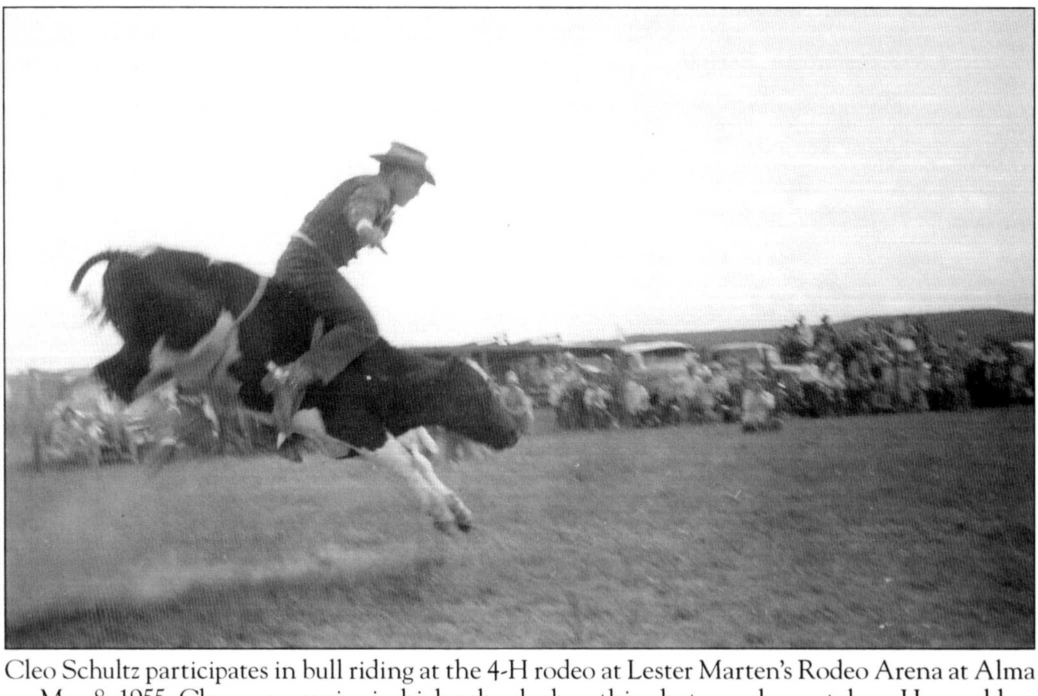

Cleo Schultz participates in bull riding at the 4-H rodeo at Lester Marten's Rodeo Arena at Alma on May 8, 1955. Cleo was a senior in high school when this photograph was taken. He would go on to participate in professional rodeos for several years. Schultz is a lifelong rancher in Volland, Kansas. (Courtesy Cleo and Julie Schultz.)

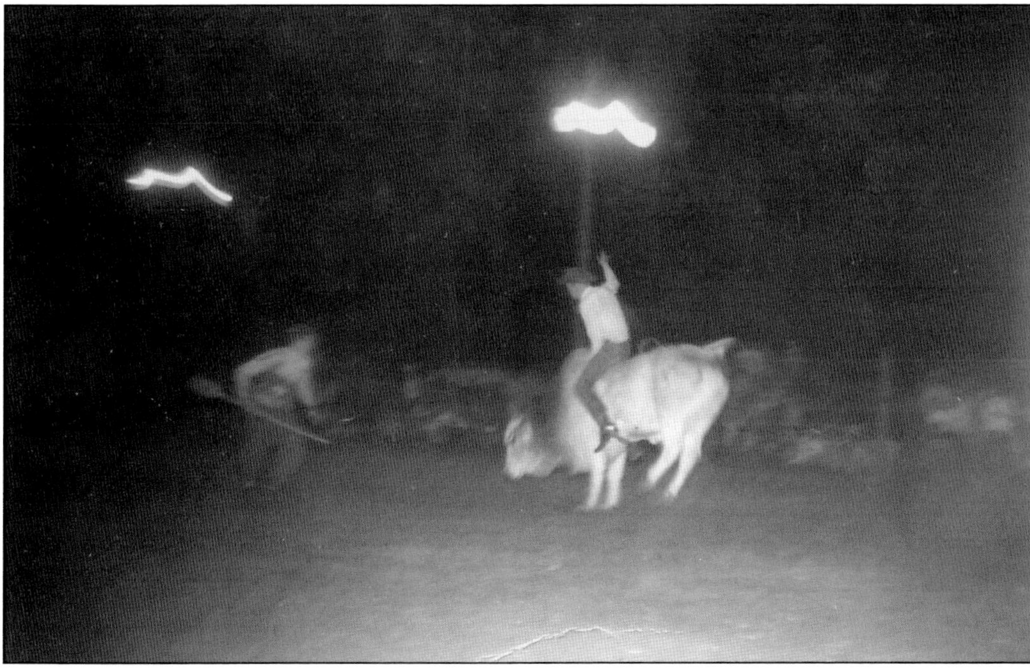

Ron Pletcher, Eskridge, Kansas, is bull riding at this night rodeo around 1959. Pletcher participated in professional rodeos during the late 1950s and 1960s. The rodeo clown to the left is poised to distract the bull when Pletcher dismounts. (Courtesy Shirley Pletcher.)

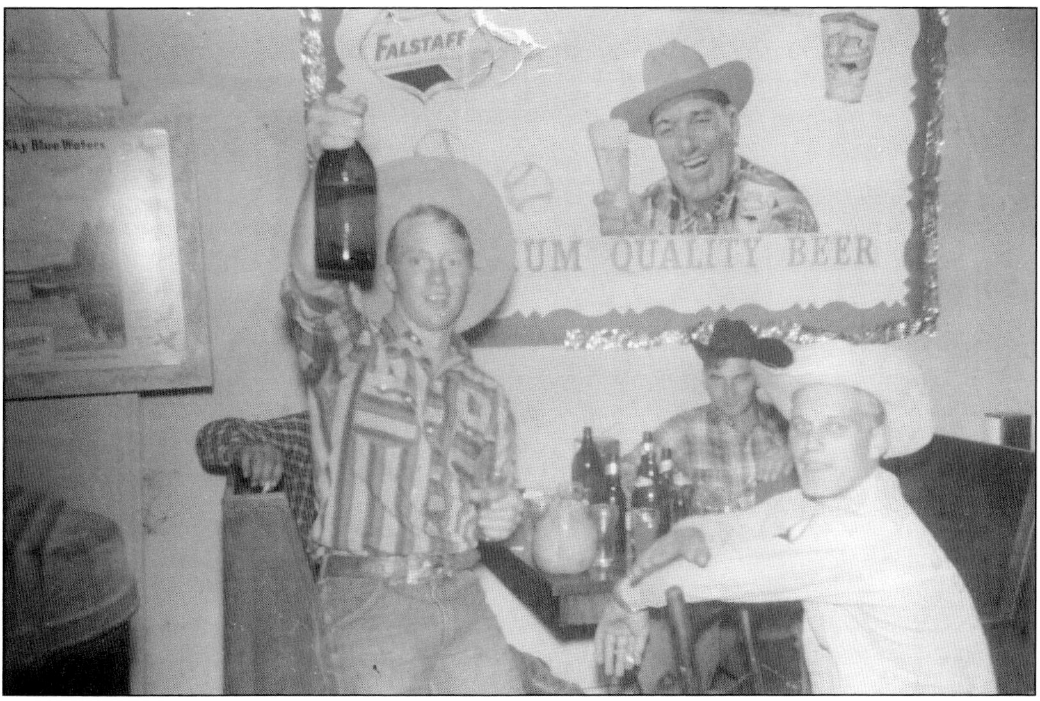

These Flint Hills cowboys stop for a small celebration after a successful rodeo, around 1959. Dale "Little Red" Wilson, left, was known to be a great storyteller, and a second, unidentified cowboy, center, and Ron Pletcher appear to be enjoying the tale. (Courtesy Shirley Pletcher.)

Discover Thousands of Local History Books Featuring Millions of Vintage Images

Arcadia Publishing, the leading local history publisher in the United States, is committed to making history accessible and meaningful through publishing books that celebrate and preserve the heritage of America's people and places.

Find more books like this at
www.arcadiapublishing.com

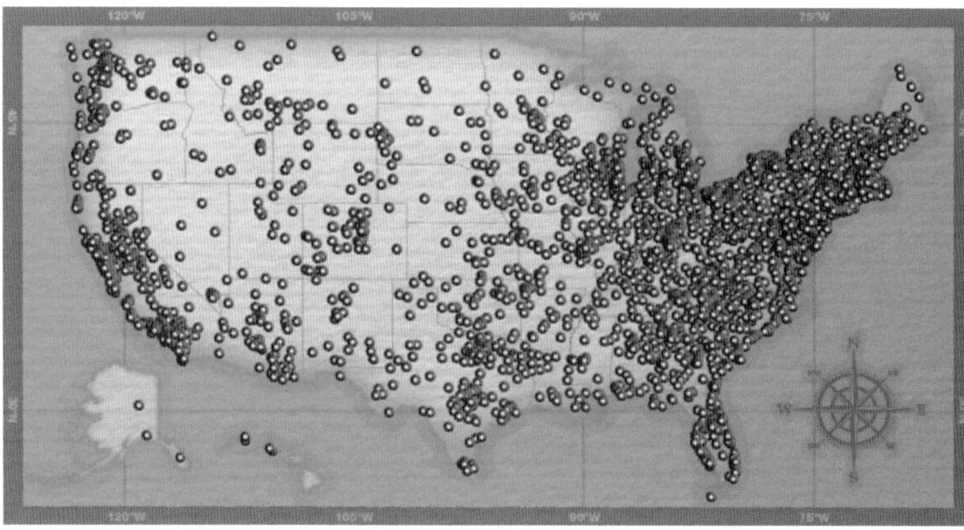

Search for your hometown history, your old stomping grounds, and even your favorite sports team.

Consistent with our mission to preserve history on a local level, this book was printed in South Carolina on American-made paper and manufactured entirely in the United States. Products carrying the accredited Forest Stewardship Council (FSC) label are printed on 100 percent FSC-certified paper.

MADE IN THE USA